D1736876

Contemporary Issues in Educational Policy and School Outcomes

a volume in
Research and Theory in Educational Administration

Series Editors:
Wayne Hoy, *The Ohio State University*
Cecil Miskel, *The University of Michigan*

Research and Theory in Educational Administration

Wayne Hoy and Cecil Miskel, Series Editors

Contemporary Issues in Educational Policy and School Outcomes

edited by

Wayne Hoy
The Ohio State University
and

Cecil Miskel
The University of Michigan

INFORMATION AGE
PUBLISHING

Greenwich, Connecticut • www.infoagepub.com

Library of Congress Cataloging-in-Publication Data

Contemporary issues in educational policy and school outcomes / edited by
Wayne Hoy and Cecil Miskel.
    p. cm. — (Research and theory in educational administration)
  Includes bibliographical references.
  ISBN 1-59311-477-X (pbk.) — ISBN 1-59311-478-8 (hardcover)
  1. School management and organization—United States. 2. Education and
state—United States. 3. Educational change—United States. I. Hoy, Wayne
K. II. Miskel, Cecil G. III. Series.
  LB2805.C6343 2006
  379—dc22

                                          2006002397

Printed in the United States of America

CONTENTS

v

EDITORS' COMMENTS

Wayne K. Hoy and Cecil G. Miskel

This book is the fifth in a series on research and theory dedicated to advancing our understanding of schools through empirical study and theoretical analysis. Scholars, both young and established, are invited to publish original analyses, but we especially encourage young scholars to contribute to this series. The current volume is similar to its predecessors in that it provides a mix of beginning and established scholars and a broad range of theoretical perspectives; in all 14 authors contributed to 9 separate but related analyses, which were selected for publication this year.

The book begins with four chapters on educational policy. The first chapter, by Tamara Young and Cecil Miskel, presents a study that examines how often state reading policy actors form coalitions, and the pervasiveness and nature of the coalitions. Not surprisingly, both governmental and nongovernmental state reading policy actors engage in a variety of alliances to influence policy outcomes. Young and Miskel point to the disparate character of the alliances and argue that they can be usefully differentiated by how the coalitions emerge. The results of the inquiry suggest that educational professionals are frequently involved in a wide variety of coalitions with many partners in an increasingly crowded policy environment, but an important question is whether participation of educational professionals in these policy coalitions is nominal or authentic.

In chapter 2, Thomas Shepley continues the analysis of coalitions in state reading policy by considering the charge that certain reading policies and instructional practices have been demonized. He examines evidence that the so-called "devil shift" explains the formation of advocacy coalitions. He concludes that "devil shift" does exist, and he argues that, although the concept fails to completely explain the genesis of advocacy coalitions, "devil shift" is a useful and relevant way to understand the formation of certain extreme coalitions.

In chapter 3, attentions shifts from reading policy to public charter school policy. Ann Allen maintains that the autonomy in public charter school policy, which is suppose to spur innovation and responsiveness to parents, tends to decrease the level of responsibility of charter schools to the general public. Public charter schools are required to maintain open and accessible board meeting; however, the results of this study suggest that autonomy overshadows the responsibility charter schools have to the larger public. Thus, an important issue in the implementation of public charter school policy becomes protecting the general public interest. Allen grapples with the ways in which public interests can be represented in public charter schools and concludes with a set recommendations that could make for greater public representation without decreasing the autonomy that promotes innovation and greater responsiveness to student needs.

Robert Slater and Mario Torres (chapter 4) introduce values as an element of politics and policy. They argue that values and values discourse have played important roles in contemporary politics. Specifically, they examine the relationship between values politics and the No Child Left Behind (NCLB) legislation. The thesis of this chapter is that values politics, a curious mix of moral and political discourse, is having an unusual and powerful effect on both foreign and domestic policy. Slater and Torres examine and discuss the moral complexity of NCLB, its consequences, and the possible impact of the emphasis of ethics and morality in educational research.

The next set of papers focuses on *school improvement and enhancing school outcomes;* these analyses also suggest the influence of accountability policy on schooling. In chapter 5, Laura Desimone examines the relationship between professional community and mathematic teaching in early elementary school. She develops a theoretical framework that integrates two theoretical perspectives—the school as a social organization and the school viewed in terms of a control and commitment framework. The empirical phase of her research tests a theoretical notion of how professional community works by dividing it into structural and social-psychological aspects and then further differentiating structural aspects into leadership and interactive teacher activities. Thus, the influence of principal leadership, teacher participation in decision making, and interactive collaborative teacher activities, as well as teachers' beliefs, shared values and sense of community are tested as paths to make instruction more challenging. The results of the study are discussed in terms of a refined theory of professional community. Desimone suggests that the power of a strong professional community is not only to foster more challenging instruction but also to move teachers to focus more on academic concerns, a proposal that is consistent with Hoy, Tarter, and Woolfolk Hoy's analysis in chapter 6. Hoy and his colleagues examine the literature on the relationship between school properties and school achievement and develop a latent school property, academic optimism, which should be related to student achievement even controlling for previous achievement, socioeconomic status, and other demographic characteristics. Academic optimism is comprised of three collective properties that work together in a united fashion to create a positive work culture. Collective efficacy provides a cognitive dimension of such a culture; faculty trust is an affective response; and academic emphasis represents a press for academic behavior. This latent construct of academic optimism is grounded in the positive psychology of Seligman and Csikszentmihalyi (2000), the social cognitive theory of Bandura (1997), the social theory of Coleman (1990), as well as the authors' own research on school climate.

Melinda Mangin in chapter 7 examines the influence of teacher leadership on instructional improvement. She studies formal teacher leaders in mathematics in five school districts. Such roles are often connected to comprehensive reform models, but in this study the roles were not part of a comprehensive model. The formal teacher leaders engaged four basic activities: modeling lessons, assisting in classroom instruction, providing materials, and facilitating group-level meetings. None of the leaders performed all four activities; each had limitations, and the influence of each was different and unequal in terms instructional improvement. Finding the right combination and balance of activities seems to be a key to instructional impact.

In chapter 8, Amanda Datnow and Vicki Parks use *Success For All*, a whole-school reform model, to explore the linkage between research and practice in a qualitative case study. Their analysis considers both the role of rigorous, quantitative research in informing the model as well as teachers' reflections on their own practices. The chapter focuses on *whose* knowledge is used and *how* it is used in the continual development of the *Success For All*. Cochran-Smith and Lytle's framework (1999) for relating knowledge and practice was a useful tool to analyze knowledge-for-practice and knowledge-in-practice. Further, the research revealed how the broader policy context shaped the Success for All reform, that is, how policy knowledge became part of reform itself. Strategies for meeting accountability demands at the state and federal levels became part of the "knowledge" of *Success For All*.

Accountability is also the backdrop of the concluding chapter of this volume. Jennifer Lin Russell (chapter 9) examines the ways in which teachers perceive that standards-based accountability policy influence their practice—both in what and how they teach. What and how much children should be expected to learn in kindergarten remain contested issues and create enduring tensions, even though kindergarten is a long-standing and institutionalized element of American public education. In spite of the fact that kindergartens are not subject to state standardized tests and are not held accountable by the state, Russell's study suggests that local districts craft their own accountability policies, which often include imposing testing requirements on kindergarten students. The widespread impact of accountability standards and its relationships with teachers' commitment and career satisfaction are discussed.

These chapters underscore the significance of educational policy in contemporary public education and in particular the impact of accountability policy on school outcomes. Public schools are increasingly being held accountable for students achieving at higher levels in both basic skills and higher-level learning outcomes. Of course, all policy is enacted by teachers in classroom and sometimes changed or distorted in the process. The challenge is to improve student outcomes without permitting accountability testing to extinguish innovation and creativity in schools.

This book series on *Theory and Research in Educational Administration* is about understanding schools. We welcome articles and analyses that explain school organizations and administration. We are interested in the "why" questions about schools. To that end, case analyses, surveys, large data base analyses, experimental studies, and theoretical analyses are all welcome. We provide the space for authors to do comprehensive analyses where that is appropriate and useful. We believe that the *Theory and Research in Educational Administration Series* has the potential to make an important contribution to our field, but we will be successful only if our colleagues continue to join us in this mission.

Wayne K. Hoy, The Ohio State University
Cecil G. Miskel, The University of Michigan
November 3, 2005

CHAPTER 1

COALITIONS IN STATE READING POLICY ISSUE NETWORKS[1]

Tamara V. Young and Cecil Miskel

Drawing extensively on the notion of issue networks and the research on coalitions in public policy, this study investigates how often state reading policy actors form coalitions; how many different coalition partners policy actors select; and what is the nature of coalitions in state reading policy issue networks. Data is drawn from interviews with 111 private and public sector policy actors involved in the development of reading policy in California, Connecticut, Michigan, and Utah. The findings of this study show that both governmental and nongovernmental state reading policy actors engage in a wide variety of collaborative alliances with numerous partners to achieve their policy objectives. The findings also demonstrate that coalitions can be differentiated by how they emerge, and government activity and previous interaction facilitate coalition activity.

Contemporary Issues in Educational Policy and School Outcomes, 1–25

NEED AND PURPOSE

The traditional educational groups and government agencies that once dominated the state educational policy process are now joined by an increasingly larger and more diverse set of organized interests concerned with K-12 education (Kaplan & Usdan, 1992; Mazzoni, 1995, 2000). This proliferation of interest groups and the growing scarcity of public resources have compelled interest groups that were previously able to operate independently to form coalitions with other groups to achieve their political goals (Baumgartner & Jones, 1993). Moreover, interest groups are not the only policy actors forming alliances, government officials are also developing coalitions to attain their policy objectives. For instance, state governors formed powerful coalitions with business groups and religious interests to promote vouchers, charter schools, and state standards (Gittell & Mckenna, 1999). In fact, so widespread are coalitions that observers of educational policy believe that "[a] web of coalitions and advocacy groups have since become ubiquitous in shaping public policy" (Kaplan & Usdan, 1992, p. 666).

Though scholars have observed that educational policy has become increasingly characterized by coalition politics, little is known about the characteristics of coalitions in the politics of education. It is not surprising that this area of literature is small. The lack of attention to coalitions has less to do with the notion of coalitions itself, but instead with an overall lack of attention to the role of interest groups in educational policy. Interest groups are an understudied aspect of educational politics (Malen, 2001). Additionally, the few studies that examine K-12 coalitions are limited in scope—analyze a single policy issue, consider the activities of a very few groups, or examine a single state (e.g., Karper & Boyd, 1988; Mazzoni & Malen, 1985). Another explanation for the dearth of information on coalitions in educational policy is that the proliferation of interest groups and the increase in both their activities and influence in educational policy have occurred over the past few decades. Thus, ad hoc coalitions and their widespread occurrence can be viewed as a relatively new phenomenon in education.

Given the limited scope of empirical evidence on coalitions in educational policy, few conclusions can be drawn about the nature and role of coalitions in educational politics. As coalitions have increasingly become a key element in the political process, dramatically changing the landscape of the politics of K-12 education, the study of coalitions has become essential to understanding how educational policies are made. Systematic data on coalitions across a wide range of groups in different states is necessary to advance our understanding of the nature and role of coalitions in the politics of education.

THE POLICY ENVIRONMENT

Because interest groups make advocacy decisions with regard to discrete issues (Hojnackni, 1997) and form coalitions when the coalition is limited to one issue or the issue is of some immediacy with a good chance of government action (Berry, 1997), we must examine interest group coalitional behavior within the context of one policy issue. Though numerous debates take place in state educational policy domains each year, the issue of reading in the early elementary grades offers fertile ground for analyzing the formation of interest group alliances in state educational policy. First, reading is fundamental to achievement. Second, the issue of reading is subsumed within discussions of equity and excellence within American schools. Reading scores, for example, highlight the achievement gaps between minority groups and white students, urban and suburban students, and English language learners and English proficient students. Third, reading policies affect a large segment of the student population, command significant fiscal resources, and affect other educational policies, such as class size, federal funding, teacher credentialing, standards, assessment, and accountability.

Additionally, although reading skills or literacy has long been considered an important topic in educational policy, reading has become a prominent issue on the policy agenda during the past decade (McDaniel, Sims, & Miskel, 2001; Miskel et al., 2003; Shepley, 2003; Young, Shepley, Miskel, & Song, 2002). Moreover, the reading reform movement in the 1990s affords an excellent opportunity to examine alliance formation within the context of a salient policy issue (Young & Miskel, 2004). Certainly, policy actors form alliances on nonsalient issues. However, nonsalient issues attract only a small number of active participants. By studying a salient issue, analysis can include the coalitional activity of a wide array of educational policy actors, providing extensive data about the range of coalitional activity. Additionally, innovative policy changes generally occur when there is heightened attention surrounding an issue (Baumgartner & Jones, 1993). Studying the prominent issue of reading will allow us to achieve a more complete understanding of policy change (Young & Miskel, 2004).

Finally, the issue of reading will serve as a rich data source for policy analysis because it permits comparative analysis. Because so many states have developed or revised reading policies in the past decade, this study makes a cross-state comparison of educational policymaking. A comparative analysis will allow us to circumvent the idiosyncratic features of one state, and generate new avenues for theory building. Furthermore, because reading methods have been debated for over a century (Ravitch, 2000) and current reading scores remain generally unchanged (Donahue,

Daane, & Grigg, 2003), it is likely that the issue of reading will appear again in the future, thereby offering a baseline for comparing interest group alliances across time.

In sum, for these reasons, reading is an excellent issue to provide empirical data for understanding coalitions in state educational policy. Accordingly, three research questions guide this study: (1) How often do state reading policy actors form coalitions? (2) How many different coalition partners are reading policy actors collaborating with to shape state reading policy? (3) What are the characteristics of coalitions in state reading policy issue networks?

THEORETICAL BACKGROUND

Issue Networks

This study presents an approach to the empirical study of alliance formation based largely on Heclo's (1978) notion of issue networks. Heclo's notion of issue networks has become a dominant paradigm for understanding interaction between and among government officials and interest groups in public policymaking in the United States. In his seminal work, *Issue Networks and the Executive Establishment*, Heclo challenged the traditional iron triangle model. The iron triangle or subgovernment perspective supposes that tight-knit powerful alliances between a limited number of participants from the executive branch, congressional committees, and peak interest groups shape policy in a particular area. Heclo argued that as a result of the growth in government activities, the increase in specialization of government units, and the proliferation of issue-conscious groups in the early twentieth century, structural arrangements in policymaking were no longer limited to the notion of iron triangles. Rather, open networks, which Heclo termed, "issue networks" (p. 102) characterized the policy decision-making process. Heclo defined an issue network as a "shared-knowledge group having to do with some aspect ... of public policy" (p. 103). Members of the issue network have a "common base of information and understanding of how one knows about policy and identifies its problems" (p. 104). According to Heclo, it is through issue networks that "policy issues tend to be "refined, evidence debated, and alternative options worked out—though rarely in any controlled, well organized way" (p. 104).

Tentative steps towards identifying and understanding issue networks in educational policy have been taken by a handful of scholars. Educational researchers have explained the proliferation of networks (Cibulka, 2001) and explored the role of networks in the diffusion of policy innovations (Kirst, Meister, & Rowley, 1984; Mintrom & Vergari, 1998). Scholars have also identified the dimensions of educational policy networks (Kirst et al., 1984) and studied policy entrepreneurs' utilization of networks (Mintrom & Vergari, 1998). Moreover, recently there has been a small but growing literature on mapping and measuring properties of reading policy issue networks (McDaniel, 2001; Miskel et al; 2003; Song, 2003; Song & Miskel, 2004; Young, 2005; Young & Miskel, 2002). Though our understanding of issue networks in state educational policy has gradually improved, a puzzle remains. How do these networks emerge? To better understand the formation and structure of issue networks in state educational policy, we need to consider the linkages, or coalitions, that comprise issue networks.

Alliances and Coalitions

Definition

Although scholars have theoretically differentiated many variations of coalitions and alliances (e.g., Berry, 1997; Hula, 1999; Knoke, 1990; Knoke & Burleigh, 1989; Loomis, 1986), in practice, studies of coalitions generally encompass the wide spectrum of coalitions that occur. Loomis (1986), for example, maintains that the concept of coalitions includes coalition building, collaboration, cooperation, or similar notions that express a joining together of interests for at least a measurable period of time. According to Loomis, this interpretation of coalition does not offer a formal model of coalition behavior, yet it represents the practices of contemporary interest groups. Like Loomis, this study does not adopt a strict definition of the terms coalition or alliance. Alliance or coalition refers to any type of collaborative activity (e.g., sharing information, exchanging resources, coauthoring a document, and cosponsoring an activity) between individual or organizational actors undertaken to advance their state reading policy agenda.

The Proliferation of Coalitions

Coalitions have been a part of American politics since its inception; however, recent changes in the political environment, such as an increase in the complexity of the policy process, the growth and decentralization of government, improved communication capabilities, and the growing politicization of interests that were either nonexistent, poorly organized, or relatively inactive have substantially increased coalitional activity in public policy (Loomis, 1986). The expansion of the interest group universe and the growing scarcity of public resources have also forced interaction among groups that were previously able to operate independently (Baumgartner & Jones, 1993). Last, with more groups and greater diversity in the types of interests that are active, there are greater opportunities for forming alliances than in decades past (Hojnacki, 1997). Indeed, a survey of national organized interests engaged in educational policy found that 98.8% of groups sometimes or normally joined coalitions to coordinate their public activities (Baumgartner & Walker, 1989).

Ad hoc Alliances

State education policy systems have experienced an eruption of coalitional activity in recent decades (Kaplan & Usdan, 1992; Mazzoni, 1995, 2000), especially of ad hoc coalitions (i.e., temporary issue-oriented coalitions that disband when the issue is resolved or members withdraw because of disinterests). Kaplan and Usdan (1992) term this proliferation of ad hoc alliances "adhocracy." Despite their transient nature, ad hoc coalitions have wielded considerable power over educational policy. For example, policy actors have temporarily joined forces to alter reading policy in California and Texas (Shepley, 2003), advocate mathematical and science curriculum reforms in California (Carlos & Kirst, 1997), promote school reforms in Chicago (Gittell, 1994), and demand tax concessions for parents of students enrolled in private schools in Minnesota (Mazzoni & Malen, 1985).

Ad hoc coalitions have also replaced traditional political alignments and steered much of the state educational reforms of the 1980s (Mazzoni, 1995, 2000). As Mazzoni indicated in his review of state educational policy during the 1980s, one of the most visible and often formidable ad hoc coalitions has been the educational alliances between political leaders and business groups. In Minnesota and New Jersey, for example, the powerful coalition between governors and business interest groups prevailed over teachers' unions over the issue of school choice (Gittell & McKenna, 1999).

Clearly, educational policymaking is increasingly characterized by coalition politics. Yet, despite the prevalence of coalitions in educational policy, we have limited empirical knowledge concerning the origins of coalitions, their activities, and their influence on state educational policies and practices. This study attempts to advance our knowledge base about coalitions in state educational politics.

METHODS

Data for this study were derived from a much larger and more comprehensive data set, The University of Michigan's State Reading Policy Project (SRPP), a study of the development of reading policy in nine states during the mid-1990s to early 2000s. The primary data sources for this study were interviews with public and private sector policy actors engaged in the formation of state reading policy. This section provides an overview of the research methods, including: sampling, data collection and management, measurement, and analysis procedures.

Population and Sampling

Alliances do not occur in an asocial context. Rather, collaborative relationships emerge within a complex political system facilitated and constrained by temporal, historical, institutional, social, and economic circumstances. Hence, to fully understand alliances, it is necessary to examine them within the context of a political microsystem—state reading policy issue networks.

States

For a number of reasons, the state level serves as an excellent locus of analysis to explore coalitional activity within educational policy. First, as more and more policy and funding power shifts from the federal government to state governments, it becomes increasingly important to understand the state policymaking process (Thomas & Hrebenar, 1992). Second, state level policy actors have initiated many of the educational reforms of the 1980s and 1990s (Fuhrman, 2001; Mazzoni, 1995, 2000; Mitchell, 1988), and subsequently state-level policymaking has become a focal point for policy activity. Finally, states have the authority to set educational policy and, as such, are the targets of interest groups' lobbying efforts.

The sample of states was obtained using a three-step process (Miskel et al., 2003). The first step involved identifying states that had been recently or were currently involved in developing reading policy initiatives during 1999 and 2000. The next step entailed narrowing the study population to obtain a range of average student achievement scores on NAEP reading tests and geographical diversity. From these criteria, nine states were selected. Out of this set of nine states, four states that had an interview response rate of at least 85% were included in this study. Limiting the study to four states enabled more detailed exploration of coalitional activity. The four state sample also provided an adequate range of state policy environments sufficient for comparative analysis.

Policy Actors

Because no generally recognized membership list of the population of policy actors existed, we followed a three-step process for selecting participants that maximized the likelihood of achieving a comprehensive list of state reading policy actors (Miskel et al., 2003; Young, 2005). First, we examined public documents related to state reading initiatives, such as, state legislation, newspapers, press releases, and journal articles. This review of public records revealed active key elected officials and their appointees or civil servants in relevant departments (e.g., department of education and state board of education), as well as representatives of important interest groups (e.g., teachers educational associations and reading associations), whom we placed on a preliminary list of study participants. Second, one or two state consultants from each state reviewed our initial list and recommend additions or deletions of specific participants. Finally, to ensure that we identified all relevant policy actors, we used a snowballing sampling technique (Goodman, 1961; Kingdon, 1995). Specifically, we asked study participants to identify other important individuals or groups actively involved in state reading policy that we had not already selected. Policy actors who had received multiple nominations for inclusion by participants were added to the study population. Given the comprehensiveness of these procedures, it is reasonable to presume that a relatively exhaustive list of relevant state reading policy actors was obtained.

With the exception of a few individual policy entrepreneurs, the policy actor was not the individual interviewed per se, rather the organizational entity the respondent represented (e.g., interest group and government agency). The average response rate across the four states was 93% (Young, 2005). Eighty-four percent (93 of 111) of the respondents represented groups outside of the state government. Nongovernmental policy actors predominantly came from a wide range of educational associations, such as: administrative and school board associations, teacher associations and unions, school districts, higher education institutions, and single-issue groups (e.g., reading associations, learning disability groups, and library associations). Interest groups concerned with education but did not primarily consist of educational professionals (e.g., businesses, business associations, citizen groups, the media, research organizations, and philanthropic foundations) were also incorporated in the sample. Sixteen (18 of 111) percent of the respondents were governmental actors. Government participants represented the governor's office, the state legislature, the state department of education, the state board of education, and a variety of government commissions and advisory boards concerned with reading policy.

Data Collection and Management

A standard open-ended structured interview schedule served as the primary data collection instrument (Miskel et al., 2003; Young, 2005).

Eight researchers representing The University of Michigan's Reading Policy Project conducted the interviews. Approximately one half of the interviews were conducted in person. The other half of the interviews were conducted over the telephone. Only one policy actor responded by e-mail. Participants were primarily interviewed during 2000–2001, but a few interviews were conducted in 2002. All the interviews were tape recorded and transcribed. To ensure anonymity, participants' names were removed from the transcripts and replaced with randomly assigned numerical codes before being stored in an Atlas.ti electronic database (Scientific Software Development, 2001).

Measurement

Research question 1.   To determine the frequency of forming coalitions, we asked nongovernmental policy actors how often they formed coalitions to influence state reading policy (i.e., never, occasionally, sometimes, and frequently). If a policy actor did not report forming a coalition, the tactic was coded as missing for that group. When more than one individual was interviewed for a policy actor entity, we computed an average rating for the organizational actor.

Research questions 2 and 3.   To gather information on coalitional activity, we asked participants to describe their involvement in state reading policymaking and to identify the policy actors with whom they had collaborated to influence state reading policy.

Analysis

Research question 1.   We generated a frequency distribution to illustrate how often nongovernmental policy actors formed coalitions to influence state reading policy. We also ran ANOVA using SPSS version 12.0 to determine if there was a significant difference in the frequency of coalition formation across the four states.

Research question 2.   To determine how many different alliance partners policy actors selected, we computed the average number of alliance partners reported by participants. Then, to allow for comparison across states, we adjusted the average number of partners for network size by dividing the average number of alliance partners by the number of potential partners—the number of actors in the state network minus one (an actor cannot form a coalition with itself). Finally, we ran ANOVA to determine if there was a significant difference in the number of partnerships (adjusted for network size) across the four states in the study.

Research question 3.   We read the interviews in their entirety and coded statements that revealed alliances between the participant and other reading policy actors. Generally, when an actor mentioned assisting, working, joining, teaming, partnering, forming alliances, establishing coalitions, and synonymous expressions, the statement was coded as alliance. To ensure that all instances of alliances had been coded, we used the text search tool of Atlas.ti (Scientific Software Development, 2001) to identify any occurrences of the terms: work, join, joint, team, partner, alliance, coalition, assist, and collaborate as well as their textual variations (e.g., join, joining, joined, etc.). We reread all text containing these expressions to make certain that all alliances were identified. After this initial coding of identifying segments of text discussing alliances, we followed the pattern coding approach outlined by Miles and Huberman (1994), which involved rereading the coded text to identify themes and clustering them into subcodes.

RESULTS

Research Question 1:   Frequency of Joining Coalitions

During the interviews, nongovernmental policy actors were asked how often they formed coalitions with other policy actors to influence state reading policy (i.e., never, occasionally, sometimes, and frequently). Table 1.1 shows the range of responses to this question. Among the 84 nongovernmental policy actors who responded to the question, 85.7% of the combined sample indicated that they formed coalitions to influence state reading policy. Furthermore, more than 3 times as many respondents in the combined sample stated that they "frequently" formed coalitions than they "never" formed coalitions. ANOVA indicated that there was no significant difference in how often groups reported forming coalitions across states.

Research Question 2:   Number of Partners

Table 1.2 indicates the average number of collaborative partners for policy actors in each state. Columns 2, 3, and 4 represent the mean and standard deviation for all policy actors, government actors only, and non-

Table 1.1.   Reading Policy Coalitional Activity of Nongovernmental Policy Actors

| State | Frequency[a] | | | |
	Never	Occasionally	Sometimes	Frequently
California (N = 30)	20.0%	13.3%	26.7%	40.0%
Connecticut[b] (N = 16)	18.8%	31.3%	18.8%	31.3%
Michigan (N = 25)	8.0%	20.0%	12.0%	60.0%
Utah[b] (N = 13)	7.7%	30.8%	7.7%	53.8%
Total (N = 84)	14.3%	21.4%	17.9%	46.4%

a.   When more than one individual was interviewed to represent a single policy actor, we computed an average rating. When the average rating did not exactly correspond to a category (i.e., never, occasionally, sometimes, and frequently), we rounded up to the nearest extant category.
b.   Some rows may not sum to 100% due to rounding.

Table 1.2.   Average Number of Collaborative Partners

| State | Actors | | | | | |
| | All | | Government | | Nongovernmental | |
	Unadjusted	Adjusted	Unadjusted	Adjusted	Unadjusted	Adjusted
California N = 39	16.21 (8.81)	.43	25.50 (6.57)	.67	14.52 (8.14)	.38
Connecticut N = 21	7.33 (4.37)	.37	15.00 (4.24)	.75	6.53 (3.61)	.33
Michigan N = 29	10.34 (6.86)	.37	19.80 (2.17)	.71	8.38 5.74	.30
Utah N = 22	7.59 (4.35)	.36	13.00 (3.81)	.62	6.00 (3.06)	.29
Total N = 111	11.29 (7.77)	.38	19.28 (6.76)	.65	9.74 (6.99)	.33

Note: Standard deviation in parentheses.

governmental actors only, respectively. As shown in Table 1.2, policy actors formed coalitions with many policy actors, on average 11 different actors when we did not adjust for network size. However, when we adjusted for network size, policy actors collaborated on average with 38% of the other actors in their state network. Moreover, once we accounted network size, governmental actors had more collaborative interaction than nongovernmental actors—more than double the number of relation-ships than nongovernmental actors in all states except California. One-way analysis of variance indicated that there was no significant difference in the number of different partners policy actors possessed across states.

Research Question 3:   Nature of Reading Policy Coalitions

Three key themes emerged from the interview data. First, alliances, regardless of the number of actors involved, tended to fall into six gen-eral categories: government-sponsored coalitions, derivative coalitions, academic collaboration, academic consulting, nontraditional actor-cen-tered alliances, and corporate partnerships. Second, coalitions varied in size, scope, membership, and activity. Lastly, government activity and previous interaction between policy actors facilitated alliance formation.

Government-Sponsored Coalition

In the first type of coalition, the government-sponsored coalition, state agencies (i.e., state board of education, state department of education, state legislature, and office of the governor) initiated and funded alliances with other government agencies as well as with nongovernmental actors with constituencies interested in the creation, implementation, evalua-tion, or modification of reading policy. In this type of coalition—often titled task force, committees, advisory boards, councils, commissions, pan-els, and partnerships—representatives of the government held the pri-mary leadership or coordinating role. In some instances, to achieve pluralism in terms of both the types of groups represented and their pol-icy preferences, government sponsors deliberately selected coalition members from a wide range of constituencies. As shown in Table 1.3, one particular prominent and diverse government-sponsored alliance was the coalition responsible for establishing the direction of reading policy in the state.

A case in point, the State Superintendent of Public Instruction-Spon-sored California Reading Task Force detailed in Table 1.4, consisted of 27 members from a wide range of stakeholders. This diverse task force included teachers, administrators, reading specialists, foundations, and businesses. A representative from a California administrators association spoke of the ideological diversity among the members of the California Reading Task Force: "She [former State Superintendent of Public Instruc-tion, Delaine Eastin] had two chairs that were different in their approaches. It was a very eclectic group. I mean, we had great difficulty

Table 1.3.   Government-initiated Reading Policy Coalitions

State	Name	Initiator	Outcome
		Coalition	
California	California Reading Task Force (27)	Convened by former State Superintendent of Public Instruction Delaine Eastin	Every Child a Reader (1995)
Connecticut	Early Reading Success Panel (31)	Mandated by state legislature	Connecticut's Blueprint for Reading Achievement: The Report of the Early Reading Success Panel (2000)
Michigan	Governor's Reading Plan Advisory Council (11)	Convened by former Governor John Engler	Recommendations to the Superintendent of Public Instruction for the Governor's Reading Plan.

Notes: The number of members in the coalition is in the parentheses. The Utah Commission on Literacy was formed after data collection for this study had been completed.

reaching agreement.... There were members from all of the different perspectives."

A Connecticut state legislature noted a similar theme of diversity with Connecticut's Early Success Reading Panel:

> I think by putting together this reading panel where we literally found the most ardent whole language supporter, the most ardent phonemic awareness supporter and put them all in a room with a bunch of people in between.... I think that did make everybody grapple with it [reading policy].

A policy actor from the Michigan Department of Education made a similar remark about John Engler's and his representatives' deliberate attempt at diversity for the Governor's Reading Plan Advisory Council:

> They also wanted to make sure that they were not only getting traditional academics but were touching on things like somebody who was versed in reading recovery or somebody who was not quite in, if you will, the main stream, but who was at least getting some sort of results.

Whether the group was pluralistic because the government sought to include a wide array of policy perspectives in the decision-making process, to thwart potential criticisms of exclusivity, or to obtain legitimacy cannot be ascertained from the interviews.

Table 1.4.   Members of the California Reading Task Force

Name	Affiliation
William Lynch, Cochair	President, William D. Lynch Foundation for Children
Bertha Pendleton, Cochair	Superintendent, San Diego City Unified School District
Harriet Borson	California State PTA
Ann Bowers	Noyce Foundation
Own Boyle	Professor, San Jose State University
Robert Climo	Vice President, TRW, Inc.
Barbara Cline	Senior Vice President, Public Affairs, Sony Pictures Entertainment
Linda Davis	Deputy Superintendent, San Francisco Unified School District
Linda Diamond	Senior Analyst, RPP International, Inc.
Carol Dixon	Senior Lecturer, University of California Santa-Barbara
Allen Felton	Teacher, North Davis Elementary School
Bill Furry	Liaison, Governor's Office of Child Development and Education (now the Office of the Secretary of Education)
Diana Garchow	Teacher, Highland Elementary School, Bakersfield
Jerry Hume	Member, California State Board of Education
Marion Joseph	Community Member, Menlo Park
Carol Katzman	Administrator, Beverly Hills Unified School District
Adria Klein	President-elect, California Reading Association
Marvin Locke	Superintendent, Tehama County Office of Education
Fannie Preston	Dean, St. Mary's College
Dolores Rains	School Board Member, Pleasant Valley School District
Rosalia Salinas	President-elect, California Association of Bilingual Educators
William Schmidt	Superintendent, Lone Pine Unified School District
Maria Souza	Parent, Discovery Bay
Stanley Swartz	Professor, California State University, San Bernardino
Ruth Tofsted	Teacher, Parsons Junior High School, Redding
Jerry Treadway	Vice-Chair, State Curriculum Development and Supplemental Materials Commission
Jean Williams	Principal, Kirk Elementary School Fresno

Source: Every child a reader: The report of the California Reading Task Force, 1995, by California Department of Education, Sacramento: California Department of Education, pp. v-vi.

Participants also viewed these diverse policy coalitions as a valuable channel for communication and a means of participation in reading policymaking. A Connecticut legislator explained: "It was through this panel that most people had input: came in and listened, had discussions, and submitted written comment and it was, everybody's philosophies I think were taken into account." Policy actors also believed that these policy coalitions signified a preoccupation with the issue of reading, increased the visibility of the issue, and indicated that the government was addressing students' reading performance. A representative from a California government agency noted the importance of the California Reading Task Force, remarking: "It was right after the superintendent's reading task force delivered their report, *Every Child A Reader*. At that point, I think all of the government's agencies involved with teachers decided there was something we really needed to do." A California reading professor and researcher remarked of the importance of the task force: "That led to the formation of a reading task force.... That gave it prominence." A representative from the Michigan Department of Education explained similarly of the Governor's Reading Plan Advisory Council:

> They wanted enough academics and enough educators on the committee that in fact they would say, not so much this committee would bless things, but that the committee would at least send up a warning flag if in fact there was something that was way out.

A Connecticut legislature explained how the Connecticut Early Reading Success Panel signified that reading was being addressed:

> We put that in our state law and to create a Reading Panel might be the way to eventually get to something that would tell us what was best practice and that we could then turn that into curriculum, get a little bit out of the phonics/whole word fight and begin to have something that was functional rather than ideological. And that's what happened.

Derivative Coalition

The second type of coalition occurring in state reading policy issue networks was the derivative coalition. Derivative coalitions were offshoots of large coalitions already in place. Stable coalitions formed by traditional educational groups (e.g., teachers associations, parent teacher associations, and administration associations) during the past few decades to address K-12 budget issues also functioned as a forum to exchange ideas about a variety of educational issues and allowed members to build or maintain relationships with colleagues. As indicated in Table 1.5, these coalitions included the teachers associations, administrative groups, the school board associations, school personnel organizations, and the state parent and teacher association. Executive directors or presidents of the organizations attended the meetings, and the chief state school officer or a representative from the state office of education were either members of the umbrella coalition or frequently attended meetings. As reading

Table 1.5.   Stable Educational Coalitions

Coalition	Members
California Education Coalition	The California Teachers Association The Association of California School Administrators The California Association of School Business Officials The California County Superintendents Educational Services Association The California Federation of Teachers (AFT-AFL-CIO) The California School Boards Association The California State Parent Teacher Association The California School Employees Association The Service Employees International Union, AFL-CIO
Connecticut Coalition for Public Education	Connecticut Association of Boards of Education Connecticut Association of Public School Superintendents The American Federation of Teachers, Connecticut The Connecticut Educators Association Connecticut Federation of School Administrators Connecticut Association of Schools The Connecticut State Parent Teacher Association Elementary and Middle School Principals Assoc. of Connecticut Connecticut Association of Schools
The Education Alliance of Michigan	Michigan Association of School Boards/Michigan Foundation for Education Leadership Michigan Education Association Michigan Business Leaders for Education Excellence Michigan Association of School Boards Michigan Association of Secondary School Principals Michigan Community College Association Association of Independent Colleges and Universities of Michigan Michigan Association of School Administrators Michigan Association of Intermediate School Administrators Michigan School Business Officials Michigan Parent Teacher Student Association Michigan Association of Public School Academies Michigan Elementary and Middle School Principals Association Michigan Federation of Teachers & School Related Personnel Michigan State University College of Education, K-12 Outreach Presidents Council, State Universities of Michigan Middle Cities Education Association Michigan Association of NonPublic Schools
Utah Education Coalition	Utah School Superintendents Association Utah Education Association Utah Parent and Teachers Association Utah Association of Secondary School Principals Association Utah School Boards Association, Utah Association of Elementary School Principals Utah School Employees Association

became a key issue on the educational policy agenda, these longstanding coalitions either undertook the issue of reading themselves or created ad hoc committees to address the issue of reading. Members of the traditional coalition would also develop smaller collaborative efforts with other members. Coalitions that result from these longstanding alliances are derivative coalitions.

Academic Partnerships and Academic Consulting

The third and fourth classifications concern reading professors and researchers—academic partnerships and academic consulting. Academic partnerships involved collegial joint-collaboration on special projects (e.g., reading centers) and scholarly endeavors (e.g., journal article). Academic consulting, in contrast, involved reading researchers partnering with organizations that required their expertise. Each state had numerous internal and external reading specialists engaged in the policy process. Internal reading pundits were affiliated with a college, university, or research groups in the state. External researchers were associated with higher education institutions or research organizations outside of the state.

Prominent researchers whose ideas supported preferred policies were well known by policy actors, and their research was often cited as evidence to validate proposed policies. Government officials sought reading specialists to testify at hearings of the state boards and state legislature. Researchers also participated in state task force or commissions, presented research, and collaborated with state departments of education. In Connecticut, for example, one external reading researcher, Marilyn Adams, and four internal reading specialists, Mary Anne Doyle (University of Connecticut), Anne Fowler (Haskins Laboratories), Pat Kleine (Eastern Connecticut State University) and Louise Spear-Swerling (Southern Connecticut State University) served on the Early Reading Success Panel. In California, Douglas Carnine and Edward Kame'enui of the University of Oregon developed the English and Language Arts Frameworks, and Louisa Moats, another external consultant, worked with the Sacramento Office of Education to devise plans for professional development that corresponded to the frameworks. In Utah, the state legislature even went so far to establish a partnership with reading researchers that they funded a reading center at the University of Utah.

Administrative and legislative agencies were not the only actors that sought out the advice of academics. Educational interest groups would invite academic scholars to present their work at conferences or professional development programs. Not all academics, however, were viewed as desirable candidates for the coalitions. Both government officials and interest groups commonly marginalized the research and advocacy efforts of researchers whose perspectives challenged the prevailing ideas. In some instances, policy actors challenged the scholarly integrity of the work of rival academics.

Nontraditional-Actor Centered and Corporate Partnerships

In the fifth and sixth categories—nontraditional-actor centered and corporate partnerships—nontraditional policy actors (e.g., citizen groups, single-issue professional education groups, and foundations) are central figures in the alliance, often initiating, coordinating, and funding the alliance. In corporate partnerships, corporations and foundations initiate partnerships with the government or school districts and fund programs that sponsor the policies or issues they support. In California, The David and Lucile Packard Foundation, for example, provided considerable funding to the Sacramento County School District's reading program, Reading Lions. The Los Angeles Times collaborated with the state department of education and several prominent reading scholars to present a reading conference for parents and educators—Read by Nine. The READY kits in Michigan received substantial funding and in-kind support from numerous corporations, including Kmart, Daimler-Chrysler, Ford Motor Company, and Walt Disney.

Coalition Diversity

Alliances across all group types varied in size, duration, scope, and activity. Coalitions could range from less than 5 members to greater than 20 members. Most reading policy alliances were ad hoc, lapsing when the purpose of the alliance had been achieved. Coalitions not only attended to the issue of reading or reading policy in general, but also focused on particular aspects of reading, including: curriculum, instructional materials, professional development, teacher education, standards, assessment, accountability, English-language learners, and students with learning disabilities. Coalitions in state reading policy networks also engaged in a wide variety of activities, including: writing reports, conducting research investigations, summarizing research, making policy recommendations, drafting specific policy, evaluating programs, submitting applications for federal grants, cosponsoring events, coauthoring articles, offering professional development programs, and providing feedback about current policies. In some instances, the primary pursuit of the alliance involved exchanging information about relevant research and proposed policies and their potential impact on students, teachers, teaching, and teacher education programs.

Facilitators of Coalitions

Previous interaction and government activity greatly facilitated alliance formation. Policy actors commonly formed alliances with those policy actors with whom they had previous contact. As policy actors, especially traditional educational and government actors, interacted with one another on a variety of educational issues, projects, and events, they established longstanding acquaintanceships, friendships, and collegial relationships. These interactions promoted collaborative activity within state reading policy issue networks. Additionally, the notion of revolving doors—officials in the public sector obtaining jobs with the private sector—is evident in state reading policy communities, particularly California (e.g., Gary K. Hart, Bill Honig, and Glen Thomas). Former state officials or employees would form coalitions with the contacts that they acquired during their tenure with the government. Government activity also promoted alliance formation in state reading policy issue networks. In particular, as government agencies formed panels to apply for federal grants and formulate policy, policy actors had the opportunity to become acquainted with other policy actors and foster relationships that led to future collaboration. Finally, government activity (e.g., holding hearings, proposing policy changes) mobilized concerned policy actors to collaborate in an effort to influence the decision-making process, promote their own policies, or challenge government solutions.

DISCUSSION AND CONCLUSIONS

Summary of Findings

The findings of this study show that both governmental and nongovernmental state reading policy actors engage in a wide variety of collaborative alliances as they seek to influence policy outcomes. These results are congruent with the larger literature on coalitions, which finds that coalitional activity is increasing across all U.S. policy domains (Hojnacki, 1997; Hula, 1999; Nownes & Freeman, 1998; Schlozman & Tierney, 1986). This study also demonstrates that educational policy actors are not only frequently forming coalitions, but are also working with numerous partners to achieve their policy objectives. Lastly, the study shows that alliances are disparate in character (i.e., size, scope, and activity) and can be differentiated by how the coalitions emerge.

Limitations

This analysis is limited by the fact that the issue analyzed is a particularly salient issue—involving numerous nongovernmental and governmental actors, heightened state and national media and public attention, considerable fiscal resources, and governmental agenda decision-making status. If interest groups behave in ways to adapt to their policy environments, then their coalition activity will depend on the issue context (Browne, 1990; Heinz, Laumann, Nelson, Salisbury, & Nelson, 1993, Laumann & Knoke, 1987; Loomis, 1986; Salisbury, Heinz, & Laumann, 1992; Schlozman & Tierney, 1986). Also absent from this study is an examination of how these coalitions affect policy outcomes. However, it is presumed that to some extent coalitional activity increases the likelihood of a policy actor achieving their aims. Establishing a relationship between coalitional activity and influence is difficult because it is a considerable empirical challenge to attribute influence to a specific influence tactic while controlling for all factors that might affect a policy outcome (Baumgartner & Leech, 1998).

Implications

The limitations notwithstanding, this study's findings have important implications for understanding coalitions in educational policy. A few researchers (e.g., Kaplan & Usdan, 1992) have urged educational professionals to join coalitions or risk further diminishing their influence on educational policy. However, the results of this study indicate that educational professionals are frequently involved in a wide variety of coalitions with many partners, including the government, who is generating policy initiatives. In brief, the policy environment is crowded not with individual policy actors competing for influence, but coalitions of policy actors competing for influence. Coalitions are vogue for twenty-first century educational politics. With coalitions being the norm for political activity, we need to discover which forms of coalitions are most and least effective and under what conditions? We also need to understand how the intent, actions, and influences of coalitions differ from the pursuits of policy actors when they act on their own (cf. Hula, 1999). We also need to understand the internal dynamics of coalitions, for example, the level of participation of educational professionals in the coalitions and their overall influence within the coalition. That is, we need determine to what extent the level of participation of educational professionals in coalitions is nominal or authentic and what factors determine authentic participation (cf. Hojnacki, 1998). Addressing these and similar questions in the future will further shed light on the role of coalitions in educational policy.

Furthermore, given the large number of policy actors, the diversity in group types, and the differences in resources and goals, as well as the broad definition of coalitions utilized in this study, it comes as no surprise coalitions exists in different forms. Though, existing research indicates that coalitions vary along a range of dimensions, such as longevity, location in the policy process, and leadership (Berry, 1997; Loomis, 1986); however, limited attention has been given to categorizing coalitions by how they emerge. By distinguishing categories of coalitions by how they develop, this study generates new questions and sets the stage for theory development on the formation of coalitions, coalition leadership, and coalition membership within the field of policy in general, and state educational policy in particular. Certainly, it is presumed that the types of coalitions revealed through this research study are not exhaustive and other dimensions will be identified.

Future Research

The next steps in understanding coalitions involve answering the who and with whom questions. That is, we must investigate who is joining coalitions and whom are they selecting as alliance partners. We must move from simply describing coalitional activity and issue networks towards predicting the formation of alliances. Future research should also examine the relationship between coalitions and the influence of the groups in the coalition over policy outcomes.

Another fruitful avenue for investigation involves exploring the different forms of coalitions. Though scholars in recent decades have begun to identify the different types of coalitions that exist (e.g., short-term versus long-term and formal versus informal), they have yet to explain how the effects of various explanatory variables for coalition formation vary when we account for different types of coalitions. A series of questions might be raised about the different forms of coalitions. How do actors' policy goals affect the type of coalition they join? How do actors' resources influence their decision to join different types of coalitions? To what extent does location or embeddedness in the network structure influence the types of coalitions in which policy actors participate? How does the policy environment facilitate or prevent the creation of certain types of coalitions? Which types of coalitions are most or least effective and when?

NOTE

1. An earlier version of this article was presented at the 2005 American Educational Research Association Meeting in Montréal, Canada. Data for this study come from The State Reading Policy Project (SRPP) affiliated with The University of Michigan. Two granting agencies sponsored the SRPP's research. The Field Initiated Studies Program, PR/Award R305T990369, Office of Educational Research and Improvement (OERI), U.S. Department of Education supported the research in five states—California, Connecticut, Michigan, North Carolina, and Texas. The Major Grants Program, Grant No. 200000269, Spencer Foundation funded parallel efforts in Alabama, Indiana, Maine, and Utah. The content does not necessarily reflect the views or policies of the OERI, the Department, any other agency of the U.S. government, or the Spencer Foundation.

REFERENCES

Baumgartner, F. R., & Jones, B. D. (1993). *Agendas and instability in American politics*. Chicago: The University of Chicago Press.

Baumgartner, F. R., & Leech, B. L. (1998). *Basic interests*. Princeton, NJ: Princeton University Press.

Baumgartner, F. R., & Walker, J. L. (1989). Educational policymaking and the interest group structure in France and the United States. *Comparative Politics, 21*(3), 273-288.

Berry, J. M. (1997). *The interest group society* (3rd ed). New York: Longman.

Browne, W. P. (1990). Organized interests and their issue niches: A search for pluralism in a policy domain. *Journal of Politics, 52*, 477-509.

California Department of Education. (1995). *Every child a reader: The report of the California Reading Task Force*. Sacramento: California Department of Education.

Carlos, L., & Kirst, M. (1997, December). *California curriculum policy in the 1990s: "We don't have to be in front to lead."* Paper presented at the annual meeting of the American Educational Research Association, Chicago, IL. Retrieved December 12, 2004, from http://www.wested.org/policy/pubs/full_text/pb_ft_cacuric.htm

Cibulka, J. (2001). The changing role of interest groups in education: Nationalization and the new politics of education productivity. *Educational Policy, 15*(1), 12-4.

Donahue, P. L., Daane, M. C., & Grigg, W. S. (2003). *The nation's report card: Reading highlights 2003* (NCES 2004-452). Washington, DC: U.S. Department of Education, Institute for Education Sciences, National Center for Education Statistics.

Fuhrman, S. H. (Ed.) (2001). Introduction. In *From the Capitol to the classroom: Standards-based reform in the states: The One Hundredth Yearbook of the National Society for the Study of Education, Part 2* (pp. 1-12). Chicago: University of Chicago Press.

Gittell, M. (1994). School reform in New York and Chicago: Revisiting the ecology of local games. *Urban Affairs Quarterly, 30,* 136-51.

Gittell, M., & McKenna, L. (1999). Redefining education regimes and reform. *Urban Education, 34*(3), 268-291.

Goodman, L. A. (1961). Snowballing sampling. *Annals of Mathematical Statistics, 32,* 148-17.

Heclo, H. (1978). Issues networks and the executive establishment. In A. King (Ed.), *The new American political system* (pp. 87-124). Washington DC: American Enterprise Institute.

Heinz, J. P., Laumann, E. O., Nelson, R. L., & Salisbury, R. H. (1993). *The hollow core: Private interests in national policy making.* London: Harvard University Press.

Hojnacki, M. (1997). Interest groups' decisions to join alliances or work alone. *American Journal of Political Science, 41,* 61-87.

Hojnacki, M. (1998). Organized interest' advocacy behavior in alliances. *Political Research Quarterly, 51*(2), 437-457.

Hula, K. W. (1999). *Lobbying together: Interest group coalitions in legislative politics.* Washington, DC: Georgetown University Press.

Kaplan, G. R., & Usdan, M. D. (1992). The changing look of education's policy networks. *Phi Delta Kappan, 73*(9), 664-672.

Karper, J. H., & Boyd, W. L. (1988). Interest groups and the changing environment of state educational policymaking: Developments in Pennsylvania. *Educational Administration Quarterly, 24*(1), 21-54.

Kingdon, J. W. (1995). *Agendas, alternatives, and public policies* (2nd ed.). New York: HarperCollins.

Kirst, M. W., Meister, G., & Rowley, S. R. (1984). Policy issue networks: Their influence on state policymaking. *Policy Studies Journal, 13,* 247-263.

Knoke, D. (1990). Organizing for collective action: *The Political Economies of Associations.* Hawthore, NY: Aldine de Gruyter.

Knoke, D., & Burleigh, F. (1989). Collective action in national policy domains: constraints, cleavages, and policy outcomes. *Research in Political Sociology, 4,* 187-208.

Laumann, E. O., & Knoke, D. (1987). *The organizational state: Social choice in national policy domains.* Madison: University of Wisconsin Press.

Loomis, B. A. (1986). Coalitions of interests: Building bridges in the balkanized state. In A. J. Cigler & B. A. Loomis (Eds.), *Interest group politics* (2nd ed., pp. 258-274). Washington, DC: Congressional Quarterly Press.

Malen, B. (2001). Generating interest in interest groups. *Educational Policy, 15,* 168-186.

Mazzoni, T. L. (1995). State policymaking and school reform: Influences and influentials. In J. D. Scribner & D. H. Clayton. (Eds.), *The study of educational politics* (pp. 53-73). Washington, DC: Falmer.

Mazzoni, T. L. (2000). State politics and school reform: The first decade of the "education excellence" movement. In N. D. Theobald & B. Malen (Eds.), *Balancing local control and state responsibility for K-12 education* (pp. 147-196). Larchmont, NY: Eye on Education.

Mazzoni, T. L., & Malen, B. (l985). Mobilizing constituency pressure to influence state education policy making. *Educational Administration Quarterly, 21*(2), 91-116.

McDaniel, J. E. (2001). *The shaping of national reading policy: Using a structural approach to examine the politics of reading*. Unpublished doctoral dissertation, University of Michigan, Ann Arbor.

McDaniel, J. E., Sims, C. H., & Miskel, C. G. (2001). The national reading policy arena: Policy actors and perceived influence. *Education Policy, 15*(1), 92-114.

Miles, M. B., & Huberman, A. M. (1994). *Qualitative data analysis: An expanded sourcebook* (2nd ed.). Thousand Oaks, CA: Sage.

Mintrom, M., & Vergari, S. (1998). Policy networks and innovation diffusion: The case of state education reforms, *The Journal of Politics, 60*(1), 126-148.

Miskel, C. G., Coggshall, J. G., DeYoung, D. A., Osguthorpe, R. D., Shepley, T. V., Song, M., & Young, T. V. (2003). *Final report: Reading policy in the states: Interest and processes*. Unpublished manuscript.

Mitchell, D. E. (1988). Education politics and policy: The state level. In N. J. Boyan (Ed.), *Handbook of research on educational administration* (pp. 453-466). New York: Longman.

Nownes, A., & Freeman, P. (1998). Interest group activities in the states. *Journal of Politics, 60*, 86-112.

Ravitch, D. (2000). *Left back: A century of failed school reforms*. New York: Simon and Schuster.

Salisbury, R. H., Heinz, J. P., Laumann, E. O., & Nelson R. L. (1987). Who works with whom? Interest group alliances and opposition. *American Political Science Review, 81*, 1217-1234.

Schlozman, K. L., & Tiernery, J. T. (1986). *Organized interests and American democracy*. New York: Harper & Row.

Scientific Software Development. (2001). *ATLAS.TI: The knowledge workbench Version WIN 4.2 (Build 059)*. Berlin, Germany: Author.

Shepley, T. V. (2003). *A tale of two giants: Coalitions and policy learning in state reading subsystems*. Unpublished doctoral dissertation, University of Michigan.

Song, M. (2003). *Influence in the reading policy domain: A cross-state social network analysis*. Unpublished doctoral dissertation, University of Michigan, Ann Arbor.

Song, M., & Miskel, C. G. (2004, April). *Exploring the structural properties of the state reading policy domain using network visualization techniques*. Paper presented at the annual meeting of the American Educational Research Association, San Diego, CA.

Thomas, C., & Hrebenar, R. (1992). Changing patterns of interest group activity: A regional perspective. In M. P. Petracca (Ed.), *The politics of interests*. Boulder, CO: Westview.

Young, T. V. (2005). *Understanding coalitions in state educational policy: The selection of alliance partners in reading policy issue networks*. Unpublished doctoral dissertation, University of Michigan, Ann Arbor.

Young, T. V., & Miskel, C. G. (2002, April). *A structural approach to understanding influence in California educational policy: An application of social network analysis to a state educational policy domain.* Paper presented at the annual meeting of the American Educational Research Association, New Orleans, LA.

Young, T. V., & Miskel, C. G. (2004, April*). Interest groups' lobbying activities in state reading policy.* Paper presented at the annual meeting of the American Educational Research Association, San Diego, CA.

Young, T. V., Shepley, T. V., Miskel, C. G., & Song, M. (2002, December). *Reading from the top: The role of Governors in reading policy agenda setting.* Paper presented at the annual meeting of the National Reading Conference, Miami, FL.

CHAPTER 2

THE DEVIL MADE ME DO IT

The Genesis of Extreme Advocacy Coalitions in State Reading Policy[1]

Thomas V. Shepley

The debate surrounding the emergence of reading instruction as part of the policy process over the past decade has included such strong accusations and powerful invectives that certain reading policies and instructional practices have been demonized. Policy scholars have suggested that these devilish characterizations are correlated with policy coalition formation and hence are a cause for the creation of advocacy coalitions. This study seeks to identify how well this concept, know as the "devil shift," explains the formation of advocacy coalitions. Interview data were collected from elite policy actors in two states. To assess the concept of the devil shift, a comparative case study approach to analyzing state reading policy subsystems was used. Findings suggest ample evidence that the devil shift does exist in the most extreme nondominant coalitions. However, data for both the California and Texas reading subsystems show that not all nondominant coalitions show evidence of the devil shift in their views. Though the devil shift fails to completely explain the genesis of advocacy coalitions, the concept is certainly a relevant way for us to understand how those on the furthest points of a policy issue feel about, or at least characterize the dominant coalition.

Contemporary Issues in Educational Policy and School Outcomes, 27–50
Copyright © 2006 by Information Age Publishing
All rights of reproduction in any form reserved.

PROBLEM, RESEARCH PERSPECTIVES, AND IMPORTANCE

The argument over how best to teach a child to read has a long history within the education community. The code-emphasis camp in this debate has tended to focus on the importance of the direct, systematic instruction of letter sounds in a hierarchical manner. Those in support of a meaning-emphasis approach to teaching reading spend more time on whole-word instruction, placing the focus on text content instead of on the hierarchical aspect of phoneme or letter-to-sound instruction. While traces of this conflict actually go back for several centuries (Aukerman, 1971), over the last few decades or so this Great Debate (Chall, 1996) about how to teach children to read has become surprisingly heated and acrimonious, turning an important dialogue into a Reading War (Ravitch, 2000).

While there is some evidence that tensions over the Reading Wars have been reduced by a focus on agreement within the reading community concerning a balanced approach to reading instruction (Song, Miskel, Young, & McDaniel, 2000), the Reading Wars opened up a whole new front in the 1990s. As reading became politicized and a focus for policy initiatives, reading instruction became a part of the policy debate. Currently, there are multiple dimensions to this complicated field surrounding reading policy, including historical (Adams, 1998; Balmuth, 1982; Chall, 1996; Ravitch, 2000), paradigmatic (Kamil, 1995; Mosenthal, 1995; Stanovich, 1990), research oriented (Flippo, 1998, 1999a, 1999b), pedagogical (Chall, 1996; Ravitch, 2000), sociopolitical (Wolfe & Poynor, 2001) and policy process (Shepley, 2003) aspects.

The debate surrounding the emergence of reading instruction as part of the policy process has been heralded by strong accusations and powerful invectives resulting in the demonization of certain reading policies and instructional practices (Coles, 2002; Moats, 2002; Simms & Miskel, 2000; Taylor, 1998). Given the ubiquitous nature of these aspersions in the policy debate, it would seem logical that these negative perceptions regarding policy actors or coalitions with differing policy positions could be an important part in understanding the policy making process generally. Sabatier and Jenkins-Smith (1993, 1999) have suggested that these devilish characterizations are correlated with policy coalition formation and hence are a cause for the creation of a policy coalition.

Advocacy Coalition Framework

Sabatier and Jenkins-Smith proposed in 1993 and revised in 1999 a generalized and testable theory of policy change called the Advocacy Coalition Framework (ACF). This framework focuses on understanding policy change through subdividing the larger policy community into sub-systems—those actors that are involved in a particular area of policy. Within subsystems, policy actors from various and diverse backgrounds group themselves into coalitions over long periods of time, glued together by similar beliefs. Each coalition works within a subsystem to put into place policies that reflect those beliefs. To enhance their efforts, coalition members learn about the policy area through research findings and real-world experiences.

The utility of the ACF has been tested in such disparate arenas as environmental, energy, airline, education and federal communications policy and has been found to be helpful in explaining policy change in not only North America, but in Europe, Asia, and Australia as well (Sabatier & Jenkins-Smith, 1999). Generally, these studies found that the ACF approach to grouping policy actors with similar policy beliefs into advocacy coalitions was a useful way of analyzing the policymaking process. None of these studies though examined in any depth the mechanism behind the genesis of advocacy coalitions within a given subsystem. As Schlager (1995) and Schlager and Blomquist (1996) have pointed out, there are actually many barriers that inhibit policy actors from working together in coalitions. These include the cost in time and resources spent on coming to a consensus decision, the difficulty in finding a policy that addresses the varying needs of coalition members and the temptation for each member of a coalition to be a free rider—to coast on the coattails of others, as it were. Given these barriers, why is it likely that policy actors with similar beliefs would work together to begin with? This posses a challenge to the foundational concepts contained within the ACF, namely that policy change can best be understood by viewing actors as members of advocacy coalitions.

Coalition Formation and the Devil Shift

In an attempt to explain the genesis of advocacy coalitions and hence bolster the framework, Sabatier and Jenkins-Smith (1999) hypothesize that aside from sharing resources, there are other significant reasons why policy actors might move beyond the difficulties of creating a coalition. One powerful reason to work in coalitions is simple fear of an opposing group's power. Sabatier, Hunter, and McLaughlin (1987) asserted that policy actors perceive what can be termed as a "devil shift" among actors with differing belief systems. What this means is that "actors perceive opponents to be stronger and more 'evil' than they actually are" (p. 450). This gives policy actors with like beliefs an incentive to work together, in order to overcome their "devilish" opponents.

Drawing on Sabatier, Hunter, and McLaughlin's (1987) concept of the devil shift, Sabatier and Jenkins-Smith (1999) posited that short-term coalition building is more likely to take place if nondominant coalition members (those not in a direct position to make policy) see their opponents, the dominant coalition members (those in a direct position to make policy), as very powerful or feel that the dominant coalition will be able to strike a near-fatal blow to their cause. Hence, Sabatier and Jenkins-Smith essentially attempt to explain some aspects of coalition genesis through the concept of the devil shift. This concept of the devil shift, while quite provocative and supported by anecdotal evidence, remains virtually untested in the policy realm as it relates to the ACF. Hence, this study examines this concept of the devil shift as a means for understanding the genesis of advocacy coalitions. With this purpose in mind, this study will be guided by the following general research question:

How well does the concept of the devil shift as part of the Advocacy Coalition Framework describe and explain the formation of advocacy coalitions?

STATE READING POLICY SUBSYSTEMS AS A TESTING GROUND

In order to assess the devil shift as an explanation for coalition formation, I chose state level reading policy subsystems as a testing ground. The topic surrounding reading policy generally and the beliefs specific to the policy field have been an area of contention for quite some time. As Aukerman (1971) has suggested, reading teachers, theorists, and scholars in the English-speaking world have for several centuries sought the most effective method for teaching children to read. Two methods of reading instruction have been the predominant approaches, one known as the code-emphasis, or phonics, approach and the other as the meaning-emphasis, or whole language, approach. Which of these instructional methods is most effective or appropriate for advances in childhood literacy has been a consistent aspect of the debate concerning reading for quite a long time.

Belief Differences in Reading Policy Subsystems

Up through the first half of the nineteenth century, reading was predominantly taught in the United States using a method that was based on instruction of phonic concepts—first teaching letter names, then letter sounds and later focusing on appropriate elocution (Ravitch, 2000; Smith, 1934). An alternate method of instruction was being advanced in

the United Statesby some of the educational reformers of the day, including Horace Mann. This whole-word method meant learning complete
words from full pieces of literature rather than learning letter sounds first.
As Ravitch (2000) contended, between 1845 and 1945, the use of the
whole-word method was slowly integrated into American reading instruction so that the sole use of the alphabetic method that characterized the
early part of the 1800s had pretty much died out by 1900. Chall (1996)
and Robinson (1987), however, argued that in the early part of the twentieth century, systematic phonics instruction was still being used in many
American classrooms, but that it was taught in combination with the
whole-word method, also known at that time as the look-say method.

With the publication of *Why Johnny Can't Read*, by Rudolph Flesch
(1955), reaction against the look-say or whole-word method became pronounced. Flesch's book, which lasted for 30 weeks on the nation's best-
sellers list, blamed the so-called literacy crisis of the 1950s on the use of
the look-say method. Flesch (1955) emphasized in no uncertain terms
that the look-say method was illogical and was the wrong way to teach
reading. As a solution to the reading problem in America, Flesch insisted
"systemic phonics is *the* way to teach reading" (p. 121, original emphasis).

At the height of these Reading Wars, the Carnegie Corporation com-
missioned Jeanne Chall to review all research in the area of reading
instruction and early reading methods (Adams, 1998; Chall, 1996; Ravitch, 2000). Chall's review concluded that direct decoding instruction
enhanced reading achievement. Even though Chall (1996) had warned
that all known reading methods produced some reading failure in children, by the late 1960s many texts adopted her recommendations concerning decoding instruction, shifting focus toward the instruction of
phonic concepts (Chall, 1996; Ravitch, 2000).

Shortly after Chall's review of the research, Frank Smith (1971) and
later Kenneth S. Goodman (1986) heralded the return of the whole-word
or look-say method, which they termed the Whole Language Philosophy.
Balmuth (1982) confirmed that Smith and Goodman's Whole Language
Philosophy was not a totally new idea but rather a direct descendant of
the earlier logographic approaches of whole-word and look-say. Defining
the Whole Language Philosophy has been a challenge to reading
researchers, partly because its proponents claim that it is more than a
reading method or approach; but rather they say it has theoretical and
political components as well (Edelsky, 1990). Bergeron's (1990) meta-
analysis and Moorman, Blanton, and McLaughlin's (1994) follow-up work
in defining whole language is very useful here. These researchers
reviewed works concerned with the Whole Language Philosophy to determine what the common aspects were. They noted that most whole language researchers point to the naturalness of reading and that literacy

instruction should enhance students' personal ownership of the text. Bergeron (1990) and Moorman et al. (1994) also emphasized that whole language practitioners resist the artificial instruction found in basal readers as well as any attempts by outside authorities to control the class curriculum. In addition, they suggested that beliefs on direct instruction of the alphabetic system vary from those who feel that this type of instruction is not necessary (Goodman, 1993; Weaver, 1994) to those who see it as a necessity for some students (Routman, 1996). Whole language instruction spread to many of the nation's classrooms through the late 1970s and into the 1980s.

There have been multiple attempts at calling a truce in the Reading Wars and an end to the Great Debate. Several studies into reading instruction have attempted to do this (Adams, 1998; Chall, 1996) with some success. This has led to a renewed battlefront, this time over the middle ground of the Reading Wars and attempts to define what has been termed a Balanced Approach. Pressley (1998) defines this as an approach that is somewhere between a bottom-up (traditional prophonics) approach to reading instruction and a top-down (whole language) one. According to Pressley, in this new approach these two constructs "are in balance" (p. 53). This attempt at a methodological solution to the Reading Wars suggests that direct instruction in phonemic awareness and phonics should be used in a systematic manner, but that the literate environment and ties between reading and writing supported by a whole language approach should be continued as well.

Which instructional technique is most effective in teaching young children to read continues to be a point of contention within reading policy communities across the United States. Researchers like Moats (2000) suggest that reading instruction that is based on the Whole Language Philosophy is at least in part responsible for poor reading achievement in the United States. She goes on to reject the call for a balanced approach, suggesting that this is simply whole language in disguise. Those researchers from the whole language camp, like Goodman (1998), deny this position, suggesting that the reading achievement levels of student in whole language classrooms are very high and that whole language has always been a balanced approach to reading instruction.

Changes in State Reading Policy Subsystems

These Reading Wars have played out in state subsystems all over the country. In the early 1990s, California policymakers and educators responded to the perception of a reading achievement problem by creating a whole host of reading policy programs and initiatives (California

Department of Education, 1995; Goodman, 1998). Nearly every branch and section of the California government dealing with education took part in the creation of these new reading policies. This broad effort to improve reading achievement was called the California Reading Initiative (CRI). During the late 1990s, Texas policymakers and educators built upon a long history of using education standards and testing by focusing on early reading as an area for investment and intervention. This led to the creation of the Texas Reading Initiative (TRI), the state model of school accountability and the student promotion policy known as the Texas Student Success Initiative (Brooks, 1997; Garner, 2000; Lindsay, 1997).

Strongly held policy beliefs concerning how best to teach reading were an intricate part of the new state policies in these two states. In California, the 1987 English Language-Arts Frameworks were largely seen as a whole language document. Legislation in California was passed requiring the use of phonics to teach reading, and the revised standards included required knowledge of decoding and phonics skills (Young, 2002). In Texas a similar transition took place, as a move toward more phonics-based instruction was encouraged by the office of the governor, the Texas Education Agency and the State Board of Education. The passage of the new state standards (TEKS), similar to changes in the California state reading standards, required knowledge of phonics skills and concepts (Shepley, 2002).

Testable Hypothesis

The extreme and vitriolic nature of the debate over the Reading Wars that has lasted for over a century (Balmuth, 1982) provides substantial evidence in the reading community for what Sabatier, Hunter, and McLaughlin (1987) called the devil shift. However, whether this aspect of the reading debate can be found in state reading policy subsystems is still unknown. While political sniping may take place in any field, for the devil shift to have importance in helping to explain the policy process as part of the ACF, it must be associated with nondominant coalition formation. Therefore, I propose to test the aspect of the ACF that incorporates the concept of the devil shift, in state reading policy subsystems. The nature and history of the debate between those who favor a whole-word (whole language) instructional method and those who favor a code-based (traditional phonics) approach leads to the following hypothesis:

Hypothesis 1:   Actors in state reading policy subsystems who are in the nondominant reading policy coalitions will characterize members of the dominant coalition as very powerful and likely to impose negative repercussions on members of the nondominant coalition.

METHODS

Sampling Procedures

The unit of analysis for this study was the state reading policy subsystems, specifically in California and Texas. Elite actors from the states of California and Texas were chosen to study for three of reasons. First, these two states are both large, with diverse student populations. In addition, both California and Texas have large urban, suburban, and rural populations. Taken together, this means that any viable educational reform initiative in California and Texas would have to be geared for a broad array of schools and student populations. Second, the education policies of California and Texas, because of the sheer size of these two educational markets, are known to influence how publishers construct the nation's textbooks. Education policy initiatives in these two states will likely influence state education policies across the nation, making California and Texas strategic in our understanding of reading policy creation across the country. Third, as Marshall and Rossman (1999) assert, it is beneficial to pick settings in which there is a high probability that data in the studied area will be found and accessed. California and Texas are two of a number of states that have initiated reform in reading policy in the past decade. However, both California and Texas have been the focus of research on reading reform. This research base provides a richer extant literature to draw from, compared to other states.

In order to delineate a sufficient policy subsystem for each state, a wide variety of policy actors who might have had an impact on reading policy were identified. Policy actors were defined as individuals working alone or in any one of the following formal or informal groups: (a) citizen groups, (b) educational associations, (c) educational institutions (e.g., K-12 school systems, higher education institutions), (d) government agencies, (e) labor unions, (f) the media, (g) noneducation associations, (h) philanthropic foundations, (i) private/for-profit firms, (j) think tanks, and (k) policy institutes.

To identify the initial sample our research group followed the procedures used by Heinz, Laumann, Nelson, and Salisbury (1993). Heinz et al. insist that individuals and groups should be selected because of their substantive concerns in setting policy. Through searches of published reports, the Internet, state archives, and newspapers, we generated initial lists of possible interviewees who had been active in state reading policy. Working with consultants knowledgeable about reading policy activities in the states, we augmented and refined these lists of interviewees. At least one individual from each of the identified interest groups or policy organizations was contacted for inclusion in the study. In addition, a snowballing (Kingdon, 1995) or sequential sampling (Heinz et al., 1993) technique was used. That is, during the interviews, individuals were asked to identify other key individuals and/or groups in the reading policy subsystem that had been omitted from the list of interviewees. Given this, the sample of policy actors was expanded to include these additional individuals and/or groups. The aim was to reach elite policy actors and their organizations in the reading policy community or those in close contact with elite policymakers who could serve as knowledgeable informants. The ultimate goal was to obtain a representative sample of the reading policy subsystems in California and Texas.

In California, representatives of 40 organizations (sometimes more than one per organization) and 6 individual actors who were acting on their own were identified as important members of the reading policy subsystem in that state. Of the 59 policy actors we contacted, 52 participated, yielding a response rate of 88%. In Texas, representatives of 42 organizations (again, sometimes more than one per organization) were identified as important members of the reading policy subsystem in that state. Of the 63 policy actors we contacted, 46 agreed to be interviewed, producing a 73% response rate. To utilize Song's (2003) and Shepley's (2003) work on the policy network in California to separate policy groups into dominant and nondominant coalitions for this study's hypothesis, alterations were made reducing the size of the sample. A total of 49 elite policy actor interviews from 37 policy organizations were used, including interviews from 13 government officials, 27 interest group members, 3 members of the media, and 6 individual actors. To separate Texas policy groups into dominant and nondominant coalitions, alterations to the Texas sample were made as well. A total of 44 elite policy actor interviews from 30 organizations were used, including interviews from 16 government officials, 27 interest group members, and 1 member of the media.

Data Collection and Management

Interview data were collected from individuals through three standard, open-ended schedules: policymakers, interest groups, and media.[2] Each potential interviewee was contacted by letter and asked to participate in the study. A letter was followed by a telephone call requesting an appointment for the interview. The interviews, generally lasting from 30 to 45 minutes, were conducted either by telephone or, when an appointment could be scheduled, in face-to-face meetings. The interviews were tape-recorded and transcribed, except for one interview in California that was conducted by e-mail and then was followed up by a phone interview for additional questions.

Interview data were digitized and stored in an electronic database. A computer software program called ATLAS.ti (Scientific Software Development, 2001) was used in building and indexing the interview database. A hermeneutic unit was created for each state to store the data related to that state's policy actor's interviews. Excel (Microsoft Corporation, 1999) was used in compiling the quantitative database. A spreadsheet was created for each state to store the data related to that state's policy actors. The interviews were assigned a number from 1 to 52 in California and 1 to 46 in Texas and will be referred to in the following sections as, for example, Texas Interview 12 or California Interview 7, abbreviated as (TX-12) and (CA-7), respectively.

The testable hypothesis of this study addresses the ACF's concept regarding the devil shift or nondominant groups expressing feelings concerning the dominant group. Responses to the following three interview questions often elicited the feelings of one policy actor about another policy actor or coalition of actors:

1. What groups or individuals have worked against you and your efforts with regard to state reading policy?
2. Which groups or individuals do you believe to be particularly influential?
3. What groups or individuals are least influential?

In this way, feelings about the dominant and nondominant coalitions were obtained from the interview data and triangulated with archival data collected on each respondent.

Narrative Coding Process

I coded each interview through the use of the computer program ATLAS.ti (Scientific Software Development, 2001). The dominant coalition was defined as the coalition in power when the interviews were conducted (Sabatier & McLaughlin, 1988). Song (2003) placed the actors in dominant and nondominant groups, equating policy actors in the core as members of the dominant coalition and members of the periphery as the nondominant coalition in each state. Shepley (2003) revised these groups for use in ACF studies based on their beliefs regarding reading instruction. The revisions resulted in a single dominant coalition in

Table 2.1.   Definitions and Narrative Examples for Devil Shift Codes

Coding Label	Coding Definition	Examples
DS About Dominant Members	Statements regarding members of the dominant coalition by members of the nondominant coalition.	"Jill Steward has vigorously attacked me many times in her columns." (CA-16)
DS About Dominant Policy	Statements made by members of the nondominant coalition characterizing the policy processes used by the dominant coalition	"I think that this reading by the third grade is a day late and a dollar short." (TX-21)

each state, but two nondominant coalitions in California and two nondominant coalitions in Texas. In the state of California, the three coalitions were identified and labeled by the researcher as the California Phonics-Leaning, Dominant (CP) Coalition, the California Balanced-Leaning, Nondominant (CB) Coalition, and the more extreme California Whole Language-Leaning, Nondominant (CWL) Coalition. In Texas, the three coalitions were identified as the Texas Phonics-Leaning Dominant (TP) Coalition, the Texas Balanced-Leaning, Nondominant (TB) Coalition and the more extreme Texas Pro-Phonics, Nondominant (TPP) Coalition.

Using these same divisions, I identified narrative statements in the interviews of elite policy actors that conveyed a complete thought related to the following coding topics: (a) characterizations of members of the dominant coalition by members of the nondominant coalitions and (b) characterizations of the policy processes used by the dominant coalition, made by members of the nondominant coalitions. Further definitions and examples of these coding topics are found in Table 2.1.

The narrative statement could be of any length, ranging from a sentence to a paragraph or two. To find information on any particular coding topic, I paid close attention to the questions discussed above but also searched for additional codable moments for each category topic throughout the interview. In addition, I systematically searched the archival data for further evidence, using the same coding topics. This information was compiled using a noncomputerized filing system that organized actor statements by coding category.

Analysis

To assess the concept of the devil shift, I rely on data from both a single and a comparative case study approach to analyzing California and Texas reading policy subsystems. Using Yin's (1994) recommended procedures, I developed evidence concerning the tested aspect of the ACF based on the convergence of a variety of data sources (interview data, policy documents, newspaper articles, Internet Web sites, etc.). Using the archival data collected on each respondent as triangulation material enhanced the overall validity of the findings for the analysis. Additional validity was sought through the referencing of all interview data cited, allowing for a full audit of the data used.

To test the hypothesis, I used a pattern-matching logic (Trochim, 1989) to compare empirically based patterns with a predicted pattern based on theory. This study's hypothesis is based on the theoretically predicted pattern known as the devil shift: that members of a coalition will regard members of the opposing coalition as strong even evil. Hence, to test the hypothesis, I looked for patterns in the two sets of coded narrative statements. Looking for themes within the text, I grouped each statement as generally negative, generally positive or neutral. If the patterns in each of the two coded sets for one state were predominantly negative in tenor, then these patterns suggest partial support for the hypothesis.

To build greater support for the concept of the devil shift, a cross-case comparison was completed as well. Similar procedures were completed in the second state, and a comparison of the results ensued. As Yin (1994) maintains, if during this type of cross-case comparison the pattern examined coincides in both cases, then the internal validity of this aspect of the case study is strengthened. Thus, if the patterns in the two coded sets for both states were predominantly negative in tenor, it would suggest full support for the hypothesis.

TESTING THE DEVIL SHIFT

Hypothesis 1 assesses the utility of the devil shift concept in explaining nondominant coalition formation within state reading subsystems. The hypothesis suggests that the devil shift is responsible for nondominant coalition formation, as those not in power tend to perceive the dominant coalition as devilish in its policy approaches and procedures. This in turn leads to coalition formation in order to combat the devilish tactics of the dominant coalition. In order to measure the devil shift effect, coded data concerning the feelings of nondominant coalition members were grouped by positive, negative or balanced stances. Trends within the coded data were tabulated and probed for narrative examples of the devil shift in reading policy.

Table 2.2.   California Nondominant Coalition Member Statements by Viewpoint and Coalition Membership

Statement Viewpoint	Statements About Dominant Membership				Statements About Dominant Policy and Processes			
	CB		CWL		CB		CWL	
	N	%	N	%	N	%	N	%
Positive	23	47	10	17	30	51	1	2
Balanced	7	14	2	3	1	2	4	7
Negative	19	39	44	80	28	47	48	91
Total	49	100	56	100	59	100	53	100

California

The sample used to test the hypothesis in the California reading subsystem was made up of the policy actors who were found to be members of the nondominant CB or more extreme CWL coalitions. The sample from the California subsystem for this hypothesis drew from 18 policy groups: 12 interest groups and 6 policy actors acting as individuals. The transcripts of California's nondominant coalition members were coded for statements about their feelings concerning the dominant coalition's membership and policy processes. Statements concerning any member or policy of the dominant coalition groups were coded and evaluated as negative, positive and balanced

Examination of the Devil Shift Concept

I divided the statements made by nondominant coalition members about members of the dominant coalition into two groups; those made by CB Coalition members and those made by CWL Coalition members. These results are presented in Table 2.2.

A majority of the statements made by members of the CB Coalition about members of the dominant coalition were either positive or partially positive. The same is true for the statements made by CB Coalition members about the dominant CP Coalition's policies and processes. While this evidence certainly refutes the existence of the devil shift within the CB Coalition, the data presented in Table 2.2 suggest strong evidence for the existence of the devil shift within the other nondominant CWL Coalition. Of the 56 statements made by members of the CWL Coalition concerning members of the dominant CP Coalition, 80% were negative in tenor. Of the statements made by CWL members about dominant policies and processes only a single statement out of the 53 was unequivocally positive.

CWL Coalition Descriptions of Dominant Members

A closer examination of the narrative statements themselves reveals that evidence of the devil shift in the CWL Coalition interviews abound. In describing members of the dominant CP Coalition, the CWL Coalition members used a variety of devilish terms. Comments made about members of the dominant coalition include describing them as "infatuated," "draconian," "defaming," "bashing" (CA-1), "unethical" (CA-22), "ignorant" and "insensitive" (CA-33). In addition, members of the CWL Coalition describe the CP Coalition members as "narrow-minded" and holding a "personal vendetta" (CA-33) that results in the CWL Coalition members feeling like they are "vigorously attacked" (CA-16) and "beaten up" (CA-33).

Themes within the narrative statements about members of the dominant coalition fall into four major groups. The first theme is that those in the CWL Coalition, felt that certain perspectives on reading instruction and reading research, namely, their own, had been ignored by members of the dominant coalition. For example, one academic suggested,

> Several of us across the state tried to say to the California Teacher's Association that this [the CRI] was not good reading policy. They were impervious. They had already made up their minds and there was nothing we could do.

(CA-01). A representative of an interest group also brought up this issue, pointing out that "a group of us actually tried to meet with the state superintendent some years ago when [the CRI] was sort of beginning. We were not successful" (CA-22). One representative of another interest group declared that members of the State Board of Education had basically said, "We hate you and we don't want to hear from you. And whatever you say means nothing to us. And we'll probably vote the opposite of whatever you say" (CA-33).

A second and similar theme running throughout the narrative statements was the feeling that politicians and interest groups were making reading policy decisions in California, not educational experts or professionals like those making up the CWL Coalition. A representative of an interest group pointed to a prominent member of the dominant coalition in particular, emphasizing, "Marion Joseph for one ... is ignoring [us] and is obviously very ignorant about the language development process" (CA-33). One academic was even clearer on this issue, arguing, "One of the first moves ... was a marginalizing of the commonly accepted leaders in the field. Basically, decisions were being made by people who are not educators" (CA-01).

A third powerful theme running throughout the narrative statements about members of the dominant coalition was a belief in the biased attitude of the California press. One academic recounted that a *Los Angeles Times* reporter mentioned during an interview that "he thought I was nuts or something like that" (CA-16). Another academic recounted how an article written by a *Los Angeles Times* reporter had run "a front-page story about how [I was teaching] contrary to law, which of course, is a defaming thing to have as a subtitle, misleading, defaming" (CA-01). A representative of an interest group recounted how "the media was not sensitive at all [... rather the media] beats us up" (CA-33).

A fourth and sometimes subtle theme within the narrative statements about members of the dominant coalition was that they are in some way unethical. References to how money is made and spent by members of the dominant coalition is one aspect of this theme. An academic pointed out that "at least three publishers that contributed to the campaign funds of our Superintendent of Instruction in California" (CA-01). This same academic went on to point out that several members of the dominant coalition worked for Open Court Publishing. A member of an interest group raised similar concerns, asserting "I think the connection between particular reading programs and particular companies is very, very dangerous ... we have some very unethical things going on" (CA-22).

CWL Coalition Descriptions of Dominant Policies

wo major themes in the narrative statements about dominant policy and processes are present. The first is that reading policy in California is fundamentally flawed, because it relies on poor causal reasoning and poor research regarding methods of reading instruction. One academic argued that the entire premise for the California Reading Initiative was flawed, reasoning "Achievement data itself doesn't support the conclusion that either scores declined nor does it support the idea that California ranked low because of its adoptions of a so-called whole language framework" (CA-24). Others members of the CWL Coalition emphasize that research pointing to the superior nature of whole language instruction was completely ignored by those dominant policymakers intent on changing reading policy in California. One academic asserted, "Well, first of all whole language is more effective, and there is tons of research to show it" (CA-01). This same academic went on to note that, "this greater body of research [showing the effectiveness of whole language] is being intentionally ignored." A representative of an interest group agreed with this assessment, confirming, "The newer reading policies in the state of California sometimes contradict some [whole language] research" (CA-33). A representative of another interest group also responded in a similar manner: "Only a very narrow band of research is being recognized by the state" (CA-22). Still another academic simply referred to California reading policy as "phonics hysteria" (CA-16).

A second theme in the responses of CWL Coalition members to the dominant coalition's reading policy was the poor use of standardized testing. One academic suggested that the use of standardized tests was "a policy that is intended to disenfranchise" (CA-01) the poor and members of ethnic minorities. Another academic argued that the money spent on statewide standardized tests would be better invested in books for school libraries, emphasizing "The state tests have taught us nothing: the scores are hopelessly confounded by many factors" (CA-16). The third academic in the CWL Coalition described the state reading policy in regard to testing as "insidious" (CA-24). A representative of an interest group in the CWL Coalition called into question the underlying norming procedures used in creating the Stanford Nine test, emphasizing that "less than 2% of the norming population were English learners, so as far as we're concerned, that's an invalid test of English learners" (CA-33). A representative of another interest group called testing in California "very dangerous" (CA-22).

Preliminary Conclusions

The results of data analysis in the California reading subsystem show partial support for the concept of the devil shift. While certainly the data do not suggest that the devil shift is the single causal factor in explaining the creation of all nondominant coalitions, there is solid evidence of the devil shift's existence in the more extreme nondominant CWL Coalition. Members of the CWL Coalition consistently described members of the dominant coalition in a strident manner, suggesting overtly that they were ignorant, scheming and unethical. Members of the CWL Coalition also point out serious flaws in state reading policy, arguing that the policies themselves are at the very least damaging and, worse, purposefully disempowering those students who are poor or members of an ethnic minority. These descriptions provide ample support for the existence of the devil shift in at least one of the California nondominant coalitions.

Texas

The sample used to test the hypothesis in the Texas reading subsystem was made up of the policy actors who were found to be members of the nondominant TB or the more extreme TPP coalitions. The sample of the Texas subsystem for hypothesis 1 drew from 16 policy groups: 15 interest groups and 1 governmental group. The transcripts of Texas's nondominant coalition members were coded for statements about their feelings concerning the dominant coalition's membership and policy processes.

Table 2.3.   Texas Nondominant Coalition Member Statements by Viewpoint and Coalition Membership

Statement Viewpoint	Statements About Dominant Membership				Statements About Dominant Policy and Processes			
	TB		*TPP*		*TB*		*TPP*	
	N	%	N	%	N	%	N	%
Positive	27	79	2	7	62	70	2	10
Balanced	3	9	2	7	5	6	1	5
Negative	4	12	23	86	21	24	17	85
Total	34	100	27	100	88	100	20	100

Examination of the Devil Shift Concept

I divided the statements made by nondominant coalition members into two groups; those made by TB Coalition members and those made by TPP Coalition members. These results are presented in Table 2.3.

Nearly 90% of the statements made by members of the TB Coalition about members of the dominant coalition were either positive or partially positive. Over three quarters of the statements made by TB Coalition members about the dominant coalition's policies and processes were at least somewhat positive. While this evidence certainly refutes the existence of the devil shift within the TB Coalition, the data presented in Table 2.3 suggest the existence of the devil shift within the other nondominant coalition, the TPP Coalition. Of the 34 statements made by members of the TPP Coalition concerning members of the dominant TP Coalition, only 4 were at all positive. The statements made by TPP members about dominant policies and processes were also overwhelmingly negative. Only 2 statements out of the 20 made concerning dominant policies and processes were unequivocally positive.

TPP Coalition Descriptions of Dominant Members

A closer examination of the narrative statements themselves reveals evidence of the devil shift in the TPP Coalition. Quite a few terms with devilish overtones were used by the TPP Coalition members in describing members of the dominant TP Coalition. Comments made about members of the dominant coalition include describing them as "unapproachable," "pawns," "full of themselves," "negative" and "unmovable" (TX-21).

A representative of one interest group in the TPP Coalition reported that members of the dominant coalition "think they're small-'g' gods" (TX-21). This same representative said that while some members of the dominant coalition had been "hoodwinked" into supporting the Texas Reading Initiative, others "just pretended to listen" to the concerns raised by members of the TPP Coalition. According to this interest group representative, the whole idea of a reading crisis in Texas had been created so that the dominant members could stay in power.

> The people who are creating the crisis are protecting the status quo, and so they say "Well, this is what's going to fix it." You know it's not the American way, but it is a way of creating a crisis so that you can come in with a solution that totally restructures the system. (TX-21)

Another member of the TPP Coalition agreed with this general assessment, observing that "most of the establishment is working against us" (TX-32). This same interest group member also went on to mention that they "don't care for most of the groups" in the dominant coalition, nor do they hold many of them "in high regard."

TPP Coalition Descriptions of Dominant Policies

A single theme runs throughout the narrative statements made by the members of the TPP Coalition: the dominant coalition's equivocal support for phonics instruction. Both members of the TPP Coalition made it clear that the dominant coalition's position on reading methods was not extreme enough in its support of phonics in early reading instruction. One interest group member insisted that "until the teachers are trained in how to teach phonics and the progressive philosophy is in some way brought into account, it's not going to get better" (TX-21). The other member of the TPP Coalition asserted nearly the exact same problem with dominant policy, contending that the major problem was "the lack of systematic instructional phonics in the early grades, along with the intransigence of the education establishment to implement that type of a curriculum and teaching strategy" (TX-32). This same interest group representative noted that while the TEKS and the TRI were a step in the right direction, the dominant policy "still leaves room for plenty of whole language."

Preliminary Conclusions

The results of data analysis in the Texas reading subsystem show partial support for the concept of the devil shift. As in California, the data do not suggest that the devil shift is the single causal factor in explaining the creation of all nondominant coalitions. However, just as in California, there is solid evidence of the devil shift's existence in the more extreme nondominant coalition; only in Texas the nondominant coalition is more extreme in its insistence on the use of phonics. Members of the TPP Coalition consistently describe members of the dominant coalition in unbecoming terms. Members of the TPP Coalition also point out that state reading policy does not go far enough to implement a phonics instructional approach while at the same time reining in whole language instructors. These descriptions by members of the Texas Pro-Phonics Coalition provide support for the existence of the devil shift in at least one of the two Texas subsystem nondominant coalitions. One interviewee's description of the Texas subsystem seems to sum up this issue well:

> Some of my fellow fundamentalist Protestants have discovered a fifth Gospel that I missed. I knew about Matthew, Mark and John. I didn't know about the Gospel of phonics. For them that's the only method. There is no other method, and anybody who deviates from that method is an agent of the devil. (TX-09)

Qualified Support for Hypothesis 1

The data presented here do not provide full support for hypothesis 1. Sabatier and Jenkins-Smith (1999) suggested that one way to explain nondominant coalition formation was through the concept of the devil shift. Data for both the California and Texas reading subsystems show that not all members of the nondominant coalitions show evidence of the devil shift in their views concerning dominant members and policies. Therefore, hypothesis 1 cannot be accepted. On the other hand, we would be unwise to completely reject the reasoning behind hypothesis 1. I found ample evidence to suggest that the devil shift does exist in the most extreme nondominant coalitions. In both California and Texas subsystems, those coalitions that support a more extreme view of reading instruction (whole language and phonics respectively) showed overwhelming evidence of the devil shift represented in their views of the dominant members and associated policies. Given this, while I cannot state that hypothesis 1 is accepted, it is responsible to suggest that in both state reading subsystems studied, the concept of the devil shift is associated with extreme coalition formation. As a result, hypothesis 1 received only qualified support.

CONCLUSIONS

One of the least tested and most criticized (Schlager, 1995; Schlager & Blomquist, 1996) aspects of the ACF deals with coalition formation. To shore up this weakness within the theory, Sabatier and Jenkins-Smith (1999) posited that the concept of the devil shift (Sabatier, Hunter, & McLaughlin, 1987) might be helpful in explaining coalition formation.

For this study, I tested the devil shift concept by proposing that actors in the nondominant reading policy coalitions will characterize members of the dominant coalition as very powerful and likely to impose negative repercussions on members of the nondominant coalitions.

While not completely explaining all coalition formation, the devil shift concept does help explain the formation of the most extreme coalitions. Of the two nondominant coalitions in each state, the coalition with the more extreme beliefs about reading showed definite signs of the devil shift. In California, a great deal of evidence supported the devil shift within the nondominant California Whole Language-Leaning (CWL) Coalition, but not the California Balanced-Leaning (CB) Coalition. The same was true in Texas, except in the case of this particular state subsystem, the strident supporters of phonics instruction, the Texas Pro-Phonics (TPP) Coalition, were the ones showing pronounced evidence of the devil shift. Members of the more moderate Texas Balanced-Leaning (TB) Coalition showed virtually no signs of the devil shift.

Consideration of Limitations

In terms of this study's attempt to capture policy beliefs, it should be noted that interviews were conducted in Texas just prior to the 2000 presidential elections. Both others and I noticed a reticence on the part of many interviewees and potential study participants to answering questions in a completely free an open manner. This reluctance to speak completely candidly could have been due to the fact that Governor Bush was in a heated battle for the presidency at that time. Members of the subsystem may not have wished to risk angering the governor or damage his chances for success in the election by critiquing his state administration. While I am confident that we were able to fairly capture the beliefs of the participants, it is unclear how much of a factor this issue played in our ability to accurately capture policy beliefs in the subsystem as a whole.

Even though this study followed a rigorous analytical approach, case studies have important limitations to consider. The most important is that the results of this study are not generalizable to other policy subsystems. In addition, the results of these case studies are not even generalizable to other state reading subsystems as those subsystems have a variety of differences that were not controlled for. Nonetheless, the findings of this study are generalizable to the Advocacy Coalition Framework as a theory of policy change. While this study can only offer limited generalizations concerning how reading policy is made in other states, at the national level or in other countries, it can be seen as a powerful test of the ACF itself and, given its rigorous nature, provides strong empirical evidence of the ACF's utility and generalizability.

The Link Between the Devil Shift and Coalition Formation

Given the results of this study, Sabatier and Jenkins-Smith's (1993, 1999) attempt to explain coalition formation appears to only help explain the formation of certain extreme coalitions in state reading policy subsystems. The concept of the devil shift was useful in explaining the formation of the more extreme TPP and CWL coalitions but did not hold up as a formative factor in the more moderate TB and CB Coalitions. Thus, the devil shift is helpful in explaining extreme coalition formation in state reading policy subsystems, but other aspects of coalition formation require further investigation. The results of this study, while confirming the place of the devil shift in the formation of extreme coalitions, provide little information that explains the formation of more moderate coalitions.

By itself, the devil shift is an inadequate response to the question of why coalitions form and coalesce. This problem of explaining the genesis of coalitions remains a serious flaw in the ACF that has yet to be repaired with the addition of new hypotheses. The devil shift does seem to play an important role in the formation of certain extreme coalitions, though. Perhaps the devil shift is noted only in subsystems where three or more coalitions exist. Perhaps the devil shift is suppressed by some mechanism within two coalition subsystems that keep more extreme members within one coalition or another or completely excluded from the subsystem all together. While the devil shift is an important aspect to understanding some portion of coalition formation in reading policy subsystems, additional assessment of this aspect of policy formation is needed in order to answer these important questions. Future researchers in this area may want to investigate the actual boundary between the dominant coalition and the more moderate nondominant coalition to look for factors that are both common and uncommon between the two.

Still, the devil shift does remain an intriguing and useful way of understanding the formation of more extreme coalitions. As we look to building the Advocacy Coalition Framework and other generalized theories of policy change, the devil shift as a concept is certainly a relevant way for us to understand how those on the furthest points of a policy issue feel about, or at least characterize the dominant coalition. While the devil shift does not successfully repair the weakness in the ACF, explaining how all coalitions form, it does help expand our understanding of how extreme coalitions form. While other policy scholars will need to work at a theoretical level to enhance this aspect of the ACF, the devil shift does add to our understanding of extreme coalition formation.

NOTES

1. This research was conducted as part of CIERA, the Center for the Improvement of Early Reading Achievement, and supported under the Education Research and Development Centers Program, PA/Award Number R3050R70004, as administered by the Office of Educational Research and Improvement, U.S. Department of Education. However, the contents of the described report do not necessarily represent the positions or policies of the National Institute on Student Achievement, Curriculum, and Assessment or the National Institute on Early Childhood development, or the U.S. Department of Education, and you should not assume endorsement by the federal government.

2. To obtain a copy of the interview schedule as well as further coding examples contact Cecil G. Miskel at the University of Michigan.

REFERENCES

Adams, M. J. (1998). *Beginning to read*. Cambridge, MA: MIT Press.

Aukerman, R. C. (1971). *Approaches to beginning reading*. New York: Wiley.

Balmuth, M. (1982). *The roots of phonics: A historical introduction*. New York: McGraw-Hill.

Bergeron, B. S. (1990). What does the term whole language mean? Constructing a definition from the literature. *Journal of Reading Behavior, 22*, 301–330.

Brooks, A. P. (1997, December 22). Bush's test-to-pass school plan called to blackboard. *Austin-American Statesman*, p. 4.

California Department of Education. (1998). *Chronology of state testing in California*. Retrieved September 3, 2002, from http://www.omsd.k12.ca.us/instruct/star/time.html

Chall, J. S. (1996). *Learning to read* (3rd ed.). New York: Harcourt Brace.

Coles, G. (2000). *Misreading reading: The bad science that hurts children*. Portsmouth, NH: Heinemann.

Edelsky, C. (1990). Whose agenda is this anyway? A response to McKenna, Robinson, and Miller. *Educational Researcher, 19*(8), 7–11.

Flesch, R. F. (1955). *Why Johnny can't read--and what you can do about it*. New York: Harper.

Flippo, R. F. (1998). Points of agreement: A display of professional unity in our field. *Reading Teacher, 52*(1), 30–40.

Flippo, R. F. (1999a). Redefining the reading wars: The war against reading researchers. *Educational Leadership, 57*(2), 38–41.

Flippo, R. F. (1999b). *What do the experts say?: Helping children learn to read*. Portsmouth, NH: Heinemann.

Garner, D. (2000). *An analysis of English/Language Arts/Reading as the foundation for public education in Texas.* Paper presented at a meeting of the Lone Star Foundation, Austin, TX.

Goodman, K. S. (1986). *What's whole in whole language?* Richmond Hill, Ontario: Scholastic.

Goodman, K. S. (1993). *Phonics phacts.* Portsmouth, NH: Heinemann.

Goodman, K. S. (1998). Who's afraid of whole language? Politics, paradigms, pedagogy, and the press. In K. S. Goodman (Ed.), *In defense of good teaching* (pp. 3–38). New York: Stenhouse.

Heinz, J. P., Laumann, E. O., Nelson, R. L., & Salisbury, R. H. (1993). *The hollow core: Private interests in national policy making.* Cambridge, England: Harvard University Press.

Kamil, M. L. (1995). Some alternatives to paradigm wars in literacy research. *Journal of Reading Behavior, 27*(2), 243–261.

Kingdon, J. W. (1995). *Agendas, alternatives, and public policies.* New York: Addison Wesley Longman.

Lindsay, D. (1997, November 12). Double standards. *Education Week,* p. 1.

Marshall, C., & Rossman, G. B. (1999). *Designing qualitative research* (3rd ed.). Thousand Oaks, CA: Sage.

Microsoft Corporation. (1999). *Excel Version WIN 9.0.2720.* Troy, NY: Microsoft Software Development.

Moats, L. (2000). *Whole language lives on: The illusion of "balanced" reading instruction.* Retrieved April 17, 2002, from http://www.edexcellence.net/library/wholelang/moats.html

Moorman, G. B., Blanton, W. E., & McLaughlin, T. (1994). The rhetoric of whole language. *Reading Research Quarterly, 29,* 309–329.

Mosenthal, P. B. (1995). Why there are no dialogues among the divided: The problem of solipsistic agendas in literacy research. *Reading Research Quarterly, 30*(3), 574–577.

Pressley, M. (1998). *Reading instruction that works: The case for balanced teaching.* New York: Guilford.

Ravitch, D. (2000). *Left back.* New York: Simon and Schuster.

Robinson, R. D. (1987). Reading teachers of the past—What they believed about reading. *Reading Improvement, 26,* 231–238.

Routman, R. (1996). *Literacy at the crossroads: Critical talk about reading, writing, and other teaching dilemmas.* Portsmouth, NH: Heinemann.

Sabatier, P. A., Hunter, S., & McLaughlin, S. (1987, September). The devil shift: Perceptions and misperceptions of opponents. *Western Political Quarterly, 41,* 449–476.

Sabatier, P. A., & Jenkins-Smith, H. C. (1993). *Policy change and learning: An advocacy coalition approach.* Boulder, CO: Westview.

Sabatier, P. A., & Jenkins-Smith, H. C. (1999). The advocacy coalition framework: An assessment. In P. A. Sabatier (Ed.), *The theories of the policy process* (pp. 117–168). Boulder, CO: Westview.

Schlager, E. (1995). Policy making and collective action: Defining coalitions in the advocacy coalition framework. *Policy Sciences, 28,* 242–270

Schlager, E., & Blomquist, W. (1996). A comparison of three emerging theories of the policy process. *Political Research Quarterly, 49*(3), 631–650.

Scientific Software Development. (2001). *ATLAS.ti: The knowledge workbench Version WIN 4.2* (Build 059). Berlin, Germay: Author.

Shepley, T. V. (2002). *Texas reading policy: Problems, processes and participants.* (Final Report). Reading Policy Project, University of Michigan.

Shepley, T. V. (2003). *A tale of two giants: Coalitions, policy-oriented learning and major change in state reading subsystems.* Unpublished doctoral dissertation, University of Michigan, Ann Arbor, Michigan.

Simms, C., & Miskel, C. (2000). *The demonization of whole language.* Paper presented at a meeting of the University Council on Education Administration, Albuquerque, NM.

Smith, F. (1971). *Understanding reading.* Hillsdale, NJ: Heinemann.

Smith, N. B. (1934). *American reading instruction: Its development and its significance in gaining a perspective on current practices in reading.* New York: Silver, Burdett.

Song, M. (2003). *Influence in the reading policy domain: A cross case study.* Unpublished doctoral dissertation, University of Michigan, Ann Arbor, Michigan.

Song, M., Miskel, C., Young, T., & McDaniel, J. (2000). *Perceived influence of interest groups in national reading policy.* Paper presented at a meeting of the University Council on Education Administration, Albuquerque, NM.

Stanovich, K. E. (1990). A call for an end to the paradigm wars in reading research. *Journal of Reading Behavior, 22*(3), 221–231.

Taylor, D. (1998). *Beginning to read and the spin doctors of science.* Urbana, IL: National Council of Teachers of Education.

Trochim, W. (1989). Outcome pattern matching and program theory. *Evaluation and program planning, 12,* 355–366.

Weaver, C. (1994). *Understanding whole language: From principles to practice* (2nd ed.). Portsmouth, NH: Heinemann.

Wolfe, P., & Poynor, L. (2001). Politics and the pendulum: An alternative understanding of the case of whole language as educational innovation. *Educational researcher, 30*(1), 15–20.

Yin, R. K. (1994). *Case study research* (2nd. ed., Vol. 5). Thousand Oaks, CA: Sage.

Young, T. V. (2002). *California reading policy: Problems, processes and participants.* (Final Report). Reading Policy Project, University of Michigan.

CHAPTER 3

REPRESENTATION IN THE AGE OF CHOICE

Implications for Policy and Research

Ann Allen

This chapter presents findings from a study examining the representative nature of public charter school policy. Findings indicate that the autonomy public charter school policy provides decreases the level of responsibility public charter school authorities and leaders exhibit to the local community, and that decrease creates a disconnect between the public charter school and its local community, sometimes leading to issues of equity in access. Implications for policy and research are presented.

INTRODUCTION

A function of public policy in a democracy is to ensure the democratic aims of society are upheld in the public sphere. Public policy in the past has created structures in the public school system that pressure school leaders to include the voice of all citizens in the school decision-making

Contemporary Issues in Educational Policy and School Outcomes, 51–73

process and in essence oblige schools to be responsible to the public they serve. The opportunity for citizens to vote on school issues, for example, casts citizens as stakeholders in the public school system and makes all citizens important to school leaders.

By keeping citizens well informed through regular newsletters, open door policies, media coverage, school television programming, and visible and accessible open meetings, administrators and school authorities preserve avenues for citizen representation in public school decision making by making the governance of public schools transparent to its public stakeholders. This transparency allows for checks on power that help to keep public programs equitable and accessible to all members of the community. In this way, public school authorities take responsibility for ensuring the public nature of public schooling.

Over the last century, however, public representation in school governance has diminished through reductions in the number of citizens who sit on local school boards, the use of special elections for school issues (Tyack, 1974; Tyack & Cuban, 1995), and the attempts to keep "politics" out of public schools (Plank & Boyd, 1994). The charter school movement takes the de-politicization of education one step further by formally removing schools from direct responsibility from the local electorate, which charter school advocates argue benefits the students, parents and schools by allowing educators to focus on the needs of their students without interference from other interests The autonomy charter school authorities have in designing and implementing their programs also allows for the innovation advocates say is needed to address the seemingly intractable problems of public schooling. As Elmore (1983) notes, such autonomy is also likely to lead to increasing variability among charter school programs. It is likely that this variability also creates inconsistencies in the way the public is represented in charter school decisions. The question remains whether the increased autonomy in charter school governance has detrimental effects on the public nature of public schooling. In other words, what, if anything, gets lost when public schooling is more accountable to a market clientele than the community in which it resides?

Scholars have been positing the detrimental effects of such policies for a decade or more (Gutmann, 1987; Levin, 1999; Plank, 1997). These authors argue that as members of a self-governing society, citizens have a stake in public school decision making because public schools are a part of the community infrastructure that affects the lives of local citizens. Others argue that public school decision making that is focused on only the students and parents enrolled in a given school may result in inequity of service to those students who are not enrolled in the school (Fiske & Ladd, 2000). Still others argue that school authorities need to be responsive to the community-at-large to ensure the school receives the support and advocacy it needs to be successful (Lutz & Merz, 1992; Stone, Henig, Jones, & Pierannunzi, 2001). Local politics, in other words, is not a bad word in education. Politics, or the debate and deliberation of multiple interests by multiple stakeholders, provides opportunities by which information is publicly disseminated to allow for a richer, more informed decision-making process. Stone et al. (2001) argue that it is the politics of education that ensures equity in educational opportunity and access in part through the advocacy that ultimately results when all stakeholders have a voice in the system.

The transition to a market approach to public schooling shifts whose voice is heard in school decision-making processes. Theoretically, the shift increases the voice of parents over the voice of other local stakeholders. Research on charter schools by Fiske and Ladd (2000) suggests that when parental voice is limited to only those parents whose children are enrolled in a given school, the inequities in public schooling are exacerbated. What results is a more segregated system of schooling.

Understanding how a shift in voice—or in other words a shift in power —affects the representation of public interests in public school governance is important to understanding how shifts in policy affect the public nature of public schooling. McCarthy (1997) warned nearly a decade ago, that moving forward with policies that redefine the "basic structure" of education calls for a more concerted effort at understanding what these changes portend. She writes:

> If the purposes and basic structure of public education in our nation are being redefined, we need to understand all implications of the decisions. We need to consider the values that are guiding educational policy into the next century because much more than public schooling is at stake. If we are not attentive, we may, by default, embrace policies that are inconsistent with democratic principles, when a majority of our citizens still believe strongly in those ideals. (p. 68)

Despite McCarthy's call, little empirical research has explored how public charter schools in the United States represent the public in school decision making. Yet it is only through empirical study that we can begin to understand the nature of representation in the age of choice. To this end, I approached a study of representation in public charter school decision making by examining how school authorities attend to the interests of citizens in four charter schools and two district schools in one Michigan city.[1]

METHODOLOGY

The study was a qualitative examination of school authorities' approach to community representation. Semistructured interviews with school administrators, board members, and neighborhood association directors were conducted across four public charter schools and two district elementary schools in one urban city in the Michigan. In addition to interviews with school leaders and neighborhood association directors, I observed school board meetings and examined documents and newspaper accounts that informed the question of how the public is represented in public school decision making.

For the study of representation in charter school decision making, I relied on a rich set of qualitative data, triangulated with interviews, observations, and document review. Using a qualitative approach provided the opportunity to examine the complexities of relationships that help explain how school leaders incorporate the interests of community stakeholders in school decisions and their reasons for doing so.

I also chose to use a case-study approach to the study of representation in public school decision making. Yin (1994) defines case-study research as inquiry that "investigates a contemporary phenomenon within its real-life context, especially when the boundaries between phenomenon and context are not clearly evident." The boundaries between public representation and public charter school decision making are not clearly defined. Charter school policy does not require formal reliance on the will of the electorate, nor does it demand any direct responsibility to a geographic community. The absence of these requirements in the policy may lead some to assume that public representation does not exist in public charter school decision making. However, to make that assumption would be to lose sight of the variability that such autonomy inevitably creates and the possibility that within that variability are charter school decision makers who choose, without a mandate, to be responsive to a larger public than the students and parents they directly serve. It is this complexity that requires a more careful, in-depth look at how public representation, responsiveness, and responsibility occur in the public charter school context.

By examining data from several different charter schools and using a comparison set of district schools, I aimed to see if similar findings are found across schools and in that way strengthen the usefulness of the study's findings. Although the data set is small, these findings indicate potential opportunities and challenges in representation that can occur as a result of autonomous public charter school policy in Michigan. These findings also may "test" the theoretical propositions of Dahl (1998), as well as Smith (2001) who posits that public charter schools have democratic potential as entities that serve to represent underrepresented groups of students.

This study takes place within the geographic boundaries of one urban school district in Michigan. Michigan is one of the nation's leaders in developing public charter schools, and Michigan's 10-year experiment with public charter school policy provides a solid base for understanding how such policy may affect the school-community relationship, specifically the representation of community in school decision making. In order to limit the confounding variables that potentially could exist with a set of schools across cities, I chose to focus my study on the school-community relationship within one urban school district. In this study, the term "community" means the citizens who reside within the boundaries of the local neighborhood public school.

My goal in selecting public charter schools was to create a data set that would allow me to see how school leaders in various types of charter schools approach public representation and more broadly engage in the school-community relations. To that end, I chose to include three elementary charter schools, one secondary charter school, and two district elementary schools. The secondary charter school is included in the study because its mission speaks directly to the question of community representation in school decision making. The school serves students in Grades 7–12.

Like the majority of public charter schools in the nation, the remaining schools in the study are elementary schools, each with a varying characteristic that may affect how the school is managed and ultimately governed. The second school in the study is a K–6 elementary school that is located in a former Catholic school building, still owned by the Catholic Church. The school aims to develop an innovative curriculum and to share that curriculum with other educators. This school also was chosen because it is the one school in the city that is chartered by the local public school district, a fact that could lead to a closer connection between the district's charter and the local community.

A third charter school was chosen because it is the only school in the city that converted from a private school to a charter school. The school's playground borders the playground of the neighborhood district elementary school, which sits directly downhill from the charter school. The charter school has been in the neighborhood for 30 years, maintaining the same administration and mission it has had for its 20 years as a private school. The school serves students in grades K–6.

The fourth school is the only charter school in the study that serves a primarily inner city African American population. It also is the only charter in the study managed by an education management organization (EMO). The EMO oversees the principal, teachers, and school staff, the general operations of the school, including instruction, accounting, maintenance, and custodial work. The curriculum is designed by the school staff with the support of EMO consultants, and professional development of educators is provided by the EMO. The EMO representative reports to the charter school board.

I chose two district elementary schools for the study based on their proximity to the charter schools in the study. The first elementary school in the study also serves the city's inner city African American population and provides a direct comparison to its charter school counterpart. The second district school in the study is the school that borders the private-conversion charter school in the study.

The respondents in this study were chosen for both their leadership roles in addressing issues of representation and responsiveness and their knowledge of these issues within the school-community context. Two school board members from each school were asked to participate in the study. In the case of the district schools, I interviewed two of the districts' school board members, who represented both of the district schools in the study. In each case, I interviewed the schools' board presidents and another board member based on the board member's availability. Including school board members as respondents in this study provided important data regarding how board members perceived their responsibility to the public as well as information on their perceptions of the relationship between public charter schools and the public-at-large.

Another set of respondents was made up of school administrators from each school in the study. In the case of two of the charter schools, I interviewed an administrative team consisting of a principal-like administrator in charge of instructional leadership and a superintendent-like administrator in charge of overall operations. Two of the charter schools have only one administrator. The district schools also have only one administrator, the school principal.[2]

Finally, in order to capture the perspective of the citizens in the neighboring communities, I interviewed the three neighborhood association directors who represented the communities in which the schools are located. Each of these directors is a public employee, and each has the task of working within the neighborhood to address citizen concerns regarding public services in the neighborhood. Putnam's work on civic engagement (1993) identifies neighborhood associations as organizations of civic engagement. Interviewing the directors of the neighborhood associations was the most systematic approach to gathering input regarding the relationship between the public charter school and the neighboring community.

Data collection for this study consisted of semistructured interviews with 22 respondents, observations of a public school board meeting for each of the five school boards in the study, and a review of approximately 20 documents related to the representation of the public in public school decision making. Data collection occurred over 4 months, from August to November 2004.

A Framework for Analysis

As I noted in an earlier essay (Allen, 2004), Dahl's (1998) conceptions of the political institutions necessary for democratic representation provides a useful framework for analyzing the representative nature of public school governance. Using such a framework, I examined the data to determine what effect market policies such as public charter schools may have on public representation. I do not suggest that findings from this small study are in anyway conclusive, but the study provides an empirical glimpse into how public school policy, and specifically charter school policy, affects public representation in school decision making and the consequences of those effects on the students and citizens not enrolled in the public charter school. Findings from the study also provide an opportunity to think more clearly about approaches to both policy and practice that could better represent the public in public school decision making.

Dahl identified six political institutions necessary for democratic representation. These institutions are: (1) Elected officials; (2) Free, fair, and frequent elections; (3) Freedom of expression; (4) Alternative sources of information; (5) Associational autonomy; (6) Inclusive citizenship. It is not unreasonable to consider these structures when thinking about the representation of public interest in school decision making. In fact, a Ford Foundation report (Hirota & Jacobs, 2003) on community engagement in public schools identified structures similar to Dahl's political institutions as important to community representation in school decision making. These basic structures of representation have traditionally been present in public school district governance (Tyack, 1974), but as educational policies aimed at creating more autonomy for public charter schools are implemented, the less representative public school decision making is likely to become. Consider these structures more closely.

Choice of Representation (Institutions 1 and 2)

By electing officials, citizens delegate the authority for decision making to representatives who act on behalf of those citizens. However, charter school policies release public charter school boards from direct citizen control through the appointment, not election, of school board members. Charter school boards are often appointed by the charter's authorizing agency—typically a public institution such as a university, community college, or public school district. However, Miron and Nelson (2002) note that in practice board members are chosen by the charter school founders and existing board members, and then presented to the authorizing agency for appointment. Write Miron and Nelson (2002): "The selection of board members by authorizers and founders, along with the selection of replacements by existing board members, serve to narrow the range of interests represented by charter school boards" (p. 33).

Access to Information

Dahl argues that effective participation is dependent on citizens' ability to access alternative and independent sources of information. Public schools are subject to freedom of information laws that make nearly all information of public concern available to citizens on request. Being under the management of private companies, however, allows some charter schools and their management companies to conceal information as property of the private organization and not as public information for citizen review, potentially limiting the public's access to information about public charter schools (Miron & Nelson, 2002).

Freedom of Expression

Whose voice is heard is an important consideration in all methods of representation. Dahl (1998) argues that freedom of expression by all citizens is necessary for effective participation. Gutmann (1987) argues for community democratic deliberation in public schools as a way to represent the interests of multiple stakeholders in public school outcomes. The open meetings laws for public schools that provide citizens the opportunity to address school authorities apply to public charter schools, but without a direct tie to the electorate and under autonomous governance, it is not clear how closely public charter school authorities attend to the precepts of public governance.

Associational Representation

Dahl's framework provides for the right of citizens to form associations that represent their interests. Examples of the types of associations that have been represented in school decision making include teachers unions, special needs students, ethnic communities such as American Indians, minority groups, low-income residents, and local senior citizen organizations. Some see charter schools as providing associational representation to children who have not been well-served in the public school districts. Smith (2001), for example, suggests the democratic potential of public charter schools is to serve as associational organizations that meet the educational needs of underserved children. Redefining "community" to be anything more than a geographic area, however, is likely to exasperate equity issues (Plank, 1997).

Inclusion

Dahl notes that democratic representation requires opportunities for all citizens to participate in decisions that affect them. By their nature, public charter schools, unlike public school districts, focus on students and parents enrolled in their school without much attention to the residents that make up the surrounding neighborhood. They do not have an elected governing board, and often do not identify with any one school community as public school districts do (Arsen, Plank, & Sykes, 1999; Miron & Nelson, 2002). As a result, charter schools may have few reasons to connect to the community beyond the parents and students they directly serve. Charter school advocates suggest this to be the key to increased responsiveness to parents (Chubb & Moe, 1990). Critics of charter schools suggest this limited scope can create a segregationist effect for students and families, limiting access to the charter schools to those who fit in (Fiske & Ladd, 2000).

FINDINGS FROM THE STUDY

Findings from the study of the four public charter schools indicate that the cautions authors have raised regarding the decrease of representation in public charter schools have merit, although evidence also suggests that the autonomy provided to public charter schools creates variability in public representation among different charter schools (Table 3.1). The variability is based in large part on the mission of the school and the school authorities. In other words, not all charter schools are the same in terms of how representative they are of public interest. However, evidence emerged from each of the four public charter schools in the study that indicates all of the public charter school authorities in the study have a much less sense of responsibility to the public-at-large than the public school authorities in the study. In addition, the autonomous nature of public charter schools appears to create a disconnect between the charter school and the citizens in its neighborhood, sometimes preventing student participation, sometimes creating barriers to citizens attendance at public meetings, and in all cases significantly reducing the level of responsibility school administrators and authorities exhibit in informing and engaging the local community.

Table 3.1.   Matrix of Schools on Dimensions of Representation

	School					
Dimensions	*District School 1*	*District School 2*	*Downtown Charter*	*District Charter*	*Inner City Charter*	*Private Conversion Charter*
Choice in Representation	✓	✓	✓	-	✓-	-
Freedom of Information	✓+	✓+	✓	✓-	✓-	✓-
Freedom of Expression	✓+	✓	✓	-	✓-	-
Associational Autonomy	+	✓+	✓	-	✓	-
Inclusive Representation	+	+	✓	-	✓	-

+ Very Strong; + Strong; Fair; - Weak; – Evidence contrary to representation

The Policies and Practices of Representation

Michigan has long been considered a local control state. The United States Constitution put the responsibility for public education in the hands of the states, and Michigan, in turn, put the responsibility of public education in the hands of local townships. Up until the early 1990s, citizens in Michigan school districts directly controlled school financing by voting on local taxes for the operations of local schools. Michigan residents continue to consider it their right to participate in the governance of their local school districts.[3] However, the local control of citizens in public school decision making has dwindled significantly in the last 10 years due to a set of educational policies that changed the politics and control of public schooling. The first of these changes had to do with Michigan's introduction of school choice policies.

Three years after Chubb and Moe (1990) published their call for public schools to be more responsive to parents, Michigan's governor and legislature began to implement a series of policies that would effectively increase parental control in public education. In 1993, Michigan became one of the first states in the nation to experiment with public charter schools. The state's charter school legislation was one of several policies implemented to increase school choice in Michigan (Arsen, Plank, & Sykes, 1999).[4]

According to the Revised School Code of Michigan, any individual or entity in the state may apply for a contract to organize a public school academy (PSA), as long as the academy is not affiliated with a church or religious organization. The policy also stipulates that PSA—which are more commonly called public charter schools—authorizers are responsible for the oversight of PSA boards of control. Individuals or entities proposing a PSA must submit a plan for board organization, including names of potential board members. PSAs must be under the oversight of a state authorizer, which can be a state university, a local community college, a local intermediate school district, or a local public school district. PSA policy stipulates that authorizers are responsible for making sure PSAs meet state and federal regulations, and authorizers are responsible for approving individuals to serve as PSA board members, although the state policy does not stipulate how such approval should occur.

While both school districts and charter schools are part of the state's public education system, and both receive public funding, the policies that direct their operations are not all the same. Arsen, Plank, and Sykes (1999) note that different policies yield different outcomes, and it is likely that the differences in the policies that direct these two types of public schools will lead to variance in how the schools relate to their local communities. For example, unlike traditional public school districts that serve a geographic service area and are responsible to the electorate within that service area, PSA's have no geographic boundaries. Policies that direct PSAs require no approval from the Michigan electorate. The only mention of the electorate in the PSA section of the School Code is if a public school district refuses to authorize a PSA. At that time, the PSA may ask for the question of authorization to be put on a ballot for a decision by the school district's electorate. Michigan's traditional public school districts boards, in contrast, are responsible to the electorate within the geographic boundaries of their school district. Voters in school districts decide who will serve as governing board members, and voters also decide issues that affect tax increases for school building funds and district organization issues such as district consolidation or annexations. Michigan PSAs by law do not have the right to ask voters for building funds; they must provide facilities from the per pupil foundation amount provided by the state.

Michigan's school choice policies and education finance restructuring together shifted the governance of public education out of the hands of the local citizen and into the hands of the parent consumer. A statement added to the School Code during the time of this shift indicates that the policies were a purposeful strategy to create a market for education aimed more at meeting what Labaree (1997) identifies as the private goals of education. The 1995 addition to the State Code, under Section 10 ("Rights of parents and legal guardians; duties of public schools") reads: "The public schools of this state serve the needs of the pupils by cooperating with the pupil's parents and legal guardians to develop the pupil's intellectual capabilities and vocational skills in a safe and positive environment." There is nothing in the State Code that speaks to the civic goals of public schooling or to the role of public schools in the local community, although the policies that govern local public school districts still maintain a level of citizen participation in school decision making through board elections for school districts and Sunshine Laws for both district and public charter schools.

Representation Depends on Individual School Mission

Evidence from the study indicates that charter school policies that do not explicitly oblige authorities to be responsive to the broader community are not sufficient in protecting the public interest in charter school decision making. When the pressures that force responsiveness are lifted, as they have been through the Michigan's School Code for Public School Academies, the responsiveness of schools to the larger community depends almost entirely on the individual interests of the individual school boards. For example, where it was a mission of the school to serve the neighborhood, there was more of an attempt to get information to neighborhood organizations. The downtown charter school, for example, leaves copies of the school's newsletters at area businesses so residents can find information about the school throughout the neighborhood, but even in this school, there is little information that goes out to residents. The neighborhood association director for this particular school noted that there has been little interaction between the neighbors and the school, and for the most part, public charter school leaders are good neighbors in that they take care of their property and are accessible, but with little information about the schools shared with the residents, residents do not see these schools as public entities that have responsibilities to the public-at-large.

The issue of an informed public was present in all the schools, although the downtown charter school appeared to have the most public reputation. Respondents saw the school as an "alternative" school for district students who cannot make it in the district schools, although the charter school administrators noted they prefer the public see them as an alternative to large schools, saying they serve all students from high achieving to those who struggle. Although information flow from the charter school to the public was much less than what was found in the public district schools, the downtown charter school had a diverse board, with no more than two parent board members at any time during its history. Board members also represented downtown neighborhood organizations, and partnerships with downtown organizations such as the local Y, local theaters, and the downtown library provided opportunities for school leaders to share information about their school with the downtown community.

Information flow to the public was even less in the other three public charter schools, although in the African American charter school public press about the school's struggle to find a permanent home helped to inform the public-at-large about the existence of the charter school. Even so, respondents from both the charter school and the neighborhoods reported very little information flows from the school to the neighborhood. The only information school leaders reported sharing with the public were recruitment fliers and an annual open house announcement. The board of this school was more diverse than the boards in the two remaining charter schools, but less diverse than the downtown school. The African American board was made up of citizens who had some connection to the church pastor that founded the school. Most of the members were members of the pastor's church, some were parents and others were community members. Where this school appeared less than open to the public was through its relationship with a private education management organization. The school's EMO representative was protective of documents and the board agenda at the public board meeting, which fit with Miron and Nelson's assessment of how EMOs have operated in the past. In addition, a local newspaper study showed the EMO charter schools to be less willing to share information with the press when asked.

These two charter schools also exhibited characteristics of what Smith (2001) called "associational democracies." Respondents from both the downtown charter school and the African American charter school indicated that part of their mission was to serve a population of students traditionally underserved, or underrepresented. By focusing their missions on these students, board members in the two schools attempted to create public institutions that extended the democratic nature of public schools by creating greater equity in accessing quality education. Evidence suggests, however, that the limited information flow to the public as well as the narrow focus of the services the schools provide limit representation to students who know about the program or who do not need special education services the schools cannot provide. In addition, when comparing the African American school with the public elementary school that serves the same neighborhood as the charter school, it is clear that the district school principal is more inclusive in her attempts to represent the entire neighborhood by advocating for all students in the inner city, and attending to the needs of the immediate neighborhood. Still, the missions of these two public charter schools to serve as associational democracies for underserved students creates a greater sense of serving the public interest than the other two public charters in the study.

Although the mission of the third public charter—the charter authorized by the public school district—was in itself in the public's interest, the insular nature of the existing board may be preventing it from representing the public it intends to serve. The district charter aims to serve the community by piloting innovative curriculum that can be shared with other educators in the district. It also aims to operate "in community" with the local neighborhood. Evidence indicates that the school is falling short on both of these goals. Very little information about this school has been shared with residents in the local community, and neighborhood respondents noted that residents do not recognize the school as a public school, but see it instead as an "independent" or "private" school. The school operates in a former Catholic school building, which is still owned by the Catholic church. The public charter school was initiated by a group out of the local Catholic college, and the public charter has formal and informal agreements with the Catholic college to provide both curriculum direction and financial management assistance. The Catholic college's finance office is the school's board treasurer. In addition, all of the school's board members—with the exception of one—have a connection to the private college that initiated the school. While the board members all noted that the school is a public school, independent of its Catholic college roots, the insular nature of the board may prevent it from being objective in addressing issues of public interest. For example, board meetings are conducted on the second floor of a building that has no elevator, and the building is locked during board meetings. At the time of my observation, a board member who forgot the code to get into the building had to resort to throwing pebbles at the second story window and yell for someone to come down and open the door so she could get in. While the practice of holding public board meetings behind locked doors could be challenged as a violation of the state's Open Meetings Act, the authorizer liaison that attends the meetings responded that she often saw that as an issue, but never addressed it with the school's board. In this particular case, the issue of access to public board meetings had a direct affect on how the board operates, and it may have contributed to the board's decision to postpone the installation of an elevator, even though it would mean students with disabilities could not attend the school. The lack of a visible public in the board room, noted the one board member who was not associated with the Catholic college, creates a sense that the public board is more of a private organization. She said:

> I think it doesn't feel very public to us. This is my own interpretation. I mean we know it's public. We know it's an open meeting. We know anybody could get the notes and look at them. We know all of that. But we don't experience any of it. I mean, there's never anybody there. It's always just us.

There's not even staff there. I think about our community college board or the public school district board, you'd have the media there and it's being recorded for television and you have staff members there. So that when you come to a contract issue or a personnel issue or legal issues, there actually is a public that will hear it. I don't think we've really confronted that.

Unlike other public charter schools in the study, the district charter school is authorized by an elected board. The fact that the charter is directly connected to the elected board seems to have little effect on its level of public representation. Data indicate that the tradition of competition and animosity between the public school district and public charter schools has contributed to a hands-off approach to district involvement in charter schools. The district liaison noted that part of the problem with disseminating the practice of the public charter is that the there still exists a resistance among public school district personnel to cooperating or collaborating with a public charter school. Respondents also noted that the district board, as the school's authorizer, is less involved in the public charter than other authorizers. While the district appoints a liaison to report back to the board, respondents note that unless citizens raise an issue about the charter school to the district board, the board remains hands-off with the charter. Unlike other authorizers in the study, the district did not include information about its public charter school on its district Web site, an indication of the variability among public charter school authorizers and the responsibility they take in ensuring public representation in public charter schools.

The board president of the private conversion school, the last of the four charter schools in the study, noted that his public school has an obligation to be responsive to all of the students in the district in part "because that is where we are drawing from," but he noted that there has been very little connection of his school to the local community. "I think we have a dim awareness of the local community and a hope—a kind of flickering hope—that we would connect with that community. But in fact that's probably in the future." The future, he said, may lie with the hiring of a new school administrator. Both board respondents from the private-conversion school noted that the administrators who were in charge of the private school are the same administrators in charge of the public charter school, and while the status of the school changed, the governance of the school remained very much the same. The board, for example, is made up entirely of parents who have students enrolled in the charter school.

Board members and school leaders at the private conversion school communicate almost extensively with the parents and students that are enrolled in the school. School administrators reported that they do not send recruitment material to residents because they have enough interest from people to call to fill whatever empty slots they have. Both neighborhood and the charter school respondents at this school noted that the public knows very little about the school, and the school is still seen as a private school. Noted a board member of the private conversion school:

> I don't know if the community sees us as an entity at all. I mean we are educating our students about the community, but I don't know that the community is really educated about us much. I don't know that people really know who we are or what we're about. I don't even know if people in my neighborhood—and I'm only two miles from the school—even really know that this school is there, or that it is a charter school.

In essence no communication to the public about school activities or offerings, no community representation on the school's board, and a long-standing reputation as a private school that remains 10 years after converting to a public charter school, the private conversion charter school showed little signs of public representation outside of opening school doors to students who choose to enroll in the public charter school. Even in this endeavor, the private conversion school conducts entrance interviews to ensure that students who choose to come to the school can agree to such edicts as a required number of parent participation hours and school practices such as bringing only healthy foods to school and calling teachers by their first names. The board president noted that school policy dictates that parents who do not heed the parent participation hours are "given the heave-ho." In this way, the school's policy takes liberties that other public schools do not have. As one of the district elementary principals noted,

> The charter schools have a way of if you don't work well with them, if things don't go smooth, they let you know that you need to go to your neighborhood school. And we've had kids return here from charters because of that. And that's one thing I believe charters need to stop (doing). If they're going to call themselves a public school, the state needs to hold them to the same standards.

Data from the public district schools clearly illuminated differences in representation between the district schools and the public charter schools. District principals noted that the public charters in their neighborhoods selected students by creating conditions for student participation. The district elementary schools, by contrast, served every student that "walked in the door." The district elementary principals also provided evidence that they served neighborhood interests by attending to the needs of all residents, including senior citizens, voters, and youth in the neighborhood who have dropped out of school. The school facilities are open and available to the community, and all citizens have access to the district board meetings. The only board meeting in the study in which members of the public attended was the district board meeting, which attracted more than 60 community members.

Interviewees from all of the public charter schools noted that the reason the public does not attend charter school board meetings is that citizens are not interested in charter schools. Yet interview data from neighborhood association directors indicate that it may not be so much a case that citizens are not interested as they are not aware that charter schools are public schools, and as public schools, citizens have a say in how these schools operate. This data corresponds to national public opinion poll data that indicates most citizens are not aware that charter schools are public schools (Vanourek, 2005). In the case of the former Catholic school, the neighborhood association director noted that most residents still believe that the school is either part of the Catholic diocese or an "independent" school. A board member from the former private elementary school that is now a public charter school made a similar statement.

Implications for Policy

Whose responsibility is it to ensure the public is informed about the public schools? Most charter school administrators and board members indicated that it is up to the public to ask for information on school issues. A common response from charter school leaders was, "The information is public. If people ask for it, we give it to them." However, if, as neighborhood directors and some of the school respondents noted and as national poll data tells us, citizens are unaware that public charter schools either exist or are public entities, how is it that they can be responsible for seeking out information about the use of public resources?

Public school authorities have a responsibility to operate in the open by disseminating whatever information is necessary for the public to understand how public charter schools use public resources and to what end. The responsibility for the dissemination of information about these public institutions must fall on the shoulders of the public authorities, whether they are elected or appointed, or risk abusing their authority and manipulating the power ceded to them for individual or private interests. Evidence in the study suggests charter school policy plays a role in the level of responsibility public authorities take for ensuring public interests are represented in charter school governance. In other words, how public policy is written dictates how well public interests will be represented.

Part of the motivation behind charter school policy was to disconnect these schools from the bureaucracy that some argue prevents school improvement and responsiveness to parents (Chubb & Moe, 1990; Hess, 1998). Charter school advocates posit that attention to too many publics cause distraction and disservice to students. In fact, many of the respondents in the study noted that the decreased level of responsibility school authorities had to the public-at-large was a benefit in being able to design and implement the kinds of programs they wanted for the students, and all the respondents indicated the ability to pick board members according to the needs of the school helped create boards that had unified goals. So what is the harm in focusing on the school itself, or in designing a school that meets a particular need? What is the danger of having a self-perpetuating board focused on similar interests? Data from the study indicate that the danger lies in the fact that without public scrutiny or representation of broader public interests, school authorities too easily neglect their public aims.

While charter school policy provides more autonomy to charter schools in part to spur innovation and responsiveness to parents, the policy does not eliminate charter schools' responsibility to the public-at-large. Public charter schools are obliged to maintain the requirement for open and accessible board meetings. However, data from this study indicate that the autonomy the charter school policy provides may overshadow the responsibility charter schools have to the larger public. Data from the study also indicate that who makes up the board of a public charter school affects how the community is represented in school decision making. When the broader community is not well-represented in school decision making, the immediate needs of the school will take precedence over more public interests like equitable access.

Protecting public interests in public schooling may require more than goodwill or good intentions on the part of charter founders and board members; it might require policies aimed at ensuring public authorities like public school board members and administrators maintain a sense of responsibility to the public-at-large. Ensuring that public schools adhere to a set of criteria, such as the dimensions of representation as defined in this study, may be a good start. Public schools that provide choice in representation, free flow of information, avenues for expression, ability for associational representation, and representation that is inclusive may do a better job representing and protecting public interests.

The issue policy makers need to consider, as articulated by respondents in the charter school study, is that choice may be a vehicle for freedom for the oppressed only if choice is accessible to all. It is the structures of democratic representation that help to ensure that public services like public schooling are delivered in fair and equitable ways, and in a manner that meets the needs and interests of the citizens they aim to serve.

Whether it is to ensure equity of service, public accountability for public dollars, or to honor the value that citizens place on democratic representation in public school decision making, the representation of community interests in public school decision making is an important and necessary component of public policy. It is apparent from this study that the variability in charter school missions and boards leads to variability in how charter schools address issues of representation. However, the overall, systematic representation of public interests in public charter schools likely will not happen without formal policies in place that oblige school authorities to be responsible and responsive to a larger community than the students and parents they directly serve.

Data from this study is far from conclusive. However, the picture of representation gathered from these schools illustrates the need to further consider the issue of citizen representation in public charter school decision making, possibly exploring ways representation can be increased while maintaining the kind of autonomy that could lead to innovation and greater responsiveness to student needs. Below are a few possibilities.

IMPLICATIONS FOR CHARTER SCHOOLS

- Increase representation of the public interest in school decisions by requiring that public school academies have some level of community representation on their school boards, determined through an open, democratic process. Public school academies might, for example, advertise for board positions in the local community as well as in regional or state newspapers. Criteria for boards, as data for this study indicate, should include an expectation of diversity in representation among board members to protect against public boards serving singular interests.

- Strengthen the role of the public charter school authorizer by delineating specific requirements for appointing and monitoring public charter school boards. The vague responsibilities for public charter school authorizers under Michigan's current policy does little to ensure that public interests are protected in charter school decision making. Without an electorate to pressure public boards into serving the public interest, it behooves the state or its appointed authorities to take on that responsibility.

- Increase access to public meetings and thereby increase opportunities for expression by enforcing laws that are already in place that oblige public charter schools to conduct all meetings in open and accessible buildings.

• Increase inclusiveness of public school academies by ensuring that all schools comply with existing laws, including laws that require public charter schools to be accessible to all students.

• Require board training for public charter school board members to ensure all board members have at least an initial understanding of their public responsibilities. Data in the study indicate that charter school board members have little training in public board work and operate from more private perspectives.

• Increase the flow of information to the larger community by requiring regular reports be published and distributed to the community at-large. Increasing information flow between public school academies and local neighborhoods will provide citizens the opportunity to examine what these schools are, what benefits they provide the community, and how citizens can contact the school's public authorities for questions or concerns.

• Increase the associational representation of public charter schools by extending opportunities for community members to use charter school buildings for the purpose of community meetings and youth activities. Creating a sense of community among the population these schools aim to serve may strengthen the support system for both the school and its students.

IMPLICATIONS FOR RESEARCH

The research from this study is only an indication of how public charter school policy affects the school-community relationship and potentially the ability of citizens to engage in school decisions that affect their lives. To date, little research has focused on the effect public charter school policies have on the school-community relationship or the representative nature of public schooling. There are many questions to be examined if we are to truly understand how major shifts in educational policy affect the school-community relationship. Questions for further research include:

• How much do citizens know about local public charter schools? Do citizens identify these schools as public, and if not, how do they define them? What expectations do citizens have for local public charter schools and how do their expectations for the local public district schools differ?

- What is the nature of information flow between public charter schools and their local communities and what effect does the level of information flow have on how local residents engage with the public charter school?
- How does the level of responsibility among school authorities in public district schools and public charter schools differ? What is the effect of that difference on the local community?
- What is the responsibility of the public charter school authorizer in ensuring public charter school boards maintain open processes for meetings and decision making? How do authorizers fulfill such responsibility?
- How can autonomy that fosters flexibility, innovation, and an ability to respond to market pressure be balanced with regulations that protect equity goals for public schooling?

Answers to these questions could help us better understand the changing relationships between school and community in the market-based systems of public schooling. Choice policies attempt to break down the expert-led, bureaucratic system of schooling that is sometimes impenetrable by the community members the system is designed to serve, but the autonomy charter school policies provide also threatens the public nature of public education.

By removing charter schools' responsibility to represent the interests of the public-at-large, we risk the removal of public schooling from the public sphere. Consequently, we risk increasing the inequities that result when the full spectrum of public interests are not represented in public decision making. Finally, public school policies that foster autonomous schools may also foster a loss of interest and support by local citizens, dissolving what has proven to be one of the most important links to the success of a school: the school's relationship to the community in which it resides.

The research from this study is an indication of how public charter school policy affects the ability of citizens to engage in school decisions that affect their lives. More empirical research is needed to surface the reality of the charter school-community relationship and the possible innovations that could contribute to a more responsible and more representative system of public schooling in the age of choice.

NOTES

1. This study was conducted as my doctoral dissertation, "Schooling in the Public Sphere: Understanding the Relationship Between the Public and the Public Charter School," through Michigan State University.

2. Since this study is school-based and not district-based, I did not interview the urban school district superintendent. Interview data from the district superintendent would likely include reflection of a district-wide perspective, which could confound the focus of this study.

3. Findings from a Michigan State University 2003 State of the State Survey indicate the majority of Michigan residents continue to want a say in local public school decisions.

4. Other policies include legislation passed in 1993 and 1994 to promote the free movement of students form district to district, first through schools of choice in which students have the opportunity to leave a home district for another, and second, by making the majority of school finances dependent on student enrollment.

REFERENCES

Allen, A. (2004). Changing governance, changing voice: Democratic representation in public school governance. In D. Walling (Ed.), *Public education, democracy, and the common good* (pp. 109–120). Bloomington, IN: Phi Delta Kappa Educational Foundation.

Arsen, D., Plank, D. N., & Sykes, G. (1999). *School choice policies in Michigan: The rules matter.* East Lansing: Michigan State University.

Chubb, J. E., & Moe, T. M. (1990). *Politics, markets, and America's schools.* Washington, DC: Brookings.

Dahl, R. A. (1998). *On democracy.* New Haven, CT: Yale University Press.

Elmore, R. (1983). Complexity and control: What legislators and administrators can do about implementing public policy. In L. Shulman & G. Sykes (Eds.), *Handbook of teaching and policy* (pp. 32–369). New York: Longman.

Fiske, E. B., & Ladd, H. F. (2000). *When schools compete: A cautionary tale.* Washington, DC: Brookings.

Gutmann, A. (1987). *Democratic education.* Princteon, NJ: Princeton University Press.

Hess, F. (1998). *Spinning wheels: The politics of urban school reform.* Washington, DC: Brookings.

Hirota, J. M., & Jacobs, L. E. (2003). *Vital voices: Building constituencies for public school reform.* New York: Academy for Educational Development, Chapin Hill Center for Children.

Labaree, D. F. (1997). Public goods, private goods: The American struggle over educational goals. *American Educational Research Journal, 34*(1), 39–81.

Levin, H. (1999). The public-private nexus in education. *American Behavioral Scientist, 43*(1), 124–137.

Lutz, F. W., & Merz, C. (1992). *The politics of school/community relations.* New York: Teachers College Press.

McCarthy, M. (1997). School privatization: Friendly or hostile takeover? In M. McClure & J. C. Lindle (Eds.), *Expertise versus responsiveness in children's worlds: Politics in school, home and community relationships* (pp. 61–69). New York: RoutledgeFalmer.

Miron, G., & Nelson, C. (2002). *What's public about charter schools: Lessons learned about choice and accountability.* Thousand Oaks, CA: Corwin.

Plank, D. N. (1997). Dreams of community. In M. McClure & J. C. Lindle (Eds.), *Expertise versus responsiveness in children's worlds: Politics in school, home and community relationships* (pp. 13–20). New York: RoutledgeFalmer.

Plank, D. N., & Boyd, W. L. (1994). Antipolitics, education, and institutional choice: The flight from democracy. *American Educational Research Journal, 31*(2), 263–281.

Putnam, R. (1993). *Making democracy work: Civic traditions in modern Italy.* Princeton, NJ: Princeton University Press.

Smith, S. (2001). *The democratic potential of charter schools.* New York: Peter Lang.

Stone, C. N., Henig, J. R., Jones. B. D., & Pierannunzi, C. (2001). *Building civic capacity: The politics of reforming urban schools.* Kansas: University Press of Kansas.

Tyack, D. (1974). The one best system: A history of American urban education. Cambridge, MA: Harvard University Press.

Tyack, D., & Cuban, L. (1995). *Tinkering toward utopia: A century of public school reform.* Cambridge, MA: Harvard University Press.

Vanourek, G. (2005). The state of the charter movement: Trends, issues and indicators. Washington, DC: Charter School Leadership Council.

Yin, R. (1994). *Case study research, design and methods.* Beverly Hills, CA: Sage.

CHAPTER 4

"VALUES" POLITICS AND NO CHILD LEFT BEHIND

Robert O. Slater and Mario S. Torres Jr.

*To serve the present age, my calling to fulfill; O may it all my powers engage
to do my Master's will! Arm me with jealous care, as in Thy sight to live,
and oh. Thy servant. Lord, prepare a strict account to give!*

—*"A Charge to Keep I Have"*

Values and values discourse have played an increasingly important role in modern politics. From Ronald Reagan to George W. Bush, values, morality and character have become ever more central in the political rhetoric. Our main point in this paper is that values politics, a curious mix of moral and political discourse in twenty-first century America, has had and is having an unusual and powerful effect on policy, both foreign and domestic. Perhaps nowhere is this effect more evident in domestic policy than in the No Child Left Behind Act. In the current context of values politics, the moral aspects of this legislation play an uncharacteristically significant role, effectively "silencing" those who would normally be vocal critics, and making its analysis and assessment both more complex and difficult.

Contemporary Issues in Educational Policy and School Outcomes, 75–85
Copyright © 2006 by Information Age Publishing
All rights of reproduction in any form reserved.

INTRODUCTION

Values and values discourse have played an increasingly important role in modern politics. From Ronald Reagan to George W. Bush, values, morality and character have become ever more central in the political rhetoric. The rise of values politics in recent decades has been fueled by the character of George W. Bush himself. This character, as everyone knows, emerged out of his struggle, in the 1980s, with binge drinking, a struggle that led him to participate in Bible-study groups in his hometown of Midland, Texas, and which led him to a religious conversion to evangelicalism. Evangelicalism is everywhere evident in Bush's life and politics (Stam, 2003). One of his favorite songs is "A Charge to Keep I Have," from which he took the title of his book. When he decided to seek the presidency he said he had been "called" to the decision by God (McClay, 2005). Soon after 9/11, in a speech to a joint session of Congress, he said that the nation must go forth "to confound the designs of evil men," because," our calling, as a blessed country, is to make the world better. Almost a decade earlier, Ronald Reagan had used a similar language of good and evil when he spoke of the "evil" Soviet empire. Back then, the use of such old-fashioned rhetoric by a man with nothing of the evangelical spirit of this president, created a furor in the press and academe. But now, a scant 10 years later, the same words met with little or no response, evidence of our shifting culture.

Our main point in this paper is that values politics, a curious mix of moral and political discourse in twenty-first century America, has had and is having an unusual and powerful effect on policy, both foreign and domestic. Rather than building the usual case (e.g., it makes economic sense) to justify policy merit, for example, the administration's approach has been to frame policies or policy stances of various kinds as a moral obligation to fulfill morally right causes. A considerable number of the Bush administration policies are defended as moral conflicts or dichotomies. For instance, in the fight against terrorism, President Bush noted to national and international audiences that the war was clearly a fight between good and evil. In an address to the nation, the President boldly remarked "You're either with us or against us in the fight against terror" (Bush, 2001). On the topic of same sex marriage, President Bush issued similar good versus evil innuendos. In a press statement in February 2004, President Bush disparaged activist local officials and judges for threatening "the most fundamental institution of civilization" (Bush, 2004). Perhaps there is no better example of packaging policy as a moral imperative than his No Child Left Behind Act, otherwise known as NCLB.

President George Bush signed NCLB into law in January 2002. It is a reauthorization of the Elementary and Secondary Education Act (ESEA) first passed during the Johnson administration in 1965 and reauthorized in 1994. The biggest component of ESEA and of NCLB as well is Title I, the federal government's principal aid program for disadvantaged students.

To say that the No Child Left Behind Act has expanded the federal role in education and become a focal point of education policy is grossly understated. "NCLB is vastly more ambitious than the original ESEA" (Hess & Finn, 2004). The goal of the original Title I was simply to provide added resources and support to schools with large populations of disadvantaged students. Ensuring that funding reached schools in need and funding was spent appropriately proved to be a burdensome venture however. The original Title I lacked the levers to force schools to rethink, reorganize, or restructure practice. It was not intended to create whole new industries or ancillary services. For all of its complexity, its underlying logic was simply "more of the same."

NCLB, on the other hand, signals a radical departure from business as usual. It insists that schools annually test students in Grades 3 through 8 in reading and math. It requires every state to track each school and school district's "adequate yearly progress" (AYP) on these tests. It demands that every school show steady improvement for not only students as a whole but for students in designated subgroups. Finally, it proposes to use sanctions and various interventions to back up its demands.

These aspects of NCLB—and they are only highlights—have by themselves unprecedented and far-reaching implications for American public schools and schooling and its leadership. Indeed, such is the scope and pervasiveness of NCLB's implications that it appears as a dramatic example on the domestic front of the evangelical vision and mission that George Bush has brought to world events. These larger events have overshadowed NCLB's importance and we are only just now beginning to see what the Bush administration has wrought for American education.

There is another aspect of NCLB, however, that makes it unlike any previous domestic policy. This aspect introduces a different force into policy analysis and critique, a force that in effect "muddies" the critique and analysis processes. This is NCLB's moral dimension. The moral aspects of NCLB play a curiously subtle but powerful role in shaping policy discourse. In part, it acts to silence and discipline traditional sources of criticism, "pulling into line" political groups whose endorsement would normally be more difficult to obtain. NCLB is masterfully packaged with captivating symbols and phrases, all defending its moral necessity. What follows is a brief examination of the moral complexity of NCLB at the federal, state, and local levels.

THE MORAL COMPLEXITY OF NCLB

The Source of NCLB's Moral Force: Closing the Achievement Gap

The primary source of the morality which both Republicans and, as we will show in the next section, even Democrats have turned to their advantage is its professed goal of closing the achievement gap between white and nonwhite students. Not even the NEA and AASA oppose this most general aspect and chief rationale of NCLB. And for good reason. A recent Phi Delta Kappa national Gallup poll is suggestive of NCLB's moral force. Findings indicate that although 68% of the public disagrees with reliance on a single test to measure student performance, 90% believe that closing the achievement is an important agenda (Phi Delta Kappa, 2005). As our society increasingly transforms itself into a twenty-first century knowledge society, school achievement, already important, becomes even more so. As the basic work of the society more and more becomes knowledge work, the correlation between school achievement and opportunities for living a self-fulfilling life become stronger. An advanced capitalist twenty-first century society stratifies its population along knowledge and technology lines: the bigger the achievement gap, the greater the stratification and inequality. The United States now has greater inequality than any other G-8 nation, and more now than it has had in the past 75 years of its history. An achievement gap left without redress can only exacerbate this problem. For a nation that claims to be a democracy, this much inequality is untenable and threatens to undermine the legitimacy of the system as whole. The achievement gap is itself an inequality (in terms of the distribution of knowledge resources), an institutional inequality that contributes to social inequality. In the context of democracy, it is prima facie immoral and can neither be justified nor countenanced.

This moral aspect of NCLB rests on its commitment to close the achievement gap in a democratic society. Its professed intent is to reduce inequality in the one institution (the public school) that is itself specifically dedicated to redressing inequalities in the larger society. School inequality is among a democracy's most morally reprehensible inequalities. We do not want democracy for its own sake but for the sake of what we hope to achieve by being democratic. That we human beings can choose how to govern ourselves is evidence of our humanity. In choosing democracy we choose not rule of the one or rule of the few but rule of the many. And we want the many to rule not in their own individual interests but in the interest of the whole. We choose this type of rule because we believe it holds more promise than its alternatives to enable each and everyone of us to live self-fulfilling lives, and to realize the full use of our powers along lines of excellence. Democracy promises not only the greatest good for the greatest number, but also that the greatest number can be good, that is, moral. But our capacity to realize ourselves, to realize our individual and unique excellences—in short, our capacity to be moral—which is to say, to be human—depends vitally on our schools and schooling. School inequality cripples our humanity and therewith our capacity to be moral. Accordingly, NCLB's commitment to eliminate this inequality is fundamentally moral.

NCLB's Size and Scope Creates Moral Complexity

The moral component of NCLB, however, is only part of a highly complex piece of legislation. As might be expected from a piece of legislation that numbers more than a thousand pages, NCLB is no single thing but many things more or less articulated within and under the general goal of closing the achievement gap between white and nonwhite students. Because of its scope and complexity, the moral aspect of NCLB can be put to various uses or marshaled to defend contradictory aspects. Those we choose to highlight in what follows are only illustrative.

THE CONSEQUENCES OF THE NCLB'S MORAL COMPLEXITY: SOME EXAMPLES

The morality of NCLB's goal to close the achievement gap undermines the effectiveness of criticism of the law and makes its complete and effective implementation appear as a moral imperative. NCLB's proponents have essentially made a claim, namely, that if properly implemented it is a law that will play a vital role in the realization of the American promise; it will significantly advance the processes of democratization in America. Given this claim and its import, particularly in the context of the present American trend toward greater inequality, any failure to fully implement NCLB, at any level, can be "spun" as nothing short of moral failure. NCLB's primary vision and rationale—the reduction of the achievement gap within and between schools—creates a moral obligation for educational leadership at all levels—federal, state, district, and school. As a consequence, criticism of NCLB is made more difficult. No one wants to go on record as opposing the elimination of the achievement gap. But this is a problem because NCLB does need critical appraisal.

The Moral Complexity of NCLB at the Federal Level

It is interesting that the moral "packaging" of NCLB has been turned by Democrats to their own ends. For example, at the federal level Senator Kennedy has argued, the law should be fully funded, something for which the Bush administration has been criticized for not doing. In the fiscal year 2002, President Bush proposed $10.3 billion for NCLB and Congress 10.4 billion. $13.5 billion was authorized. In 2003, the figures were $11.3, $11.7 and $16 billion respectively. In 2004, the figures were $12.3, $12.3, and $18.5 billion respectively. So far over the 3 years since the law's signing the President has proposed $33.9, Congress $34.4 billion, and $48 billion has been authorized. Of this $48 billion total authorization only $34.4 billion has been appropriated—a shortfall of more than $13 billion or about a year's worth of funding (Hardy, 2004).

Now, it is true that for every federal program authorization levels are ceilings not floors, maximum expenditure levels not minimum. Nonetheless, given the import of NCLB, the claims, tacit and explicit made for it, and the current context of inequality, it is relatively easy for the Democrats to argue that the administration has a moral obligation to fund this program at its authorization levels. While a failure to do so could and perhaps should be characterized as a moral failure, the core machinery of NCLB has effectively withstood sharp criticism from federal legislators. NCLB is masterfully packaged with captivating symbols and phrases, all defending its moral necessity. Statements issued by President Bush and the former Education Secretary Rod Paige illustrate the sizable burden critics bear in mounting a political attack on NCLB. The President issued the following justification for NCLB:

> This educational divide is caused by the soft bigotry of low expectations. Many excuses have been offered, but the result is still the same. Students are more likely to stop believing in themselves if they think adults have stopped believing in them. This is unacceptable. Our government must speak for disadvantaged children who have been unheard and overlooked. They are the children who were hidden behind the averages and shuffled from class to class, grade to grade, without receiving the attention they needed and deserved. We need No Child Left Behind. (Bush, 2004).

Secretary Rod Paige issued a similar moral harkening as he likened the school choice provisions in NCLB to "emancipation" allowing students to "throw off the chains of a school system that has not served them well" (Paige, 2004). In sum, these moral symbols and phrases have for all intents and purposes shielded NCLB's core machinery from acerbic political criticism.

At its inception, the legislation earned strong bipartisan support, especially from prominent Senators Edward Kennedy from Massachusetts and Connecticut Senator Joe Lieberman. While 2004 democratic presidential hopefuls Howard Dean and Wesley Clark readily envisaged the legislation's failure, Lieberman in particular refused to toe the democratic line (Zernike, 2004). During a 2004 debate in Iowa, Lieberman maintained that "anybody who says they're going to pull back and repeal No Child Left Behind is turning their back on the students, and particularly the low-income students, of America" (Zernike, 2004). At a later point during 2004 Presidential campaign, even Senator and Democratic presidential candidate Kerry criticized the legislation's budgeting shortfall but clearly demonstrated support for legislation's philosophical intent (Dobbs, 2004).

The serve and volley like commentary at the federal level suggests if not confirms that NCLB is unlike any previous domestic policy. NCLB is equipped with a moral defense system which permits it to deflect and at times overcome even the most rational criticism, which is most notably its lack of full funding. Problems encountered by states and local governing units in its implementation reveal another level of moral complexity.

The Moral Complexity of NCLB at the State Level

State governments (i.e., governors, state education agencies, etc.) undoubtedly face enormous challenges in meeting the requirements of NCLB. In addition to budgetary concerns, state governments assume the tall responsibility of putting in place the infrastructure enabling federal guidelines to be met and local educational agencies to comply. NCLB in short involves unprecedented coordination and action between and among all levels of government. Unlike past education reform agendas pressed primarily by ambitious governors (e.g., minimum testing requirements, decentralization, etc.), NCLB originated through federal, not state action. While some states viewed NCLB as an intrusion into what was thought for more than a century to be strictly a matter of state and local control, others cherished the opportunity to build political cache and push for change.

To be sure, states' motives for either embracing or resisting NCLB are complicated and difficult to make out. However, evidence seems to suggest a large measure of governors substantially support the core moral principles of NCLB. Fusarelli's (2005) study on gubernatorial reactions to NCLB showed that despite considerable opposition to some of its details, most governors seemed to embrace its core purpose but for dissimilar justifications. Fusarelli argues that governors by and large endorse NCLB for reasons such as broadening political influence, the level of consistency with already established state educational goals, and a fear of sanctions to name only some. For instance, as Fusarelli found, governors such as Michigan governor John Engler seized on NCLB's moral message (i.e., "leave no child behind") in an effort to rally political support, but rarely cited the legislation specifically when calling for educational change. Other governors such as Montana Republican governor Judy Martz and New Mexico Democratic governor Bill Richardson called attention to problematic issues associated with rural state compliance but hesitated to categorically denounce it (Fusarelli, 2005). Even as the unintended consequences or flaws of NCLB continue to emerge, its moral dimensions routinely soften attempts at harsh criticism.

The moral dimension of NCLB has also effectively "pulled into line" political groups whose endorsement would normally be more difficult to obtain. For example, in a recent report on the status of NCLB at the state level, the Education Commission of the States (2004) makes the following five recommendations: (a) Embrace NCLB as a civil rights issue; (b) ensure performance growth of all students, not just low-performing students; (c) reassess adequate yearly progress; (d) strengthen highly qualified teacher requirements; and (d) build state and local capacity. As a whole, the five recommendations clearly support rather than reject the legislation. The civil rights orientation of the first recommendation alone confirms that NCLB be endorsed by the states as a moral rather than a professional obligation. However, it is also apparent that these appeals for moral duty conceal and subdue legitimate technical criticisms of the legislation. At no other level is this suppression more perceptible than with local educational agencies.

The Moral Complexity of NCLB at the Local Level

At no other level are the morally defended but increasingly problematic practicalities of NCLB more exposed than at the local level. Local education agencies bear the onus of NCLB's implementation. Unlike former federal reform initiatives, its consequences for failing to meet expectations are punitive and threatening. All the same, NCLB is ambitious in purpose and impressive in scope. Without question, the details of the legislation have predictably confused and frustrated a fair amount of local school officials leaving some to wonder whether its full implementation is realizable.

Historically, school districts have relied largely on traditional national coalitions (e.g., American Association of School Administrators, the National Education Association, and the American Federation of Teachers) to speak on their behalf. NCLB presents an unusual challenge though. Its moral packaging seemingly makes it less disposed to criticism from powerful interest groups. Moreover, its moral dimension has made it especially challenging for interest organizations such as the NEA and AFT to coalesce and agree on a common strategy to confront the issues (Torres, 2004). With groups divided, NCLB's moral defense system has managed up to this point to conceal problems and suppress local criticism.

The Role of Educational Research?

Ethics and ethical behavior have become hot topics in educational administration (Starrat, 1994), and the moral aspects of NCLB may play well into this movement. The heightened concern for ethics and morality in educational administration research comes through in recent research by Whitney Sherman and Margaret Grogan (2003) on superintendents' responses to the achievement gap. This paper illustrates well the interest among educational researchers in the combination of scientific research and ethical critique of the status quo. As these authors point out, "Although a superintendent alone cannot restructure a school system to make it more equitable for all children, he or she can establish the importance that all students achieve success and set the tone for change" (p. 224). The authors make the normative point that "To effect change, superintendents must use a combination of political acumen and moral reasoning."

With this rationale, Sherman and Grogan interview 15 superintendents in the state of Virginia, eight women and seven men. They used Robert Starrat's conceptual framework which "forces educators to confront the moral issues involved when schools disproportionately benefit some groups in society and fail others (Starrat, 1994, p. 47). What they found is that superintendents had minimal knowledge of the achievement gap and that very little was being done about it. Moreover, only about one-third of the superintendents interviewed "gave importance to and showed insight into the notion of a gap in test scores at all. Of these, only two spoke of specific strategies that they were using to eliminate the gap" (p. 231). When the achievement gap was brought to their attention the superintendents deferred to their school boards.

It is still to early to tell what impact the emphasis on ethics and morality in research of this type will have on administrative behavior. Nonetheless, the two sources of emphasis on morality, one research, and the other policy, can be made to converge. We should not be surprised to see district level politics affected accordingly, with new political coalitions developing around an education policy that were it not for its moral component would probably never serve as a source of political polarities.

SUMMARY AND CONCLUSIONS

It is much too early to assess NCLB's impact and future. The political use of NCLB's moral aspects will undoubtedly be rendered less effective by the practicalities of its implementation in the coming years once the key requirements go into full effect. Technical issues like the adequate yearly progress and the highly qualified teacher requirements are already exposing weaknesses and shortcomings, which are raising serious doubts about the legislation, its moral aspect notwithstanding. To date, at least 10 state teacher collective bargaining organizations and or school districts have filed a lawsuit against the U.S. Department of Education upon various grounds (Lewis, 2005). But at least for now, NCLB's moral packaging seems to have enabled it to weather the storm longer than its opponents initially predicted.

REFERENCES

Bush, G. W. (2004, February 24). *President calls for constitutional amendment protecting marriage.* Retrieved September 1, 2005, from http://www.whitehouse.gov/news/releases/2004/02/print/20040224-2.html

Bush, G. W. (2004). The essential work of democracy. *Phi Delta Kappan, 86*(2), 144, 118–121.

Bush, G. W. (2001, November 6). *Bush says it is time for action.* Retrieved September 1, 2005, from http://archives.cnn.com/2001/US/11/06/ret.bush.coalition/index.html

Dobbs, M. (2004, October 20). Kerry competes to claim issue of reform; Democrat criticizes Bush policy for its implementation but not the law itself. *The Washington Post*, p. A4.

Education Commission of the States. (2004). *Report to the nation: State implementation of the No Child Left Behind Act.* Denver, CO: Author.

Fusarelli, L. (2005). Gubernatorial reactions to No Child Left Behind: Politics, pressure, and education reform. *Peabody Journal of Education, 80*(2), 120–136.

Hardy, L. (2004). The high cost of NCLB. *American School Board Journal, 191*, 7

Hess, F., & Finn, C. (2004). Inflating the life rafts of NCLB. *Phi Delta Kappan, 86*, 34–58.

Lewis, A. C. (2005). States flee NCLB. *The Education Digest, 71*(1), 68–69.

McClay, W. (2005) Bush's calling. *Commentary, 119*, 49–53.

Paige, R. (2004, January 28). *Paige calls vouchers "educational emancipation."* Retrieved September 1, 2005, from http://www.cnn.com/2004/EDUCATION/01/28/paige.choice.ap/

Phi Delta Kappa. (2005, September). *Thirty-seventh annual Phi Delta Kappa/Gallup poll of the public attitudes towards the public schools.* Retrieved September 1, 2005, from http://www.pdkintl.org/kappan/k0509pol.htm

Stam, J. (2003). Bush's religious language. *Nation, 277*(21), 27.

Sherman, W., & Grogen, M. (2003). Superintendents' response to the achievement gap: An ethical critique. *International Journal of Leadership in Education, 6*(3), 223–237.

Starratt, R. (1994). *Building an ethical school: A practical response to the moral crisis in schools.* London: Falmer Press.

Torres, M. S. (2004). Best interests of students left behind? Exploring the ethical and legal dimensions of United States federal involvement in public school improvement. *Journal of Educational Administration, 42*(2), 249–269.

Zernike, K. (2004, January 12). No Child Left Behind brings a reversal: Democrats faulta federal education plan. *The New York Times*, p. A16.

CHAPTER 5

TOWARD A MORE REFINED THEORY OF SCHOOL EFFECTS

A Study of the Relationship Between Professional Community and the Teaching of Mathematics in Early Elementary School

Laura M. Desimone

This study uses nationally representative data from the Early Childhood Longitudinal Study (ECLS) to refine a theory of professional community. Specifically, the study examines how professional community influences mathematics instruction in kindergarten and first grade by (1) distinguishing structural from social-psychological aspects of professional community, (2) dividing structural aspects of professional community into leadership and interactive activities, and then (3) applying these distinctions to the theoretical underpinnings of a commitment and control framework in organizations. Results support the hypotheses that collaboration and professional development foster more challenging mathematics instruction, and mediate the relationship between leadership and mathematics instruction. There is little support for the hypothesis that social-psychological professional community mediates the relationship of collaboration and professional develop-

Contemporary Issues in Educational Policy and School Outcomes, 87–133
Copyright © 2006 by Information Age Publishing

ment with mathematics instruction. Implications for theories about the relationship between professional community and mathematics instruction are discussed.

INTRODUCTION

School organization is a popular target for school change efforts, but our theoretical understanding of *how* school organization affects teaching and learning is limited. Empirical tests of hypothesized theoretical relationships are even rarer; but there is a body of work on teacher's professional community that has advanced our thinking about the links between the social organization of schools and teaching and learning. This study builds on that previous work and extends it in several ways.

First, the study integrates two theoretical perspectives—schools as social organizations and Brian Rowan's (1990) commitment and control framework—to study the relationship between professional community and teacher's use of conceptual instruction in mathematics. Second, the study refines and empirically tests a theoretical notion of how professional community works by dividing it into structural and social-psychological aspects, and by further dividing the structural aspects into leadership and interactive teacher activities. The theory set forth suggests that interactive activities mediate the relationship between leadership and instruction, and that social-psychological sense of community mediates the relationship between structural aspects of professional community and teacher's instruction. The third extension is the testing of the theory on a nationally representative sample of students in the early grades (from the Early Childhood Longitudinal Study, http://nces.ed.gov/ecls), which is touted as one of the most effective points of intervention for at-risk students (e.g., Knapp, 1997; Shore, 1997; Slavin, Karweit, & Madden, 1989). This builds on previous foundational work that was primarily conceptual or conducted on case studies or localized samples, and focused on upper elementary, middle, or high school (e.g., Bryk, Lee, & Holland, 1993; Louis & Marks, 1998).

A SOCIAL ORGANIZATIONAL PERSPECTIVE ON SCHOOLING

Moving from the seminal works of Coleman et al. (1966) and Jencks (1972) showing weak school effects on student achievement, Sorensen and Hallinan (1977) arguably made the first attempt to conceptually link the effects of school and schooling with the process of learning. Their theoretical conception identified school effects as operating through opportunity to learn (Carroll, 1963), student aptitude, and student effort. Bidwell and Kasarda (1980) then elaborated on Sorensen and Hallinan's (1977) social organizational perspective on schooling by focusing on how relationships among social structure, resources, and individual attributes affect learning; one of Bidwell and Kasarda's (1980) influential views was that "formal organizational milieus" (for example, information flow, interpersonal relationships, working routines, and communication transfer) could affect the outcomes of schooling by ensuring teachers' conformity with the school's or district's instructional policy.

With grounding in these early theoretical ideas, scholars of schools as organizations called for studies to help explain how the organizational design of schools affects teaching and learning (Rowan, Bossert, & Dwyer, 1983). Barr and Dreeben (1988) were among the first to apply social organization theory to studies of schooling, showing how the organization of classroom instruction—the assignment, pace, and content of different reading groups, for example—affected student achievement in reading. Also pioneers in the study of schools, Bryk and Driscoll (1988) demonstrated associations of aspects of teachers' work and relationships, which could be considered components of Bidwell and Kasarda's (1980) "milieus," with teaching and learning. These lines of work fostered a major stream of research on professional community.

Professional Community

Bryk and Driscoll's (1988) and Rosenholtz's (1985, 1989) research was central to establishing the premise that professional community—broadly defined to include dimensions such as collaborative planning time, professional development, teacher decision making, shared goals, shared vision, teacher commitment, and sense of collective responsibility for student learning—can influence teaching and learning. Building on this work, Kruse, Louis, and Bryk (1994) showed that positive school outcomes were related to specific aspects of professional community, particularly a collective focus on student learning, collaboration, teacher empowerment, and autonomy. Kruse and her colleagues separated what they considered conditions or precursors for professional community, such as communication structures, school autonomy, supportive leadership, trust and respect, and teacher decision making, from characteristics of professional community, which they defined by such factors as a focus on student learning, deprivitization of practice and engaging in reflective dialogue (Louis & Marks, 1998; Louis, Marks, & Kruse, 1996; Louis, Kruse, & Associates, 1995).

Newman and Wehlage (1995) related student achievement to a similar conception of professional community, including the collective reinforcement of goals, clear shared purpose and responsibility for student learning, and engaging in collaborative activity. Lee and Smith (1996) also showed a link between student achievement and professional community, defined as collective responsibility for student learning, staff cooperation, and control over classroom and school work conditions.

Despite variation in how scholars operationalize professional community, the core idea seems consistent across studies: professional community represents leadership that is supportive of change, is focused on a clear vision for the school, and provides teachers with a role in decision making about the school and the classroom. Professional community also represents interactive, collaborative activities that require teachers to engage with each other around issues of curriculum and instruction, as well as positive social-psychological beliefs and attitudes towards teachers' work life, such as support, respect, and commitment.

Thus, a series of well-designed studies in the past 2 decades has demonstrated a link between professional community, in its various forms, and student achievement. This raises a major question: *How* does professional community influence student achievement?

One notion, for which there is some evidence, is that professional community influences student achievement indirectly through instruction (Creemers & Reezigt, 1996; Sorenson & Hallinan, 1977; Stringfield & Slavin, 1992). For example, Newman and Wehlage (1995) and Louis and Marks (1998) concluded that their measure of professional community had a positive relationship with student performance through teachers' increased use of "authentic" pedagogical strategies, such as having students construct knowledge and communicate their understanding of that knowledge.[1] Similarly, Taylor, Pearson, Clark, and Walpole (1999) found that in the context of teaching reading, teacher collaboration led to teaching in small groups, which fostered the use of more effective teaching strategies such as more engaging instruction—leading, in turn, to increased student achievement.

The idea that professional community impacts teachers' instruction is consistent with the research that has highlighted how teachers' work context shapes their use of instructional strategies and activities (Little, 1993; McLaughlin, 1994; Talbert & McLaughlin, 1993). Teaching is considered a complex task requiring high levels of skill and motivation, and an effective school organization capitalizes on a teacher's ability and motivation to improve performance (Rowan, 1994). In a continued effort to understand the influence of professional community, this previous empirical work leads to the question: How does professional community influence teaching?

TOWARD A MORE REFINED THEORY OF THE EFFECTS OF PROFESSIONAL COMMUNITY ON TEACHING

To help answer this question—and in the process refine theory about links between professional community and the classroom—two research areas are bridged. First, current theoretical ideas that consider the broad, multi-dimensional nature of professional community are refined by dividing professional community into two components: structural aspects and social-psychological aspects. Structural aspects are then further divided into two dimensions, one related to leadership and the other related to interactive, collaborative teacher activities. Second, this newly created professional community dichotomy (i.e., structural vs. social-psychological) is bridged with Rowan's (1990) theory of a continuum of school organization—from commitment to control oriented—to suggest that challenging "conceptual" instruction is more likely to take place in schools high on professional community ("commitment" environments) than in "control"-oriented schools, which tend to focus on procedural instruction. The next section describes the evolution of these two approaches, and the hypotheses generated from bridging them.

Structural Aspects of Professional Development

For this theory-building exercise, structural aspects of professional community are considered to be those factors representing how a teacher's worklife is organized or structured. This includes the role of principals and teachers in leadership and decision making, as well as the form that teacher interactions take.

Leadership

Principal leadership. Key aspects of principal leadership that may help foster professional community include principals buffering teachers from outside pressures such as parents, districts, and resource issues; setting clear goals and following through on them; and providing a supportive environment for change (Firestone & Wilson, 1983; Leithwood, Leonard, & Sharratt, 1998; Little, 1982; Louis, Kruse, & Associates, 1995; Newmann & Wehlage, 1995; Rosenholtz, 1985, 1989). Buffering teachers from outside influences allows them to focus on instruction; setting clear goals allows them to develop coherent strategies around a particular target; and being supportive of change provides a safe environment for trial and error in trying out more complicated teaching strategies.

Teacher participation in decision making. Democratic approaches to leadership that involve teachers are characteristic of positive professional communities (Little, 1982; Newmann, Smith, Allensworth, & Bryk, 2001). Rosenholtz (1985, 1989) explains that one way teacher decision making may work to improve instruction is that the decision-making process moves teachers away from arbitrary or automatic reactions toward deliberate evaluation, suggestions, discussion, and modifications related to the nature and purpose of instruction. This is consistent with organizational theories that suggest including employees in the decision making allows performance to become more dependent on employee skills and motivation (Rowan, Chiang, & Miller, 1997).

Further, participation in decision making about teaching fosters more self-confidence in teachers (Lee, Dedrick, & Smith, 1991; McNeil, 1988; Mohrman, Cooke, & Mohrman, 1979; Newmann, Rutter, & Smith, 1989; Rosenholtz, 1989) and allows them to develop an increased sense of ownership regarding instructional goals—a key component to implementing instructional change (e.g., Datnow, 2000; McLaughlin & Marsh, 1978).

Interactive Activities

Leadership-related issues are only one component of the structural aspects of professional community. Another key aspect describes the structural arrangements that provide teachers with opportunities to collaborate and interact.

Collaboration. The opportunity to interact around instruction is a central component of professional community. More effective instruction may occur in schools where teachers engage in reflective discussion about their practice (Smith, Lee, & Newmann, 2001) and have an opportunity to collaborate (Rutter, Maughan, Mortimore, Ouston, & Smith, 1979; Little, 1982; Newmann & Wehlage, 1995). Working with other teachers on lesson plans and curricula allows teachers to share their ideas and pass along their successful experiences (Bird & Little, 1986). Such collaborations increase access to technical resources and expertise that can help teachers implement more challenging instruction; in other words, teacher collaboration may increase teachers' opportunity to learn (Kilgore & Pendleton, 1993). Collaborative work may also help teachers forge common goals, develop mutual respect for each other (Bird & Little, 1986; Rosenholtz, 1985), develop a sense of cohesiveness (Bridges & Hallinan, 1978), increase motivation and commitment (Newmann et al., 2001), and enhance their sense of mutual support for each other (Louis, Kruse, & Associates, 1995).

Professional development. In-service professional development activities can also be a productive form of teacher collaboration. Activities that provide teachers with an opportunity to observe or be observed, obtain feedback from other teachers, or work with other teachers in learning new content or pedagogical strategies can be powerful community-building mechanisms, as well as useful ways of increasing teachers' knowledge and skills (Bird & Little, 1986; Cohen & Ball, 1990a; Cohen, McLaughlin, & Talbert, 1993; Garet, Birman, Porter, Yoon, & Desimone, 2001; Loucks-Horsley, Hewson, Love, & Stiles, 1998; Newmann et al., 2001). Such opportunities to learn from each other are crucial to teachers' efforts to successfully adopt reform-oriented practices such as conceptual instruction (Cohen & Ball, 1999) and have been shown to be related to increased use of such practices (Desimone, Garet, Birman, Porter, & Yoon, 2002).

Social-Psychological Aspects of Professional Community

Next, the social-psychological aspects of professional community are considered. Unlike structural aspects, social-psychological aspects do not represent roles or actions; instead, the beliefs and attitudes of teachers—as reflected by, for example, shared vision, shared responsibility, and mutual respect—represent the social-psychological factors that are consistent with the idea of professional community.

Sense of community. The important social-psychological aspects of professional community are characterized by shared values, a shared sense of the school's mission, and mutual respect (Bryk, Easton, Kerbow, Rollow, & Sebring, 1993; Cohen, 1988; Cohen, McLaughlin, & Talbert, 1999; Firestone & Rosenblum, 1988; Lee & Smith, 1996). Feeling respected and being part of a school with a shared mission can increase teacher commitment (Firestone & Pennel, 1997). A value consensus may not be related to better teaching, and may enforce traditional teaching standards (e.g., Anyon, 1981; McLaughlin & Talbert, 1993), but shared respect might also convey a feeling of unity and belonging among peers that counteracts the fragmentation of teachers' work and helps teachers manage the demands associated with more challenging types of teaching (Newmann, Rutter, & Smith, 1989).

Structural Versus Social-Psychological Aspects of Professional Community

While scholars have not explicitly divided professional community into structural and social-psychological aspects, the theoretical base and design of several important studies supports such a distinction. The structural features of professional community—such as shared decision making and collaborative planning—have been used to predict what is termed here as social-psychological aspects of professional community, including teachers coalescing around a shared vision and taking collective responsibility for student learning (Lee & Smith, 1995; Little, 1990; Louis, Marks, & Kruse, 1996; Newmann & Wehlage, 1995; Rosenholtz, 1985, 1989). Previous work has also used social-psychological aspects of professional community to predict teachers' instruction (Louis & Marks, 1998; Newmann & Wehlage, 1995) and conceptualized dimensions of support for professional community as either "structural" or "social and human resources" (Louis, Kruse, & Associates. 1995). These studies have not, however, explicitly and systematically divided professional community into structural and social-psychological aspects in order to empirically examine their direct and indirect relationships with instruction.

Building on theory that links professional community to more challenging instruction, this study suggests how such links may operate. It is hypothesized that supportive, focused principal leadership and teacher decision making foster interactive professional development (i.e., activities where teachers actively interact) and other collaborative activities, in turn fostering positive social-psychological sense of community, which then directly influences teachers' capacity and choices about instruction and moves them toward covering more challenging content. Figure 5.1 illustrates the theoretical underpinnings of these relationships; the dotted lines represent current theory and the bold lines reflect the refinement that this analysis tests. Thus, in addition to hypothesizing direct relationships between professional community and teaching, which current theory supports, this analysis tests for mediating effects—specifically, that interactive, collaborative activities mediate the effect of leadership on teaching, and that sense of community mediates the effects of both leadership and interactive, collaborative teacher activities on instruction.

Linking the Structural/Social-Psychological Dichotomy With Rowan's Commitment and Control Framework

Previous theory provides a strong foundation on which to build a more detailed conceptual understanding of how professional community affects teaching. Specifically, Rowan (1990) applied structural contingency theory to schools, positing that the most appropriate organizational form depends on the kind of work an organization does. Rowan describes two main features of school organization on which schools may vary: (1) a "commitment" environment that fits the idea of professional community described earlier, where the school emphasizes shared responsibility for work, shared commitment to a common set of goals, lateral communication and shared power in decision making; and (2) a "control" environment where there is a clear hierarchy with top-down control and individualized (not collaborative) work. Most schools have aspects of both

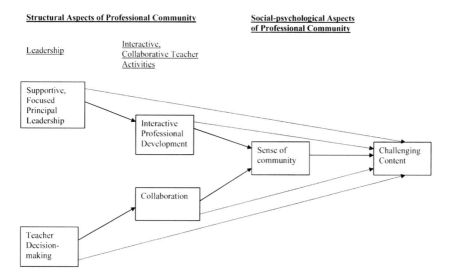

Structural Aspects of Professional Community

Social-psychological Aspects of Professional Community

Leadership

Interactive, Collaborative Teacher Activities

Supportive, Focused Principal Leadership

Interactive Professional Development

Collaboration

Teacher Decision-making

Sense of community

Challenging Content

Note: Dotted arrows reflect current theories. Bold arrows reflect refinement of current theory that (1) separates professional community into structural and social-psychological aspects, (2) separates structural aspects into leadership and interactive, collaborative activities, (3) suggests that leadership has its effect on instruction partially through collaborative activities and social-psychological sense of community and (4) suggests that collaborative activities have their effect on instruction partially through sense of community.

Figure 5.1. A refined theory of professional community.

of these types of organization, but are usually stronger in one than the other. These two organizational forms have also been characterized, respectively, as "communal" and "bureaucratic."

Rowan (1990) suggests that the nature of teaching varies across these two organizational settings. Routine, clear-cut work—as represented by procedural, direct instruction techniques—is better managed with specialization and a clear hierarchy, while flexible, nonroutine work—as represented by project-centered or conceptual teaching—is better managed with lateral, open communication. Conceptual approaches to teaching may result from communal organizational settings, or they may be the source of the communal organization (Rowan, 1995). For example, when faced with new and challenging tasks, teachers may be more likely to seek help from their colleagues. Based on these ideas, one would hypothesize that instruction characterized by direct, procedural content would be more likely to occur and more successful in a control-oriented school, whereas instruction characterized by conceptual content would be more common and more effective in a school with more of the "commitment" form (e.g., Bryk & Driscoll, 1988; Rowan, 1990).

HYPOTHESES

This study attempts to refine theoretical ideas about the relationship between professional community and teaching, as well as between organizational forms and teaching (Rowan, 1990), by (1) distinguishing structural from social-psychological aspects of professional community, (2) dividing structural aspects into leadership and interactive activities, and then (3) applying these distinctions to the theoretical underpinnings of Rowan's commitment and control framework.

The first hypothesis establishes the general relationship between instruction and professional community—specifically, that *the stronger the professional community, the more likely teachers are to implement conceptual approaches to instruction in the classroom.* This hypothesis is grounded in research that points to school structures and organizations as powerful mechanisms for shaping teachers' work lives and influencing their choices about both pedagogy and content (e.g., Elmore & Associates, 1990; Smith, Lee, & Newmann, 2001). To effectively use conceptual techniques, teachers must build their content knowledge—and they need support from their principal and fellow teachers as they undertake the risks, trial and error, and new learning required for conceptual teaching (e.g., Cohen, McLaughlin, & Talbert, 1993). Unless they feel a part of a strong professional community working toward a common goal, teachers may tend to maintain the individualism of their instruction and thus the status quo, which is predominantly procedural instruction.

The second hypothesis is that *structural aspects of professional community can be divided into leadership and interactive teacher activities; interactive, collaborative activities mediate the effect of leadership on the extent to which teachers implement conceptual instruction in the classroom.* For example, in schools with supportive principals who establish a clear vision and where teachers have opportunities to participate in decision making, teachers are more likely to establish mechanisms to interact, such as collaborative work groups and joint planning. Through these joint planning and collaborative endeavors, teachers build their knowledge and skills, fostering an increased use of more challenging instruction in their classrooms. These relationships are illustrated in Figure 5.1. While the theory being tested hypothesizes a particular causal ordering, temporal antecedence cannot be determined from the data analysis. Further, it is reasonable to consider that teachers with a proclivity to use conceptual approaches might foster a more communal type of professional community (e.g., Rowan, 1995). The potential nonrecursive relationship between teaching and professional community does not, however, interfere with the fundamental focus here on studying whether particular aspects of professional community are related to specific types of instruction.

The third main hypothesis is that *social-psychological aspects of professional community mediate the effects of structural aspects on the extent to which teachers cover challenging content.* For example, teachers foster a sense of shared vision and mutual respect via collaboration in planning the curriculum or in addressing the needs of individual students; this in turn motivates them to build their knowledge and skills and provides them with the support they need to increase their use of challenging content in the classroom.

Mathematics Instruction

This study focuses on mathematics, a subject targeted in the federal No Child Left Behind Act of 2001 and used as an international benchmark for the relative standing of U.S. students (e.g., Schmidt, McKnight, & Raizen, 1997; Stevenson & Stigler, 1992; Stigler & Hiebert, 1999). Evidence suggests that teacher practices differ by subject area (Stodolsky & Grossman, 1995), which supports the separate study of teaching practices by subject.

Rather than attempt to define instruction in all its depth and complexity (Cohen, Raudenbush, & Ball, 2003; Good & Brophy, 2000), this study instead focuses on one aspect of instruction: content, which is defined to include topics (e.g., counting, time) and type of learning required (e.g., memorization, communicating understanding). This choice is based on a pragmatic need to develop a measurable definition of instruction, as well as evidence that the content of instruction has thus far proven a stronger predictor of student achievement than pedagogical techniques have (e.g., Barr & Dreeben, 1983; Cooley & Leinhardt, 1980; Pellegrino, Baxter, & Glaser, 1999; Porter, Kirst, Osthoff, Smithson, & Schneider, 1993; Rowan & Miracle, 1983).

The distinctions between types of instruction used in this paper are grounded in the mathematics reform literature of the past 2 decades that focuses on the difference between "procedural" and "conceptual" knowledge, and suggests an increased emphasis on conceptual instruction is a potentially powerful strategy for increasing student achievement (see Loveless, 2001).

Reform scholars argue that the prevailing view of mathematics that has dominated K–12 education has involved mostly rules and procedures (Goodlad, 1984; Stake & Easley, 1978), with a focus on computational and algorithmic procedures that involve following predetermined steps to compute correct answers (Romberg, 1983). Student learning goals are usually memorization, recitation, and demonstration of facts, definition, and procedures (Smith, Lee, & Newmann, 2001).

In contrast, "conceptual" teaching in mathematics—also called "higher-order instruction," "teaching for understanding," and "authentic teaching"—is supported by much research (see Carpenter, Fennema, & Franke, 1996; Cohen & Ball, 1990b; National Council of Teachers of Mathematics, 1989; Spillane & Zeuli, 1999). Scholars state that through reasoning and argument (Lampert, 1992), as well as through conversations about mathematics, students learn from one another and gain insights that are not possible through procedural techniques (Brown & Campione, 1990; Brown, Collins, & Duguid, 1989; Simon, 1986). Conceptual teaching is often characterized as focusing more on higher-order thinking, such as synthesizing, estimating, explaining, hypothesizing, engaging in substantive conversation, and making connections to everyday situations than on simple manipulation of numbers to compute the right answer (Ball, 1993; Cobb, 1988; Lampert, 1986, 1990; Ma, 1999; National Council of Teachers of Mathematics, 1989, 1991; Newmann & Wehlage, 1995; Schifter & Fosnot, 1993)— for example, understanding the idea of place value, rather than just memorizing "where the decimal goes."

Debates persist about the appropriate balance between conceptual and procedural instruction in mathematics; it has not yet been determined which mix of content with which students has what effect over what duration of time under what circumstances (see Gamoran, Secada, & Marrett, 2000; Loveless, 2001; Shouse, 2001). However, many studies have documented achievement benefits from increased use of conceptual techniques in mathematics, using different definitions of conceptual instruction, and studying different grade levels (e.g., Carpenter, Fennema, Peterson, Chiang, & Loef, 1989; Cobb et al., 1991; Gamoran, Porter, Smithson, & White, 1997; Hiebert et al., 1996, 1997; Lee, Smith, & Croninger, 1997; Silver & Lane, 1995). Research also shows that conceptual techniques might be especially beneficial to disadvantaged students (e.g., Knapp, Shields, & Turnbull, 1992; Smith, Lee, & Newmann, 2001). Some studies, though, offer evidence in support of an emphasis on direct, procedural instruction (e.g., Geary, 2001; Slavin, Madden, Karweit, Livermon, & Dolan, 1990).

This study does not intend to contribute to the debate on the relative importance of conceptual versus procedural instruction. The decision to focus on conceptual instruction is based on evidence that (1) most mathematics students in the United States receive predominantly traditional, procedural instruction in mathematics (Hiebert, 1999;

Schmidt, McKnight, & Raizen, 1997), and so there is no need to increase the use of procedural instruction; (2) compared to their high and mid-achieving counterparts, low-achieving students receive less conceptual and more procedural instruction on average (Knapp & Shields, 1990; Kozma & Croninger 1992; Smith, Lee, & Newmann, 2001); and (3) most reformers advocate for at least a balance of procedural and conceptual instruction (Gamoran et al., 1997; Mullis, 1997; Smith, Lee, & Newmann, 2001), if not more of an emphasis on conceptual.

METHOD

Data

The study uses data from the National Center for Education Statistics (NCES) (National Center for Education Statistics, 2000) Early Childhood Longitudinal Study (ECLS), a nationally representative longitudinal sample of students who were kindergartners in 1998. The kindergarten sample is based on a national sample of schools with kindergarten programs. Because the ECLS followed students, teachers and schools were sampled in the first grade only if they included one or more ECLS-K children in their classrooms (NCES, 2004).

The ECLS' nested design of students in classrooms in schools, as well as its multidimensional measures of professional community and teaching, make it a good resource for testing the theoretical propositions presented here. The ECLS currently provides 2 years of data on a national multistage probability sample of 19,000 kindergartners and first graders in 3,000 classrooms in 1,000 schools (the public-use third-grade student achievement data became available in the summer of 2004). The ECLS conducted teacher surveys (93% response rate), principal surveys (69%), and parent interviews (85%) each year (NCES, 2000).

This study examines kindergarten and first grade teachers within schools using teacher and principal surveys from the "restricted-use" version of the ECLS. These data allow the linking of students to classrooms and schools. Since initial analyses of separate kindergarten and first-grade samples showed very similar results, and theory does not suggest that professional community would work differently in different early elementary school grades, the sample was pooled. Teacher-level variables are calculated from teacher questionnaires and classroom averages of student characteristics; school-level characteristics are calculated from administrator surveys and school averages of student characteristics. After choosing teachers with complete data on instruction, a total of 4,742 teachers and 969 schools are included in the analysis.

The Quality of Survey Data

The variables in this analysis are taken from teacher self-report surveys. As with every type of data collection, surveys have limits; however, careful examination of the research literature offers support for the use of surveys to measure instruction and other school-related activities. For example, the problem of teachers being inclined to answer in socially desirable ways (Burstein, McDonnell, Van Winkle, Ormseth, Mirocha, & Guitton, 1995) is less of a problem with anonymous surveys than in focus groups or interviews where they are in a more public forum (Aquilino, 1994; Dillman & Tarnai, 1991; Fowler, 2002). Also, when survey questions do not seek judgments of quality but rather accounting of behaviors, as the instruction questions on the ECLS do, social bias decreases and the validity and reliability of teacher self-report data can be quite high (Mullens & Gayler, 1999; Mayer, 1999).

Research has also shown that survey measures of teaching—especially composite measures like the ones used in this study—are effective in describing and distinguishing among different types of teaching practices and how often they are used, though not in measuring dimensions of teaching such as teacher-student interaction and teacher engagement (Herman, Klein, & Abedi, 2000; Mayer, 1999; McCaffrey, Hamilton, Stecher, Klein, Bugliari, & Robyn, 2001). Further, several studies have shown that teacher self-report surveys are highly correlated with classroom observations and teacher logs, and that one-time surveys about the content and strategies that teachers emphasize are quite valid and reliable in measuring teachers' instruction (Mullens, 1995; Mullens & Gayler, 1999; Mullens & Kasprzyk, 1996, 1999; Schmidt, McKnight, & Raizen, 1997; Shavelson, Webb, & Burstein, 1986; Smithson & Porter, 1994). The proper use of survey data to measure instruction also includes clarifying effect size claims and avoiding claims of causality from nonexperimental survey data (e.g., Rowan, Corenti, & Miller, 2002), both of which this study does. Further, surveys are considered appropriate for estimating a range of instructional approaches and providing estimates of their relationships with other key school and student-level variables (e.g., Cohen, Raudenbush, & Ball, 2003; Raudenbush, Rowan, & Cheong, 1993). While the ECLS survey data are limited in depth, they provide a good opportunity to test in a national sample the relationships that smaller studies have found between professional community and instruction.

MEASURES

The structural aspects of professional community are measured by three variables that represent leadership—supportive, focused principal leadership, teacher decision making about the school, and teacher decision making about the classroom—and two variables that represent teacher interactions—teacher collaboration and interactive professional development opportunities. The social-psychological aspect of professional community is measured by a variable that represents sense of shared mission and mutual respect. Appendix A describes each measure in the analysis and provides the alpha reliability of each composite of 3 or more items. Table 5.1 provides the standardized mean, standard deviation, and minimum and maximum value for each of the main independent and dependent variables.

Most of the variables are composite measures comprised of several items. Composites were developed based on the literature, then tested through confirmatory factor analysis to ensure that the items in each composite were measuring the same latent construct. Each professional community variable is measured at the teacher level, to account for the reality that there is substantial within-school variation on professional community (e.g., Newmann, King, & Youngs, 2000; Rowan, Chiang, & Miller, 1997).

Control Variables

Teachers' experience, knowledge, and skills have been associated with their ability and proclivity to use conceptual approaches to teaching (Ball, 1991; Putnam & Borko, 1997), and have been identified as mediators of the relationship between school organization and instruction (e.g., Cohen & Ball, 1990a, 1999; Louis & Marks, 1998). Thus, the analysis controls for teachers having a bachelor's or higher degree in mathematics, the number of mathematics courses taken in college, type of certification, years of experience, and whether teachers are in their first or second year of teaching. Further, there is evidence to suggest that teachers use conceptual approaches more often with higher-achieving students and procedural approaches more often with lower-achieving students (e.g., Smith, Lee, & Newmann, 2001; Snow, Burns, & Griffin, 1998; Turnbull, Welsh, Heid, Davis, & Ratnofsky, 1999), so student achievement at the start of the school year is controlled to help account for any variation in teachers' instruction that might be due to their responses to the class's achievement background. The amount of time in school (full-day kindergarten) and the time spent on math instruction are also controlled.

Table 5.1.   Standardized Descriptive Statistics

	Mean	SD	Minimum	Maximum
Teacher-Level Variables (n = 4,742)				
Professional Community				
Structural Aspects				
Leadership				
Supportive, focused, principal leadership	0.00	0.85	-3.13	1.09
School decision making	-0.01	0.98	-2.01	1.38
Classroom decision making	-0.01	0.99	-3.94	0.75
Interactive Activities				
Collaboration	-0.02	0.71	-.169	2.52
Interactive professional development	-0.01	0.63	-0.86	1.25
Social-Psychological Aspects				
Sense of Community	-0.01	0.78	-4.21	1.09
Teacher Background Characteristics				
Teaching Experience	-0.00	1.00	-1.27	3.89
1st or 2nd Year Teacher	.12	.32	0	1
No BA in mathematics	0.01	0.09	0.00	1.00
BA in mathematics	0.26	0.44	0.00	1.00
More than a BA in mathematics (masters or additional mathematics classes)	0.67	0.47	0.00	1.00
Math teacher courses taken	-0.01	1.00	-1.59	2.02
No certification	0.02	0.13	0.00	1.00
Emergency certification	0.09	0.28	0.00	1.00
Alternative certification	0.02	0.12	0.00	1.00
Regular certification	0.50	0.50	0.00	1.00
Advanced certification	0.33	0.47	0.00	1.00
Fall IRT score	-0.08	1.00	-2.28	1.94
Full day kindergarten	.29	.44	0	1
Time spent on math	23.09	10.08	0	45
Class < 27	.10	.29	0	1
1–10% LEP	.77	.40	0	1
1–10% spec. ed.	.94	.23	0	1
% minority in class	.43	.35	0	1
Instruction				
Basic	10.09	4.35	0.00	21.67
Algorithmic	7.04	4.26	0.00	21.67
Relational	8.37	4.63	0.00	21.67
Conceptual	7.53	4.68	0.00	21.67
School Background Variables (n = 969)				
Private school	0.24	0.43	0.00	1.00
Percent free lunch	0.37	0.48	0.00	1.00
School size	-0.00	1.00	-1.87	5.70

Note: Dummy variables have a minimum of 0 and maximum of 1; standardized variables have a mean of 0 and standard deviation of 1; each item in a composite was standardized, then used to create the composite.

School- and class-level demographic factors are correlated with the features of professional community (e.g., Cohen, McLaughlin, & Talbert, 1993), as well as with different types of instruction (Knapp, Shields, & Turnbull, 1992)—so the analysis controls for school poverty (free and reduced price lunch), percent minority students (Black or Hispanic) students in the class, and the percent of Limited English Proficient (LEP) and special education students in the class. In addition, because professional community has been associated with small schools (e.g., Lee & Smith, 1996) and research suggests private schools have different selection, organization, teacher, and community characteristics (Coleman, Hoffer, & Kilgore, 1982), the analysis controls for school and class size and whether the school is private or public. Finally, since instruction is expected to become more challenging in later grades, the analysis controls for class level (i.e., kindergarten or first grade).

Instruction

Teachers' instruction is dynamic and complex (e.g., Cobb, Wood, Yackel, & McNeal, 1992, 2001; Good & Brophy, 2000; Lehrer, Lee, & Jeong, 1999). While there are certainly many nuances not captured in this analysis, the measures used have adequate construct, face, and predictive validity; the composites are sufficiently reliable (with alpha reliabilities from .60 to .87); and the measures are consistent with the literature in terms of distinguishing topics and cognitive demands at increasingly challenging levels for early mathematics learners (e.g., Clements & Sarama, 2004). As such, the measures are instructive for the goal of this study: to test a relationship between professional community and increasingly challenging instruction. Though using alternative and more complex notions of challenging content and other important dimensions of instruction such as teacher-student interactions (Cohen, Raudenbush, & Ball, 2003) is beyond the scope of this study, such investigations would be a natural follow-up to the work reported here.

Reasonable dimensions of the content of instruction were derived from the literature on mathematics teaching and learning described earlier, standards for high-quality early elementary mathematics education (Clements & Sarama, 2004), descriptions of the "average" content taught in kindergarten and first grade (e.g., Denton & West, 2002), and consultation with nationally recognized experts in early mathematics. Based on a synthesis of this information, the ECLS measures of instruction were divided into four categories in order of increasing focus on more challenging content: basic, algorithmic, relational, and conceptual. Confirmatory factor analysis was conducted to check the validity of the constructs. Details on how each measure is constructed are in the appendix.

Relative amount of conceptual instruction. The expectation is that most teachers teach a substantial amount of basic instruction in both kindergarten and first grade, and a substantial amount of algorithmic instruction in first grade; so the hypothesis testing here should focus on how well professional community variables predict conceptual (and relational) teaching, with basic and algorithmic teaching as comparison points. This is a reasonable approach, but it assumes that teachers have to "trade off" time spent on one type of content with time spent on another; for example, more time on conceptual instruction would mean less time on basic instruction. However, the ECLS survey questions do not ask teachers to account for 100% of their instructional time with each of the four types of instruction; instead, teachers indicate how many times a day/week/month they cover particular content, which does not force trade-offs.

The descriptive data was examined to suggest the extent to which trade-offs were being made. Correlations of the four different dimensions of instruction described above range from .44 to .68 (see Table 5.2); further, comparisons of scatterplots of each type of instruction (not shown) reveal only small tradeoffs. An examination of the mean for each type of instruction for low, medium, and high levels on each of the professional community variables (see Appendix A) indicate that basic instruction is the most common, conceptual is the least common, and as values of professional community increase, teachers engage in more conceptual instruction.

A new instruction variable was created to test the sensitivity of results to the trade-off assumption. To "control" for possible high levels of other types of instruction when predicting conceptual instruction, an additive dependent variable was created. As instruction becomes more challenging, the weight increases. So, the weight for basic = 1, algorithmic = 2, relational = 3, and conceptual = 4. In effect, this variable measures the relative amount of conceptual teaching, given the amounts of other types of teaching. The empirical reasonableness of this "hierarchy" of types of instruction is supported by the HLM (hierarchical linear modeling) results for the control variables (reported in Tables 5.3, 5.4, and 5.5). For example, as classroom mean achievement and teachers' content knowledge (as measured by number of mathematics courses taken) increases, teachers are more likely to use relational and conceptual approaches.

The original response categories for all types of instruction were 1 = never, taught at a higher grade level, or children should already know; 2 = once a month or less; 3 = 2 or 3 times a month; 4 = once or twice a week; 5 = 3 of 4 times a week; and 6 = daily. For ease of interpretation, the instruction variables and the collaboration variable—which is on the

Table 5.2. Correlation of Main Independent and Dependent Variables

	Leadership	School-Level Decision Making	Class-Level Decision Making	Interactive Professional Development	Collabora-tion	Sense of Community	Basic	Algorithmic	Relational	Conceptual
Supportive, focused, principal leadership	1.00									
School-level decision making	.37***	**1.00								
Class-level decision making	.19***	.30***	1.00							
Interactive professional development	.11***	.09***	0.02	1.00						
Collaboration	.07***	.08***	.02**	0.23***	1.00					
Sense of community	.48***	.31***	.21***	0.06***	0.09***	1.00				
Basic	.07***	-0.03**	.00	0.17***	0.15***	0.03**	1.00			
Algorithmic	.02*	-0.02+	-.00	0.10***	0.14***	0.01	0.56***	1.00		
Relational	.08***	0.00	0.01	0.16***	0.17***	0.06***	0.68***	0.44***	1.00	
Conceptual	.07***	-0.01	0.00	0.18***	0.22***	0.06***	0.50***	0.53***	0.54***	1.00

+ = $p < .10$, * = $p < .05$, ** = $p < .01$, *** = $p < .001$

same scale—are converted to frequency per month. Thus, the new scale is $1 = 0$ times per month; $2 = 1$ time per month; $3 = 2.5$ times per month; $4 = 6$ times per month; $5 = 1\ 5.16$ times per month; and $6 = 21.6$ times per month.

Analysis

Three models are used to test the three main hypotheses. All three models test the first hypothesis: that all types of professional community are associated with increased use of conceptual and relational instruction. The first and second models test the second hypothesis: that interactive activities mediate the effects of leadership on the extent to which teachers use conceptual instruction. To test this hypothesis, the first model regresses the five different measures of instruction—basic, algorithmic, relational, conceptual, and relative amount of conceptual—on (1) school and teacher-level measures of supportive, focused leadership, and (2) school- and teacher-level teacher participation in school and classroom-level decisions. This analysis provides evidence of the extent of the direct relationship between aspects of leadership and instruction. The second model then adds the interactive activities—collaboration and interactive professional development—to the estimation. If the size and/or significance of the leadership variables decreases significantly from the first to the second model, this will suggest that part of the effect of leadership on instruction is mediated through interactive teacher activities.

The third model tests the third hypothesis that the social-psychological aspects of professional community mediate the effects of the structural aspects. So, in the third model, the variable measuring social-psychological aspects of professional community is added to the estimation; if the coefficients for leadership or interactive activities decrease or lose their significance, this is an indication that social-psychological aspects of professional community mediate the relationship between structural aspects of professional community and instruction.

All analyses were conducted using HLM, which separately estimates coefficients for each level of the system (i.e., school and teacher). This method reduces the aggregation bias inherent in regression models that use variables at different levels in the same equation (Bryk & Raudenbush, 1988). The multilevel modeling technique used here "is an elegant method for examining differences between groups in individual-level effects" (Gamoran, Secada, & Marrett, 2000), but does not address causal ambiguities; suggestions about causal ordering are derived from previous work. A longitudinal sample of teachers (ECLS follows students, not teachers) would be more appropriate for identifying temporal antecedents to teachers' instruction; such a study would also be able to address how the instability of instruction may influence results (Cohen & Ball, 1999). Still, the analysis here can provide a solid foundation for refining ideas about professional community, especially given the nature of the national sample.

In the analysis, school is level 2 and teachers are level 1. A random intercepts model was used at both level 1 and level 2. Mean substitution is used for missing data on the independent variables; dummy variables were created to flag variables for which there were 10% or more missing, and these dummy variables were then entered into the model to indicate whether missing data introduces bias in the results. Cases with missing data on the dependent variables were dropped. To check the sensitivity of the results to substituting the mean for missing values, the multiple imputation method was also used. Because results from the multiple imputation analysis were nearly identical to the mean substitution results in terms of significance (a few of the coefficients were 10–15% larger in the mean substitution), the results of the more straightforward method of mean substitution are reported.[2]

RESULTS

Table 5.2 contains the correlations of the main independent and dependent variables in the study. With the exception of the two teacher decision-making variables, all professional community variables are significantly correlated with types of instruction. These correlations forecast later findings from the multilevel models that the two teacher decision-making variables are the weakest predictors of instruction. On the whole, the correlations show that multicollinearity between the independent and dependent variables is not a concern.

Consistent with prior research (e.g., Bryk & Raudenbush, 1988), the variance decomposition (see Tables 5.3, 5.4, and 5.5) shows more within- than between-school variation in professional development and teaching. The models explain between 10 and 17% of the between-school variance in different types of instruction.

Hypothesis 1:   Professional community fosters teachers' use of challenging content in the classroom.

As mentioned earlier, examination of the means for each type of instruction by low, medium, and high levels of professional community (reported in Appendix A) provide support for the idea that more challenging instruction is more common in schools with higher levels of professional community. In fact, Table A1 shows that use of all types of instruction increases as professional community increases. Higher levels of professional community are often associated with more of an increase in conceptual than other types of instruction, but differences between types of instruction are generally not statistically significant.

Moving from this precursory mean analysis to the HLM analysis predicting instruction (reported in Tables 5.3, 5.4, and 5.5), results show that some, but not all, structural and social-psychological aspects of professional community predict the increased use of conceptual instruction. Results also indicate that professional community variables predict other types of instruction, though often at weaker levels. In Model 1 (Table 5.3), teacher-level supportive, focused principal leadership predicts a .27 ($p <$ .001) standard deviation increase in algorithmic instruction, compared to a .49 ($p < .001$) standard deviation increase in conceptual instruction—a statistically significant difference. Translating these coefficients into a more interpretable metric, when supportive, focused principal leadership changes from 3.97 (about "agree") to 4.92 (about "strongly agree"), there is a corresponding increase in algorithmic teaching of one fourth of a day each month ($b = .27$),[3] compared to almost half a day's increase in conceptual teaching per month ($b = .49$).

Supportive, focused principal leadership also predicts a .38 ($p < .001$) standard deviation increase in basic instruction, which is not statistically different from its predictive power for conceptual. In Models 2 (Table 5.4) and 3 (Table 5.5), supportive, focused leadership predicts more of an increase in the more conceptual than procedural types of instruction, but the differences are small. School-level decision making is insignificant in model 1 (Table 5.3), but is associated with decreased use of all types of instruction except algorithms in models 2 (Table 5.4) and 3 (Table 5.5). Classroom-level teacher decision-making variables are insignificant across all of the models.

As expected, teacher-level collaboration and professional development generally are stronger predictors of conceptual and relational than basic and algorithmic, though differences are quite small. For example, collaboration predicts a .98 ($p < .001$) standard deviation increase in conceptual and a .92 ($p < .001$) standard deviation increase in relational teaching, compared to a .79 ($p < .001$) and .59 ($p < .001$) standard deviation increase in basic and algorithmic instruction respectively. Translating these coefficients into a practical metric, an increase from 2.99 to 4.19 in the number of days per month spent collaborating—basically an increase of 1 day per month—corresponds to an increase of a little less than 1 day per month of conceptual (.98) and relational (.92) teaching, about three fourths of a day per month of basic instruction (.79) and about half a day's increase in algorithmic teaching (.59).[4]

Table 5.3. Model 1, HLM Results Using Leadership and Teacher Decision Making to Predict Instruction

Variable	Basic		Algorithmic		Relational		Conceptual		Relative Amt. of Conceptual	
	Beta	Se	Beta	Se	Beta	Se	Beta	Se	Beta	Se
Intercept	7.73***	0.43	4.26****	0.38	6.56***	0.46	4.59***	0.46	5.43***	0.37
Teacher Level										
Professional Community										
Structural Aspects										
Leadership	0.38***	0.08	0.27***	0.07	0.43***	0.09	0.49***	0.08	0.42***	0.07
School-level decision-making	-0.12+	0.07	-0.02	0.06	-0.05	0.08	-0.09	0.08	-0.06	0.06
Classroom-level decision making	-0.12	0.07	0.07	0.06	0.07	0.08	0.11	0.08	0.09	0.06
Teacher Background Characteristics										
Yrs. of teaching experience	-0.28	0.07	-0.25***	0.06	-0.25**	0.08	-0.01	0.08	-0.16*	0.06
1st or 2nd year teacher	-0.16	0.21	-0.16	0.19	0.00	0.23	0.24	0.22	0.08	0.17
No BA in math[a]	2.46***	0.91	2.97***	0.82	1.4	0.94	0.51	0.73	1.47***	0.71
BA in math	0.04	0.15	0.16	0.13	-0.28+	0.16	-0.31*	0.16	-0.17	0.12
Math teacher courses taken	-.43***	0.06	0.26***	0.06	0.47***	0.07	0.45***	0.07	0.42***	0.05
No certification[b]	-0.19	0.61	-0.68	0.45	-0.48	0.63	0.45	0.56	-0.27	0.49
Emergency certification	0.02	0.25	-0.04	0.22	-0.25	0.27	-0.11	0.26	-0.13	0.21
Alternative certification	0.77	0.59	-.89	0.55	0.04	0.58	0.31	0.61	-0.13	0.50
Regular certification	-0.19	0.18	-0.11	0.16	-0.29	0.20	-0.17	-.19	-0.40	0.15

Fall IRT score	-0.21	0.16	-0.55***	0.14	-0.07	0.17	0.74	0.16	0.37**	0.13
Full day kindergarten	1.85***	0.24	0.80***	0.20	1.48***	0.24	1.25***	0.23	1.28***	0.18
Time spent on math	0.09***	0.01	0.08***	0.01	0.08***	0.01	0.08***	0.01	0.08***	0.01
Class < 27	-0.11	0.32	-0.33	0.27	-0.23	0.31	0.01	0.28	-0.14	0.23
1–10% LEP	-0.20	0.19	-0.24	0.17	0.13	0.19	0.04	0.20	-0.02	0.15
1–10% spec. ed.	-0.36	0.25	-0.24	0.24	0.34	0.28	-0.10	0.29	-0.02	0.23
% minority in class	0.56*	0.26	-0.42+	0.24	0.07	0.27	0.33	0.27	0.30	0.22
School-Level Demographics										
Private school	0.08	0.25	-0.02	0.23	-0.51*	0.26	-0.63	0.24	-0.40*	0.20
Percent free lunch	0.20*	0.09	0.08	0.08	0.05	0.09	0.00	0.09	0.05	0.07
School size	0.30***	0.08	0.21	0.08	0.25***	0.08	0.38***	0.08	0.30***	0.07
Variance Component										
Level 1 variance	14.97		11.06		17.92		16.64		10.68	
Level 2 variance	1.88***		1.97***		1.71***		1.91***		1.26***	
d.f.	963		963		963		963		963	
Chi-square	1,551		1,796		1,390		1,452		1,473	
Deviance	26,513		25,221		27,271		26,980		24,902	
d. f.	2		2		2		2		2	

Table 5.4. Model 2, HLM Results Using Leadership, Teacher Decision-Making, Interactive Professional Development and Collaboration to Predict Instruction

Variable	Basic		Algorithmic		Relational		Conceptual		Relative Amt. of Conceptual	
	Beta	se	beta	se	beta	se	beta	se	beta	se
Intercept	7.75***	0.42	4.26***	0.38	6.58***	0.45	4.61***	0.44	5.45***	0.35
Teacher Level										
Professional Community										
<u>*Structural Aspects*</u>										
Leadership										
Supportive, focused, principal leadership	0.29***	0.08	0.22**	0.07	0.34***	0.09	0.38***	0.08	0.33***	0.07
School-level Decision making	-0.20**	0.07	-0.06	0.06	-0.14+	0.07	-0.19*	0.08	-0.15*	0.06
Class-level Decision making	0.12	0.07	0.07	0.06	0.07	0.07	0.10	0.07	0.09	0.06
Interactive Activities										
Professional development	0.73***	0.11	0.30**	0.09	0.76***	0.12	0.87***	0.11	0.71***	0.09
Collaboration	0.79***	0.10	0.59***	0.08	0.92***	0.11	0.98***	0.10	0.87***	0.08
Teacher Background Characteristics										
Teaching Experience	-0.24***	0.07	-0.23***	0.06	-0.20**	0.08	0.04	0.08	-0.11+	0.06
1st or 2nd year teacher	0.05	0.21	-0.28	0.19	-0.23	0.22	-0.02	0.22	-0.14	0.17
No BA in math[a]	2.23	0.84	2.81***	0.8	1.15	0.92	0.20	0.68	1.22+	0.67
BA in math	0.10	0.14	0.20	0.13	-0.21	0.15	-0.23	0.15	-0.11	0.12
Math teacher courses taken	0.33***	0.06	0.20***	0.06	0.36***	0.07	-0.33***	0.07	0.32***	0.05

No certification[b]	0.02	0.58	-0.52	0.45	-0.22	0.06	0.34	0.52	-0.03	0.45
Emergency certification	0.06	0.25	-0.01	0.22	-0.20	0.27	-0.05	0.26	-0.08	0.21
Alternative certification	0.66	0.56	0.85	0.54	-0.07	0.54	0.19	0.57	0.30	0.46
Regular certification	-0.18	0.18	-0.01	0.16	-0.27	0.19	-0.14	0.19	-0.17	0.15
Fall IRT score	-0.23	0.15	-.54***	0.14	-0.09	0.16	0.72***	0.16	0.36***	0.13
Full day kindergarten	1.83***	0.23	0.79***	0.20	1.47***	0.24	1.24***	0.22	1.27***	0.18
Time spent on math	0.08***	0.01	0.07***	0.01	0.08***	0.01	0.07***	0.01	0.08***	0.01
Class < 27	-0.2	0.31	-0.39	0.27	-0.30	0.31	-0.06	0.29	-0.21	0.23
1–10% LEP	-0.26	0.29	-0.28+	0.17	0.04	0.18	-0.05	0.19	-0.09	0.15
1–10% Spec. Ed.	-0.20	0.24	-0.13	-.24	0.52+	0.27	0.09	0.28	0.14	0.22
% minority in class	-.63*	0.26	0.48*	0.24	0.14	0.27	0.41	0.26	0.37+	0.21
School-Level Demographics										
Private school	0.39	0.24	0.21	0.23	-0.16	0.25	-0.25	0.23	-0.07	0.19
Percent free lunch	0.20*	0.009	0.09	0.08	0.05	0.09	0.00	0.08	0.05	0.07
School size	0.27***	0.08	0.19*	0.08	0.23**	0.08	0.35***	0.08	0.27***	0.06
Variance Component										
Level 1 variance	14.46		10.86		17.3		15.93		10.14	
Level 2 variance	1.79***		1.95***		1.57***		1.65***		1.11***	
d.f.	963		963		963		963		963	
Chi-square	1,540		1,804		1,372		1,400		1,437	
Deviance	26,321		25,118		27,069		26,721		24,615	
d.f.	2		2		2		2		2	

+ = $p < .10$, * = $p < .05$, ** = $p < .01$, *** = $p < .001$; [a]suppressed category = advanced degree in math; [b]Suppressed category is advanced certification.

Table 5.5. Model 3, HLM Results Using Leadership, Teacher Decision-Making, Interactive Professional Development, Collaboration, and Social-Psychological Sense of Community to Predict Instruction

Variable	Basic		Algorithmic		Relational		Conceptual		Relative Amt. of Conceptual	
	Beta	se	Beta	se	beta	se	beta	se	Beta	se
Intercept	7.77***	0.42	4.29***	0.38	6.6***	0.45	4.63***	0.44	5.47***	0.35
Teacher Level					L					
Professional Community										
<u>Structural Aspects</u>										
Leadership										
Supportive, focused principal leadership	-0.22*	0.09	0.19*	0.08	0.25**	0.09	0.32***	0.09	0.26***	0.07
School-level decision making	-0.21**	0.07	-0.07	0.00	-0.16*	0.07	-0.21**	0.08	-0.17**	0.06
Class-level decision making	0.11	0.07	0.07	0.06	0.05	0.07	0.09	0.07	0.08	0.06
Interactive Activities										
Professional development	0.73***	0.11	0.30**	0.09	0.77	0.12	0.87***	0.11	0.71***	0.09
Collaboration	0.78***	0.11	0.58***	0.08	0.90***	0.10	0.97***	0.10	0.85***	0.08
<u>Social-Psychological Aspects</u>										
Sense of community	0.18+	0.09	0.09	0.09	0.09*	0.12	0.16+	0.09	0.17*	0.08
Teacher Background Characteristics										
Teaching experience	-0.26***	0.07	-0.24***	0.06	-0.22**	0.08	0.03	0.08	-0.13*	0.06
1st or 2nd year teacher	-0.04	0.21	-0.27	0.19	-0.22	0.23	0.00	0.22	-0.13	0.17
No BA in math[a]	2.28**	0.84	2.87***	0.80	1.20	0.92	0.27	0.68	1.28+	0.67

BA in math	0.09	0.14	0.19	0.13	-0.22	0.15	-0.25+	0.15	-0.12	0.12
Math teacher courses taken	0.33***	0.06	0.20***	0.06	0.37***	0.07	0.34***	0.07	0.32***	0.05
No certification[b]	0.02	0.58	-0.52	0.44	-0.22	0.59	0.35	0.52	-0.02	0.45
Emergency certification	0.08	0.25	0.00	0.22	-0.17	0.27	0.19	0.57	0.31	0.46
Alternative certification	0.67	0.56	0.85	0.53	-0.06	0.54	0.19	0.57	0.31	0.46
Regular certification	-0.18	0.18	-0.10	0.16	-0.26	0.19	-0.13	0.19	-0.17	0.15
Fall IRT score	-0.24	0.15	0.54***	0.14	-0.11	0.16	0.71***	0.16	0.34**	0.13
Full Day kindergarten	1.82***	0.23	0.79***	0.2	1.45***	0.24	1.23***	0.22	1.26***	0.18
Time spent on math	0.08***	0.01	0.07***	0.01	0.08***	0.01	0.07***	0.01	0.08***	0.01
Class < 27	-0.21	0.31	-0.38	0.27	-0.32	0.31	-0.06	0.29	-0.22	0.23
1–10% LEP	-0.26	0.19	-0.29+	0.17	0.30	0.18	-0.06	0.19	-0.10	0.15
1–10% Spec. Ed.	-0.21	0.24	-0.14	0.24	0.51+	0.27	0.08	0.28	0.13	0.22
% Minority in class	0.63*	0.26	0.48*	0.24	0.15	0.27	0.42	0.26	0.08***	0.01
School-Level Demographics										
Private school	0.35	0.24	0.19	0.23	-0.21	0.25	-0.28	0.23	-0.11	0.19
Percent free lunch	0.20*	0.09	0.09	0.08	0.05	0.09	0.01	0.08	0.06	0.07
School size	0.28***	0.08	0.20**	0.08	0.24**	0.08	0.36***	0.08	0.28***	0.06
Variance Component										
Level 1 variance	14.45		10.84		17.29		15.92		10.13	
Level 2 variance	1.77***		1.95***		1.56***		1.64***		1.1***	
d. f.	963		963		963		963		963	
Chi-square	1,536		1,807		1,370		1395		1,432	
Deviance	26,307		25,102		27,053		26705		24,598	
d. f.	2		2		2		2		2	

+ = $p < .10$, * = $p < .05$, ** = $p < .01$, *** = $p < .001$

[a]Suppressed category = advanced degree in math; [b]Suppressed category is advanced certification.

This pattern is similar for teacher-level professional development and holds true for Model 3, when social-psychological professional community is added. In several cases, interactive professional development does a significantly better job of predicting conceptual than basic; for example, in both Models 2 and 3 (Tables 5.4 and 5.5), interactive professional development predicts a .73 (p < .001) standards deviation increase in basic instruction, compared to a .87 (p < .001) increase in conceptual instruction. This translates into an increase in professional development from 1.4 days per month to 1.87, corresponding to an increase of .73 days per month in basic instruction and an increase of .87 days in conceptual instruction.[5]

As for the direct relationship between social-psychological professional community and the different types of instruction, Model 3 shows that controlling for the structural aspects of professional community, social-psychological aspects predict a .09 (p < .05) increase in relational instruction, and a .17 (p < .05) standard deviation increase in relative amount of conceptual instruction (relationships with basic and conceptual instruction are only significant at the .10 level). This means that an increase in social-psychological community from "agree" to "strongly agree" predicts an increase of about one fourth of a day more relational teaching and one fifth of a day more relational instruction and relative amount of conceptual instruction per month. These effects are weaker than for professional development and collaboration. Sense of community is a much weaker predictor of instruction than supportive, focused leadership, interactive professional development, or collaboration.[6]

> Hypothesis 2: In considering the structural aspects of professional community, interactive, collaborative activities mediate the effect of leadership on increasing teachers' use of challenging content in the classroom.

Comparing Tables 5.3 and 5.4 shows that interactive, collaborative activities have direct relationships with instruction, and they also mediate the relationship between all types of instruction and supportive, focused principal leadership and school-level decision making. Specifically, relationships between supportive, focused principal leadership and all types of instruction decrease moderately when the interactive activities variables are added to the model. For example, teacher-level supportive, focused principal leadership goes from predicting a .49 (p < .001) standard deviation increase in conceptual instruction and a .43 (p <.001) standard deviation increase in relative conceptual instruction in Model 1 to predicting only a .38 (p < .01) standard deviation increase in conceptual instruction and .34 (p < .001) increase in relative conceptual instruction in Model 2. The relationships with algorithmic and relational instruction also decrease when collaboration and interactive professional development are added.

The school-level decision-making variables that did not predict instruction in Model 1 (Table 5.3) become significant negative predictors when interactive activities are added in Model 2 (Table 5.4). It could be that once professional development and collaboration are controlled, the more school decision making becomes a proxy for having a leadership role at the school, which results in teachers spending less time on instruction.

> Hypothesis 3: The social-psychological aspects of professional community mediate the effects of structural aspects of professional community on teachers' use of challenging content.

The third hypothesis can be examined by comparing Models 1, 2, and 3 in Tables 5.3, 5.4, and 5.5. Results suggest that social-psychological aspects of professional community may mediate the effects of supportive, focused leadership, but not the effects of school-level decision making, collaboration, or professional development.

The addition of social-psychological aspects of professional community to the estimation reduces the predictive power of supportive, focused principal leadership for all types of instruction, especially relational and relative amount of conceptual, only negligibly (by .02 or less). Interactive professional development and collaboration remain basically unchanged. Thus, in this analysis, instruction and social-psychological aspects of professional community mediate the relationship between instruction and supportive, focused principal leadership but not the relationship between instruction and school-level decision making or instruction and interactive collaborative activities.[7]

DISCUSSION

Though most of the effect sizes in this analysis are small (see Rosenthal & Rosnow, 1984), there are some effects of moderate practical size—for example, a 1 day per month increase in collaboration results in a 1 day per month increase in conceptual teaching. In addition, since only about 10–20% of the variance in instruction is due to school-related variables, the coefficients here that explain between 25% to a full standard deviation change in teaching are substantial enough to suggest a meaningful relationship, adequate for drawing tentative conclusions about the theory being tested.

A sophisticated understanding of the relationship between school- and classroom-level factors acknowledges that there are most likely important bidirectional, indirect, and interactive effects (e.g., Cohen & Ball, 1999; Cohen, Raudenbush, & Ball, 2003; Elmore, Peterson, & McCarthey, 1996; Gamoran, Secada, & Marrett, 2000). Competing theories hypothesize that teaching may drive organization instead of the other way around (e.g., Elmore, Peterson, & McCarthey, 1996; Rowan, 1995; Rosenholtz, 1985), given that teaching practice is to a large extent shaped by teachers' prior ideas and teaching behaviors (also Cohen, 1990; Cohen & Hill, 2000). Unfortunately, bidirectionality cannot be examined, since the study does not follow teachers over time. It is noted that a longitudinal study of teachers would provide a natural follow-up to the current analysis, and the possibility of nonrecursive and interactive effects should be considered in the interpretation of the results. Also, unmeasured variables may explain part of the professional community effects; for example, the effect might be partly explained if schools high on professional community were also more likely to offer rewards, or have explicit policies about conceptual instruction.

Interpretation of Findings

Results offer some support for the first two hypotheses. Findings support the first hypothesis, that professional community fosters more challenging instruction, but more generally, professional community supports all types of instruction; class-level decision making was the only professional community variable that never significantly predicted instruction. The second hypothesis was that structural aspects pertaining to leadership operate primarily through their relationship with fostering teacher interactions and positive social-psychological community. Findings show that interactive and social-psychological aspects of community do explain some (but not all) of the relationship between leadership and instruction. But there is little support for the third hypothesis, that those structural aspects of professional community representing teacher interaction have part of their effect through the social-psychological aspects of professional community.[8]

Some but not all aspects of professional community predict more conceptual instruction. Results of this analysis support the idea that teachers are more likely to cover more challenging content in the classroom if they work in an environment where the principal is supportive and has a clear vision for the school, and where they interact with other teachers—observing, receiving feedback, and engaging in dialogue about instructional practices—to plan and strategize collaboratively (e.g., Smith, Lee, & Newmann, 2001). In other words, "commitment"-oriented environments are more likely to have more challenging instruction (Rowan, 1990)—but teachers in this study in commitment–oriented schools are also more likely to spend time on procedural instruction.

In the current analysis, findings suggest that teacher decision making does not have a direct relationship with instruction, but may work indirectly through teacher interactive activities. Decision making about school-level policy was negatively predictive of most types of instruction when interactive activities were included in the analysis. Supplemental analyses show that teacher decision making has a small but significant relationship with both interactive professional development and collaboration. These results may suggest that in schools where teachers have more decision-making authority, they may be more likely to design and participate in professional development activities that require collaboration and interaction, which themselves have a direct positive relationship with the use of more challenging instruction (as well as procedural instruction).

Class-level decision making is never a significant predictor of instruction. These results are consistent with earlier work suggesting teacher decision making is not sufficient for establishing professional community (Louis & Marks, 1998), and that it has either a weak or no direct association with instruction (e.g., Conley, 1991; Lee & Smith, 1996; Malen, Ogawa, & Kranz, 1990; Murphy & Beck, 1995; Newman, Rutter, & Smith, 1989). One hypothesis is that involvement in school-level policy setting is distracting to teachers, since it often is not directly related to classroom teaching (Johnson, 1990).

Interactive, collaborative aspects of professional community mediate the effects of principal leadership on instruction. The relationship between a principal's supportive, focused leadership and teachers' instruction becomes smaller when collaboration and interactive professional development and are added to the estimation model. This provides support for the initial theoretical notions set forth here—that structural aspects of professional community can be divided into leadership and interactive, collaborative activities, and that leadership's effects on instruction are mediated by the actual activities in which teachers engage. Results offer some support for the hypothesis that the reason supportive, focused leadership might facilitate more challenging instruction is in part because such leadership involves the creation of organizational structures that allow teachers to interact with each other around curriculum and instruction (according to Rowan, 1990, a more "commitment"-oriented environment is more likely to have opportunities for teachers to work with each other). This in turn builds the knowledge and skills teachers need to implement more challenging instruction, and also increases their motivation and commitment to implementing such instruction (e.g., Datnow, 2000). However, even after adding interactive activities, supportive, focused principal leadership has independent positive relationships with all types of instruction, indicating that teacher interactions do not explain all of the effect of leadership.

Social-psychological professional community mediates supportive, focused principal leadership, but not collaboration or interactive professional development. These findings are consistent with the view that teachers' opportunity to learn, such as in collaborative planning and interactive professional development, is crucial to improving their instructional capacity (Cohen & Ball, 1999; Smith, Lee, & Newmann, 2001).

Previous views that collegial interactions contribute to a strong feeling of belief in community, making teachers more focused and thus more effective (Little, 1982; Meyer & Cohen, 1971; Rosenholtz, 1985) could still be true. It could be that certain aspects of social-psychological professional community are more important than others, for example, collective responsibility for student learning, which was not measured in this analysis. Also, sense of community perhaps has its influence through teacher efficacy, or through behaviors consistent with teacher commitment—such as increased teacher attendance and retention—which are beyond the scope of this analysis. It would be instructive to further explore how other variables might mediate the relationship between sense of community, instruction, and student achievement.

While results generally support a positive relationship between professional community and more challenging instruction, results differentiating the four forms of instruction are not as strong as the theory anticipated. This is probably due in part to the modest correlation among the four dependent variables and to the complexities involved in trying to distinguish four separate content levels of instruction in a multigrade analysis (e.g., the algorithmic variable is more advanced for kindergarten than first graders). To some extent the inclusion of the weighted variable that measures amount of conceptual instruction relative to other types of instruction accounted for these challenges.

But the findings also suggest another hypothesis, appealing for its relevance to this theory-building exercise: that some of the influence of professional community, especially in disadvantaged schools, could be to focus teachers on instruction—any type of instruction—and away from discipline, paperwork, and other nonacademic concerns. Nearly 2 decades ago, Brophy and Good (1986) pointed out the importance of teachers focusing on any type of instruction versus not actively teaching at all. This would explain why the professional community variables are significant predictors of basic and algorithmic as well as relational and conceptual instruction. Such a notion is consistent with the proposition set forth by Lee, Smith, and Croninger (1997) in their analysis of high-school organization. They suggested that school organization might have its effect not only on individual teacher practice, but through a "willingness of schools to adopt and stick to policies and practices that move them away from bureaucracies toward communities with a strong academic focus" (p. 141). Thus, it could be that much of the power of strong professional community is not only to foster more challenging content, but to move teachers away from spending time on nonacademic concerns so they can focus on any type of content.

Future Directions for Research

The analysis here provides support for Rowan's (1990) application of contingency theory to schooling, which establishes the importance of organizational commitment strategies for mediating the effectiveness of professional community on teachers' instruction. The next step in developing an even more refined theory of how professional community affects teaching and learning is to apply Rowan's view that organization improves the *effectiveness* of particular teaching practices; that is, to examine the extent to which professional community influences the *effectiveness* of instruction on student achievement. Such a study might examine the extent to which conceptual teaching is more strongly linked to student achievement in schools with strong professional community (commitment-oriented) than in control-oriented schools. This line of work would also be informed by analyses that model structural/organizational interactions with teaching (Lee & Bryk, 1989); and a study of a longitudinal sample of teachers would be an appropriate way to help tease out the time-ordering (e.g., Rogosa, 1995).

A strength of this study is that it focuses on kindergarten and first grade, at a time when more and more research is showing the importance of good teaching in the early grades (Snow, Burns, & Griffin, 1998). However, the relationship between professional community and instruction might differ in later elementary grades; examining these relationships in a national upper-elementary sample with multiple conceptions or dimensions of professional community would also be informative. Further, research should continue to be sensitive to the finding that teachers within the same school have different experiences in terms of professional community.

Conclusion

In seeking to refine a theory of how professional community influences teaching, this study of kindergarten and first grade suggests that (1) conceptual instruction is more likely to occur in schools with supportive, focused leadership, teacher collaboration, and interactive professional development; this is consistent with Rowan's (1990) hypothesis that conceptual teaching is more likely in commitment-oriented schools; (2) collaboration and interactive professional development mediate some but not all of the relationship between supportive, focused leadership and conceptual teaching, and (3) social-psychological professional community mediates some but not all of the relationship between supportive, focused principal leadership and instruction, but does not mediate the relationship between collaboration and professional development and instruction.

Developing a more detailed theoretical view of how professional community influences teachers' use of particular types of instruction has the potential to help us better understand the links between schools and classrooms. Refining our conceptions of how schools work can serve as a theoretical foundation for modeling and testing efforts to improve and equalize teaching and learning for all students.

Appendix A. Mean Frequency of Instruction Types by Level of Professional Community

	Basic			Algorithmic			Relational			Conceptual		
	B25	M50	T25	B25	M50	T25	B25	M50	T25	B25	M50	T25
Leadership	3.97	4.0	4.16	3.18	3.12	3.25	3.76	3.83	4.01	3.48	3.49	3.66
School-level teacher decision making	4.04	4.03	4.3	3.19	3.15	3.13	3.86	3.86	3.85	3.57	3.52	3.50
Class-level teacher decision making	4.05	4.07	4.06	3.20	3.18	3.17	3.50	3.52	3.52	3.44	3.43	3.47
Collaboration	3.89	4.02	4.20	2.94	3.18	3.35	3.67	3.85	4.06	3.25	3.54	3.80
Interactive professional development	3.87	4.05	4.25	2.98	3.20	3.33	3.69	3.87	4.05	3.27	3.57	3.79
Social-psychological sense of community	4.01	4.01	4.15	3.20	3.14	3.21	3.81	3.83	4.03	3.49	3.51	3.67

B25 = Bottom 25%; M50 = Middle 50%; T25 = Top 25%

Appendix B.   Unstandardized Descriptive Statistics for Professional Community Variables

	Mean	SD	Minimum	Maximum
Teacher-Level Variables				
Supportive, Focused Principal Leadership	3.97	.81	1	5
School-Level Teacher Decision Making	3.36	1.15	1	5
Class-Level Decision Making	4.35	.84	1	5
Interactive Professional Development	1.40	.30	1	2
Collaboration	2.99	.86	1	6
Social-Psychological Sense of Community	4.14	.62	1	5

ACKNOWLEDGMENT

This work was supported by the Spencer Foundation National Academy of Education Post-doctoral Fellowship Program.

NOTES

1. As described in Newman, Marks, and Gamoran (1996), authentic pedagogy is defined as instruction that requires (1) the construction of knowledge; (2) disciplined inquiry (which includes building on the student's prior knowledge base, requiring demonstration of an in-depth understanding. and elaborated communication; and (3) the material to have value beyond school.

2. Though mean substitution produces unbiased estimates of coefficients in regression analyses if the data are missing at random, it does lead to lower estimates of standard errors (Allison, 2001). Multiple imputation permits estimates of all cases, even missing data on the dependent and independent variables. This method has the benefit of generating unbiased and efficient estimates, and provides better estimates of standard errors than mean substitution does (Allison 2001). Multiple imputation analysis assumes that data are missing at random; five data sets can be sampled from the original data set with randomly imputed values for the missing data. The SAS multiple imputation procedure was used to generate the missing data; these five imputed data sets were then used to conduct the multilevel analysis 5 times, generating five sets of coefficients and standard errors. These results were merged using the HLM software; Rubin's (1987) algorithms were used to calculate unbiased and efficient estimates of coefficients and standard errors (Allison, 2001).

3. The standard deviation of the leadership variable is .85 (see Table 5.1). To determine how much of a standard deviation change is equal to 1, divide 1 by .85, which is 1.17. Thus, for an increase of 1.17 standard deviations of leadership, there will be an increase of .27 in algorithmic instruction. To translate this into a change in leadership on the 5-point scale, using the unstandardized means and standards deviations reported in Appendix B

(mean = 3.97, SD = .81), a rise of 1.17 standard deviations changes the value of leadership from 3.97 to (3.97 + 1.17* .81), or 4.92. Thus, a coefficient of .27 (see Table 5.4, Model 1) indicates that a change from 3.97 to 4.92 on the leadership scale corresponds to an increase of .25 days more of algorithmic teaching.

4.   A coefficient of .98 (see Table 5.5, Model 2) means that for an increase of 1.4 standard deviations (.71 is the standard deviation of collaboration, and 1/.71 = 1.4) of collaboration there will be an increase of about a day (.98) per month of conceptual teaching. So a rise of 1.4 standard deviations changes the value of collaboration from 2.99 (unstandardized mean) to 4.19 (i.e., 2.99 + 1.4 *. 86, where .86 is the unstandardized standard deviation of collaboration). Thus, a coefficient of .98 indicates that when teachers increase their collaboration from 2.99 days per month to 4.19 days per month, there is a corresponding increase of .98 days of conceptual teaching.

5.   A rise in interactive professional development of 1.58 standard deviations (1/.63 = 1.58, where .63 is the standard deviation of professional development) changes the value of professional development from 1.40 (unstandardized mean) to 1.87 (1.40 + 1.58 * .30, where .30 is the unstandardized standard deviation). Thus the coefficient of .73 means that when teachers increase the number of types of interactive professional development they participate in from 1.4 (between 1 and 2 activities) to 1.87 (about 2 activities), there is an increase of .73 days of basic instruction per month, and an increase of .87 days of conceptual instruction (.73 and .87 are the coefficients in Model 2 in Table 5.5). Recall that the professional development scale is comprised of an index of four different types of interactive activities, and response categories are 0 = no and 1 = yes, so teachers can score a low of 0 (participates in no interactive professional development) and a high of 4 (participates in all 4 types of interactive professional development) on the composite.

6.   An increase from 4.14 (unstandardized mean) to 4.92 (4.14 + 1.28 * .61, where 1.28 = 1/.78, the standardized standard deviation) roughly corresponds to a change from "agree" to "strongly agree," where 4 = agree and 5 = strongly agree.

7.   This is not to say that interactions and social-psychological perceptions are not correlated; supplemental analyses show that teacher-level collaboration and interactive professional development do have a small direct relationship with social-psychological professional community.

8.   In fact, supplemental analyses show structural aspects of professional community explain much of the relationship between social-psychological sense of community and instruction.

REFERENCES

Allison, P. D. (2001). *Missing data.* Thousand Oaks, CA: Sage.

Anyon, J. (1981). Social class and school knowledge. *Curriculum Inquiry, 11,* 3–45.

Aquilino, W. S. (1994). Interview mode effects in drug surveys. *Public Opinion Quarterly, 58*(2), 210–240.

Ball, D. L. (1991). Research on teaching mathematics: Making subject matter knowledge part of the equation. In J. Brophy (Ed.), *Advances in research on teaching: Teacher's knowledge of subject matter as it relates to their teaching practices* (Vol. 2., pp. 1–48). Greenwich, CT: JAI Press.

Ball, D. L. (1993). With an eye on the mathematical horizon: Dilemmas of teaching elementary school mathematics. *The Elementary School Journal, 93*(4), 373–397.

Barr, R., & Dreeben, R. (1983). *How schools work.* Chicago: University of Chicago Press.

Barr, R., & Dreeben, R. (1988). The formation and instruction of ability groups. *American Journal of Education, 97*(1), 34–64.

Bidwell, C. E., & Kasarda, J.D. (1980). Conceptualizing and measuring the effects of school and schooling. *American Journal of Education, 88*(4), 401–430.

Bird, T., & Little, J. W. (1986). *Instructional leadership in eight secondary schools.* Final report to the National Institute of Education. Boulder, CO: Center for Action Research.

Bridges, E., & Hallinan, M. (1978). Subunit size, work system interdependence, and employee absenteeism. *Educational Administration Quarterly, 14*(2), 24–42.

Brophy, J., & Good, T. (1986). Teacher behavior and student achievement. In M. Wittrock (Ed.), *Handbook of research on teaching* (pp. 340–370). New York: Macmillan.

Brown, A., & Campione, J. (1990). Communities of learning and thinking, or a context by any other name. *Contributions to Human Development, 21,* 108–126.

Brown, J., Collins, A., & Duguid, P. (1989). Situated cognition and the culture of learning. *Educational Researcher, 18*(1), 32–42.

Bryk, A. S., & Driscoll, M. E. (1988). *The high school as community: Contextual influences and consequences for students and teachers.* Madison, WI: National Center on Effective Secondary Schools, University of Wisconsin.

Bryk, A. S., Lee, V. E., & Holland, P. B. (1993). *Catholic schools and the common good.* Cambridge, MA: Harvard University Press.

Bryk, A. S., Easton, J. Q., Kerbow, D., Rollow, S. G., & Sebring, P. A. (1993). *A view from the elementary schools: The state of reform in Chicago.* Chicago: Consortium on Chicago School Research.

Bryk, A., & Raudenbush, S. (1988). Toward a more appropriate conceptualization of research on school effects: A three-level hierarchical linear model. *American Journal of Education, 97*(1), 65–107.

Burstein, L., McDonnell, L. M., Van Winkle, J., Ormseth, T., Mirocha, J., & Guitton, G. (1995). *Validating national curriculum indicators.* Santa Monica, CA: RAND.

Carpenter, T. P., Fennema, E., & Franke, M. L. (1996). Cognitively guided instruction: a knowledge base for reform in primary mathematics instruction. *The Elementary School Journal, 97,* 3–20

Carpenter, T. P., Fennema, E., Peterson, P. L., Chiang, C., & Loef, M. (1989). Using knowledge of children's mathematics thinking in classroom teaching: An experimental study. *American Educational Research Journal, 26*(4), 499–531.

Carroll, J. (1963). A model of school learning. *Teachers College Record, 64,* 722–733.

Clements, D. H., & Sarama, J. (Eds.). (2004). *Engaging young children in mathematics: Standards for early childhood mathematics education.* Mahwah, NJ: Erlbaum.

Cobb, P. (1988). The tension between theories of learning and instruction in mathematics education. *Education Psychologist, 23*(2), 97–103.

Cobb, P., Wood, T., Yackel, E., & McNeal, B. (1992). Characteristics of classroom mathematics traditions: An interactional analysis. *American Educational Research Journal, 29*(3), 573–604.

Cobb, P., Wood, T., Yackel, E., Nicholls, J., Grayson, W., Trigatti, B., & Perlwitz, M. (1991). Assessment of a problem-centered second-grade mathematics project. *Journal for Research in Mathematics Education, 22*(1), 3–29.

Cohen, D. K. (1988). Knowledge of teaching: Plus que ca change.... In P. W. Jackson (Ed.), *Contributing to educational change* (pp. 27–84). Berkeley, CA: McCutcheon.

Cohen, D. K. (1990). A revolution in one classroom: The case of Mrs. Oublier. *Educational Evaluation and Policy Analysis, 12*(3), 311–329.

Cohen, D., & Ball, D. (1990a). Policy and practice: An overview. *Educational Evaluation and Policy Analysis, 12*(3), 347–353.

Cohen, D., & Ball (1990b). Relations between policy and practice: A commentary. *Educational Evaluation and Policy Analysis, 12*(3), 249–256.

Cohen, D., & Ball, D. (1999). *Instruction, capacity, and improvement.* CPRE Research Report Series, RR-43. University of Pennsylvania: Consortium for Policy Research in Education.

Cohen, D., & Hill, H. (2000). *Learning policy: When state education reform works.* New Haven, CT: Yale University Press.

Cohen, D. K, McLaughlin, M. W., & Talbert, J. (Eds.) (1993). Introduction: New visions of teaching. In *Teaching for understanding: Challenges for policy and practice.* San Francisco: Jossey-Bass.

Cohen, D. K., Raudenbush, S. W., & Ball, D. L. (2003). Resources, instruction, and research. *Educational Evaluation and Policy Analysis, 25*(2), 119–142.

Coleman, J. S., Campbell, E. Q., Hobson, C. J., McPartland, J., Mood, A. M., Weinfeld, F. D., et al. (1966). *Equality of educational opportunity.* U.S. Office of Education. Washington, DC: USGPO.

Coleman, J. S., Hoffer, T., & Kilgore, S. (1982). *High school achievement: Public Catholic and private schools compared.* New York: Basic Books.

Conley, S. (1991). Review of research on teacher participation in school decision making. In G. Grand (Ed.), *Review of research in education 17* (pp. 225-265). Washington, DC: American Educational Research Association.

Cooley, W. W., & Leinhardt, G. (1980). The instructional dimensions study. *Educational Evaluation and Policy Analysis, 2*(1), 7–25.

Creemers, B., & Reezigt. G. (1996). School level conditions affecting the effectiveness of instruction. *School Effectiveness and School Improvement, 7*(3), 197–228.

Datnow, A. (2000). Power & politics in the adoption of whole school reform models. *Educational Evaluation and Policy Analysis, 22*(4), 357–374.

Denton, K., & West, J. (2002). *Children's reading and mathematics achievement in kindergarten and first grade.* Washington, DC: National Center for Education Statistics.

Desimone, L., Garet, M., Birman, B., Porter, A., & Yoon, K. (2002). How do district management and implementation strategies relate to the quality of the professional development that districts provide to teachers? *Teachers College Record, 104*(7), 1265–1312.

Dillman, D. A., & Tarnai, J. (1991). Mode effects of cognitively designed recall questions: A comparison of answers to telephone and mail surveys. In P. N. Beimer, R. M. Groves, L. E., Lyberg, N. A. Mathiowetz, & S. Sudman (Eds.), *Measurement errors in surveys* (pp. 367–393). New York: Wiley.

Elmore, R., & Associates (1990). *Restructuring schools: The next generation of educational reform*. San Francisco: Jossey-Bass.

Firestone, W., & Pennell, J. (1997). Designing state-sponsored teacher networks: A comparison of two cases. *American Educational Research Journal, 34*(2), 237–266.

Firestone, W. A., & Rosenblum, S. (1988). Building commitment in urban high schools. *Educational Evaluation and Policy Analysis, 93*, 285–299.

Firestone, W. A., & Wilson, B. L. (1983). *Using bureaucratic and cultural linkages to improve instruction: The high school principal's contributions*. Philadelphia: Research for Better Schools.

Fowler, F. J., Jr. (2002). *Survey research methods. Applied social research methods series* (3rd ed., Vol. 1). Thousand Oaks, CA: Sage.

Gamoran, A., Porter, A. C., Smithson, J., & White, P. A. (1997). Upgrading high school mathematics instruction: Improving learning opportunities for low-achieving, low-income youth. *Educational Evaluation and Policy Analysis, 19*(4), 325–338.

Gamoran, A., Secada, W. G., & Marrett, C .B. (2000). The organizational context of teaching and learning: Changing theoretical perspectives. In M. T. Hallinan (Ed.), *Handbook of the sociology of education* (pp. 37–63). New York: Kluwer.

Garet, M., Birman, B., Porter, Yoon, K., & Desimone, L. (2001). What makes professional development effective? Analysis of a national sample of teachers. *American Education Research Journal, 38*(3), 915–945.

Geary, D. C. (2001). A Darwinian perspective on mathematics and instruction. In T. Loveless, *The great curriculum debate: How should we teach reading and math?* (pp. 85–107). Washington, DC: Brookings.

Good, T. L., & Brophy, J. (2000). *Looking in classrooms* (8th ed.). Reading, MA: Longman.

Goodlad, J. I. (1984). *A place called school: Prospects for the future*. New York: McGraw-Hill.

Herman, J., Klein, D., & Abedi, J. (2000). Assessing students' opportunity to learn: Teacher and student perspectives. *Educational Measurement: Issues and Practice, 19*(4), 16–24.

Hiebert, J. (1999). Relationships between research and the NCTM standards. *Journal for Research in Mathematics Education, 30*, 3–19.

Hiebert, J., Carpenter, T. P., Fennema, E., Fuson, K., Human, P., Murray, H., Olivier, A., & Wearne, D. (1996). Problem solving as a basis for reform in curriculum and instruction: The case of mathematics. *Educational Researcher, 25*(4), 12–21.

Hiebert, J., Carpenter, T. P., Fennema, E., Fuson, K., Wearne, D., Murray, H., Olivier, A., & Human, P. (1997). *Making sense: Teaching and learning mathematics with understanding.* Portsmouth, NH: Heinemann.

Jencks, S. (1972) *Inequality.* London: Penguin

Johnson, S. M. (1990). *Teachers at work: Achieving success in our schools.* Boston: Basic Books.

Kilgore, S. B., & Pendleton, W. W. (1993). The organizational context of learning: Framework for understanding the acquisition of knowledge. *Sociology of Education, 66*(1), 63–87.

Knapp, M. (1997). Between systemic reforms and the mathematics and science classroom: The dynamics of innovation, implementation, and professional learning. *Review of Educational Research, 67*(2), 227–266.

Knapp, M. S., & Shields, P. M. (Eds.). (1990). *Better schooling for children of poverty: Alternatives to conventional wisdom* (Vol. 2). Washington DC: U.S. Department of Education, Office of Planning, Budget, and Evaluation.

Knapp, M. S., Shields, P. M., & Turnbull, B. J. (1992). *Academic challenge fro the children of poverty: Summary report.* Washington, DC: U.S. Department of Education.

Kozma, R., & Croninger, R. (1992). Technology and the fate of at-risk students. *Education and Urban Society, 24*(4), 440–453

Kruse, S., Louis, K., & Bryk, A. (1994). Building professional community in schools. In *Issues in restructuring schools, No. 6.* Madison: University of Wisconsin, Center on Organization and Restructuring of Schools.

Lampert, M. (1986). Knowing, doing and teaching mathematics. *Cognition and Instruction, 3*(4), 3, 5–342.

Lampert, M. (1990). When the problem is not the question and the solution is not the answer: Mathematical knowing and teaching. *American Educational Research Journal, 27*, 29–63.

Lampert, M. (1992). Practices and problems in teaching authentic mathematics. In F. Oser, A. Dick, & J. L. Patry (Eds.), *Effective and responsible teaching: The new synthesis* (pp. 295–313). San Francisco: Jossey-Bass.

Lee, V. E., & Bryk, A. S. (1989). A multilevel model of the social distribution of high school achievement. *Sociology of Education, 62*, 172–192.

Lee, V., Dedrick, R., & Smith, J. (1991). The effect of the social organization of schools on teachers' self-efficacy and satisfaction. *Sociology of Education, 64*, 190–208.

Lee, V. E., & Smith, J. B. (1995). Effects of high school restructuring and size on gains in achievement and engagement for early secondary school students. *Sociology of Education, 68*, 241–270.

Lee, V. E., & Smith, J. B. (1996). Collective responsibility for learning and its effects on gains in achievement for early secondary school students. *American Journal of Education, 104*, 103–147.

Lee, V. E., Smith, J. B., & Croninger, R. G. (1997). How high school organization influences the equitable distribution of learning in mathematics and science. *Sociology of Education, 70*, 128–150.

Lehrer, R., Lee, M., & Jeong, A. (1999). Reflective teaching of logo. *Journal of the Learning Sciences, 8*(2), 245–289.

Leithwood, K., Leonard, L., & Sharratt, L. (1998). Conditions fostering organizational learning in schools. *Educational Administration Quarterly, 34*(2), 243–276.

Little, J. W. (1993). Teachers' professional development in a climate of educational reform. *Educational Evaluation and Policy Analysis, 15*(2), 129–151.

Little, J. W. (1990). The persistence of privacy: Autonomy and initiative in teachers' professional relations. *Teachers College Record, 91*(4), 509–536.

Little, J. W. (1982). Norms of collegiality and experimentation: Workplace conditions of school success. *American Educational Research Journal, 19*(3), 325–340.

Loucks-Horsley, S., Hewson, P. W., Love, N., & Stiles, K. (1998) *Designing professional development for teachers of science and mathematics.* Thousand Oaks, CA: Corwin.

Louis, K. S., & Marks, H. M. (1998, August). Does professional community affect the classroom? Teachers' work and student experiences in restructuring schools. *American Journal of Education, 106*(4), 532–575. (EJ 576 587)

Louis, K., Marks, H., & Kruse, S. (1996). Teachers' professional community in restructuring schools. *American Educational Research Journal, 33,* 757–798.

Louis, K. S., & Kruse, S., & Associates. (1995). *Professionalism and community: Perspectives on reforming urban schools.* Thousand Oaks, CA: Corwin.

Loveless, T. (Ed.) (2001). *The great curriculum debate: How should we teach reading and math?* Washington, DC: Brookings.

Ma, L. (1999). *Knowing and teaching elementary mathematics: Teachers' understanding of fundamental mathematics in China and the United States.* Mahwah, NJ: Erlbaum.

Malen, B., Ogawa, R., & Kranz, J. (1990). What do we know about school-based management? In W. H. Clune & J. F. White (Eds.), *Choice and control in American education* (Vol. 2., pp. 289-342).) New York: Falmer.

Mayer, D. P. (1999). Measuring instructional practice: Can policymakers trust survey data? *Educational Evaluation and Policy Analysis, 21*(1), 29–45.

McCaffrey, D., Hamilton, K., Stecher, B., Klein, S., Bugliari, D., & Robyn, A. (2001). Interaction among instructional practices, curriculum, and student achievement: The case of standards-based high school mathematics. *Journal for Research in Mathematics Education, 22*(5), 493–517.

McLaughlin, M. W. (1994). Somebody knows my name. In *Issues in restructuring schools* (Issue 7, pp. 9–11). Madison, Wisconsin: Center on Organization and Restructuring of Schools, University of Wisconsin.

McLaughlin, M. W., & Marsh, D. D. (1978). Staff development and school change. *Teachers College Record, 80*(1), 69–94.

McLaughlin, M., & Talbert, J. (1999). *Professional community and the work of high school teaching.* Chicago: University of Chicago Press.

McNeil, L. (1988). *Contradictions of control: School structure and school knowledge.* New York: Routledge & Kegan Paul.

Meyer, J., & Cohen, E. (1971). *The impact of the open-space school upon teacher influence and autonomy: The effects of an organizational innovation.* Stanford, CA: Stanford University. (ERIC Document Reproduction Service No. ED062291)

Mohrman, A. M., Cooke, R. A., & Mohrman, S. A. (1979). Participation in decision making: A multidimensional perspective. *Educational Administration Quarterly, 15*(3), 97–113.

Mullens, J. (1995). *Classroom instructional processes: A review of existing measurement approaches and their applicability for the teacher follow-up survey* (NCES 95–15). Washington, DC: National Center for Education Statistics.

Mullens, J. E., & Gayler, K. (1999). *Measuring classroom instructional processes: Using survey and case study field test results to improve item construction.* Washington, DC: U.S. Department of Education, Office of Educational Research and Improvement.

Mullens, J., & Kasprzyk, D. (1996). Using qualitative methods to validate quantitative survey instruments. In *1996 proceedings of the section on survey research methods* (pp. 638–643). Alexandria, VA: American Statistical Association.

Mullens, J., & Kasprzyk, D. (1999). *Validating item responses on self-report teacher surveys.* Washington, DC: U.S. Department of Education.

Mullis, I. V. S. (1997). *Benchmarking to international achievement: TIMSS as a starting point to examine student achievement* (ORAD-97-1025). Washington, DC: Office of Educational Research and Improvement.

Murphy, J., & Beck, L. G. (1995). *School-based management as school reform: Taking stock.* Newbury Park, CA: Corwin Press.

National Center for Educational Statistics (NCES). (2004). *Early childhood longitudinal survey: Frequently asked questions.* Retrieved June 17, 2004, from http://nces.ed.gov/ecls/KinderFAQ.asp?faq=4

National Center for Education Statistics (NCES). (2000). *Early childhood longitudinal study—Kindergarten base year: Data files and electronic codebook.* Washington DC: Author.

National Council of Teachers of Mathematics. (1989). *Curriculum and evaluation standards for school mathematics.* Reston, VA: Author.

National Council of Teachers of Mathematics. (1991). *Professional standards for the teaching of school mathematics.* Washington, DC: Author.

Newmann, F., King, M., & Youngs, P. (2000). Professional development that addresses school capacity: Lessons from urban elementary schools. *American Journal of Education, 108*(4), 259–299.

Newmann, F., Smith, B., Allensworth, E., & Bryk, A. (2001). *School instructional program coherence: Benefits and challenges.* Chicago: Consortium on Chicago School Research.

Newmann, F., Rutter, R., & Smith, M. (1989). Organizational factors that affect school sense of efficacy, community, and expectations. *Sociology of Education, 62,* 221–238.

Newmann, F., & Wehlage, G. (1995). *Successful school restructuring: A report to the public and educators by the Center on Organization and Restructuring of Schools.* Madison: Board of Regents of the University of Wisconsin System.

Pellegrino, J. W., Baxter, G. P., & Glaser, R. (1999). Addressing the "two disciplines" problem: Linking theories of cognition and learning with assessment and instructional practice. *Review of Research in Education, 24*(9), 307–353.

Porter, A. C., Kirst, M. W., Osthoff, E. J., Smithson, J. L., & Schneider, S. A. (1993, October). *Reform up close: An analysis of high school mathematics and science classrooms.* Madison: University of Wisconsin-Madison.

Putnam, R., & Borko, H. (1997). Teacher learning: Implications of new views of cognition. In B. J. Biddle, T. L. Good, & I. F. Goodson (Eds.), *The international handbook of teachers and teaching* (pp. 1223–1296). Dordrecht, The Netherlands: Kluwer.

Raudenbush, S., Rowan, B., & Cheong, Y. (1993). The pursuit of high order instructional goals in secondary schools: Class, teacher and school influences. *American Educational Research Journal, 30*(3), 523–553.

Rogosa, D. R. (1995). Myths and methods: "Myths about longitudinal research," plus supplemental questions. In J. M. Gottman (Ed.), *The analysis of change* (pp. 3–65). Hillsdale, NJ: Erlbaum.

Romberg, T. (1983). A common curriculum for mathematics. In G. D. Fenstermacher & J. Goodlad (Eds.), *Individual differences and the common curriculum* (pp. 121–159). Chicago: National Society for the Study of Education.

Rosenholtz, S. (1989). Workplace conditions that affect teacher quality and commitment: implications for teacher induction programs. *Elementary School Journal; 89*(4), 421–439.

Rosenholtz, S. (1985). Effective schools: Interpreting the evidence. *American Journal of Education, 93*(3), 352–388.

Rosenthal, R., & Rosnow, R. (1984). *Essential of behavioral research: Methods and data analysis.* New York: McGraw Hill.

Rowan, B. (1990). Commitment and control: Alternative strategies for the organizational design of schools. *Review of Research in Education, 16*, 353–389.

Rowan, B. (1994). Comparing teachers' work with work in other occupations: Notes on the professional status of teaching. *Educational Researcher, 23*, 4, 17-21.

Rowan, B., Bossert, S. T., & Dwyer, D.C. (1983). Research on effective schools: A cautionary note. *Educational Researcher, 12*(4), 24–31.

Rowan, B. (1995). Learning, teaching, and educational administration: Toward a research agenda. *Educational Administration Quarterly, 31*(3), 344–354.

Rowan, B., Chiang, F., & Miller, R. (1997). Using research on employees' performance to study the effects of teachers on students' achievement. *Sociology of Education, 70*, 256–284.

Rowan, B., Correnti, R., & Miller, R. (2002). *What large-scale survey research tells us about teacher effects on student achievement: Insights from the Prospects study of elementary schools.* Philadelphia: Consortium for Policy Research in Education.

Rowan, B., & Miracle, A. (1983). Systems of ability grouping and the stratification of achievement in elementary schools. *Sociology of Education, 56*, 133–144.

Rubin, D. B. (1987). *Multiple imputation for nonresponse in surveys.* New York: Wiley.

Rutter, M., Maughan, B., Mortimore, P., Ouston, J., & Smith, A. (1979). *Fifteen thousand hours: Secondary schools and their effects on children.* Cambridge, MA: Harvard University Press.

Schifter, D., & Fosnot, C. (1993). *Reconstructing mathematics education: Stories of teachers meeting the challenge of reform.* New York: Teachers College Press.

Schmidt, W. H., McKnight, C. C., & Raizen, S. A. (1997). *A splintered vision: An investigation of U.S. science and mathematics education.* Boston: Kluwer.

Shavelson, R. J., Webb, N. M., & Burstein, L. (1986). Measurement of teaching. In M. Wittrock (Ed.), *Handbook of research on teaching* (3rd ed., pp. 1-36). Washington, DC: American Educational Research Association.

Shore, R. (1997). *Rethinking the brain: New insights into early development.* New York: Families and Work Institute.

Shouse, R. (2001). The impact of traditional and reform-style practices on student mathematics achievement. In T. Loveless (Ed.), *The great curriculum debate: How should we teach reading and math?* (pp. 108–133). Washington, DC: Brookings.

Silver, E., & Lane, S., (1995). Can instructional reform in urban middle schools help students narrow the mathematics performance gap? Some evidence from the QUASAR project. *Research in Middle Level Education Quarterly, 18*(2), 49–70.

Simon, M. (1986). The teachers' role in increasing student understanding of mathematics. *Educational Leadership, 43,* 40–43.

Slavin, R. E., Madden, N. A., Karweit, N. J., Livermon, B. J., & Dolan, L. J. (1990). Success for all: First-year outcomes of a comprehensive plan for reforming urban education. *American Educational Research Journal, 27*(2), 255–278.

Slavin, R., Karweit, & Madden, N. (Eds.). (1989). *Effective programs for students at risk.* Needham Heights, MA: Allyn & Bacon.

Smith, J., Lee, V., & Newmann, F. (2001, January 2001). *Instruction and achievement in Chicago elementary schools: Improving Chicago's schools.* Chicago: Consortium on Chicago School Research.

Smithson, J. L., & Porter, A. C. (1994). *Measuring classroom practice: Lessons learned from efforts to describe the enacted curriculum—The reform up close study.* CPRE Research Report Series #31. Madison: University of Wisconsin, Consortium for Policy Research in Education.

Snow, C., Burns, M., & Griffin, P. (1998). *Preventing reading difficulties in young children.* Washington, DC: National Research Council. National Academy Press.

Sorensen, A. B., & Hallinan, M. (1977). A reconceptualization of school effects. *Sociology of Education, 50,* 272–289.

Spillane, J., & Zeuli, J. (1999). Reform and teaching: Exploring patterns of practice in the context of national and state mathematics reforms. *Educational Evaluation and Policy Analysis, 21*(1), 1–27.

Stake, R., & Easle, J. (1978). *Case studies in science education* (No. 038-000-00377-1). Washington, DC: U.S. Government Printing Office.

Stevenson, H., & Stigler, J. (1992). *The learning gap: Why our schools are failing and what we can learn from Japanese and Chinese education.* New York: Summit Books.

Stigler, J. W., & Hiebert, J. (1999). *The teaching gap: Best ideas from the world's teachers for improving education in the classroom.* New York: The Free Press.

Stringfield, S., & Slavin, R. (1992). A hierarchical longitudinal model for elementary school effects. In B. P. M. Creemers & G. J. Reezigt (Eds.), *Evaluation of educational effectiveness* (pp. 35–69). Groningen, The Netherlands: ICO.

Stodolsky, S. S., & Grossman, P. (1995). The impact of subject matter on curricular activity: An analysis of five academic subjects. *American Educationl Research Journal, 32,* 227–250.

Talbert, J. E., & McLaughlin, M. W. (1993). Understanding teaching in context. In D. Cohen, M. McLaughlin, & J. Talbert (Eds.), *Teaching for understanding: Challenges for policy and practice* (pp. 167–206). San Francisco: Jossey-Bass.

Taylor, B. M., Pearson, P. D., Clark, K. F., & Walpole, S. (1999). *Beating the odds in teaching all children to read*. (CIERA Report #2-006). Ann Arbor: CIERA/University of Michigan.

Turnbull, B., Welsh, M., Heid, C., Davis, W., & Ratnofsky, A.C. (1999). *The longitudinal evaluation of school change and performance (LESCP) in Title I schools: Interim report to congress*. Washington, DC: Policy Studies Associates/Westat.

CHAPTER 6

ACADEMIC OPTIMISM
OF SCHOOLS

A Second-Order Confirmatory
Factor Analysis

Wayne K. Hoy, C. John Tarter, and Anita Woolfolk Hoy

Since the Coleman report, researchers, educators, and policy makers have searched for school-level properties that are positively related to school achievement. The quest has been difficult because the negative power of low socioeconomic factors simply overwhelms most school properties by either dampening or eliminating their positive effects. Three school properties, however, have emerged that are consistently related to school achievement, even controlling for SES and other demographic characteristics: collective efficacy, trust, and academic emphasis. This inquiry reviews that research, examines the commonalities of the three school properties, and then theorizes and demonstrates that there is a general construct formed by collective efficacy, faculty trust in parents and students, and academic emphasis. We label this general construct, academic optimism and relate it to other work on optimism and positive psychology.

Contemporary Issues in Educational Policy and School Outcomes, 135–157
Copyright © 2006 by Information Age Publishing
All rights of reproduction in any form reserved.

The Coleman report conclusion that "only a small part of [student achievement] is the result of school factors, in contrast to family background differences between communities" (Coleman et al., 1966, p. 297) shocked the educational research establishment. Since that landmark study, however, the association between socioeconomic factors (SES) and student achievement has been a consistent finding in educational research. Nevertheless, researchers, educators, and policy makers alike have been reluctant to conclude that schools have little or no effect on student achievement. Instead the quest has turned to the identification of school factors that make a difference in achievement, regardless of student socioeconomic status.

The discovery of such factors has been difficult because the power of SES simply overwhelms most school variables; that is, when researchers control for SES, the relationships between other factors and achievement typically evaporate. For example, although administrators do not believe it, the weight of the evidence suggests little or no direct relationship between principal leadership and student achievement (Hallinger & Heck, 1996). There are, however, a few school-level characteristics that consistently predict student achievement, even when controlling for socioeconomic factors. In particular, three organizational properties seem to make a difference in student achievement: the academic emphasis of the school, the collective efficacy of the faculty, and the faculty's trust in parents and students.

ACADEMIC EMPHASIS OF SCHOOLS

The first organizational property that is important in fostering student achievement is academic emphasis. Academic emphasis is the extent to which the school is driven by a quest for excellence—a press for academic achievement. High, but achievable goals are set for students; students respect intellectual accomplishments; and students are conscientious about their school work; that is, they are cooperative in activities in class and complete their homework outside class (Hoy & Miskel, 2005; Hoy, Tarter, & Kottkamp, 1991).

The first studies to suggest that a collective organizational property, the academic emphasis of the school, was positively and directly related to student achievement in high schools while controlling for SES were conducted by Hoy and his colleagues (Hoy, Tarter, & Bliss, 1990; Hoy, Tarter, & Kottkamp, 1991). Studies using other measures of school effectiveness (e.g. measures of commitment) also showed that academic emphasis, controlling for SES, was related to effectiveness. Later, researchers demonstrated the same positive relationship between academic emphasis and student achievement for middle schools, again controlling for socioeconomic factors (Hoy & Hannum, 1997; Hoy & Sabo, 1998).

For elementary schools, the results are the same as for high and middle schools. Using hierarchical linear modeling and controlling for SES as well as other demographic characteristics such as school size, student race, and gender, Goddard, Sweetland, and Hoy (2000) found that academic emphasis was a critical collective property of schools that explained higher student achievement in both mathematics and reading. The authors concluded, "elementary schools with strong academic emphases positively affect achievement for poor and minority students" (p. 698).

Finally, a recent study (Alig-Mielcarek & Hoy, 2005) that examined the influence of the instructional leadership of the principal and the academic press of the school also demonstrated the significance of academic emphasis in explaining student achievement, even controlling for SES. Using structural equation modeling to test the proposed model, the researchers found that academic press, not instructional leadership, was the crucial variable explaining achievement. In fact, instructional leadership worked indirectly, not directly, through academic press to influence student achievement.

The results of these studies show that regardless of methodology—multiple regression, structural equation modeling, or hierarchical linear modeling—and whether the settings are elementary, middle, or high schools, the results are consistent: academic emphasis is a key variable in explaining student achievement, even controlling for socioeconomic status, previous achievement, and other demographic variables.

COLLECTIVE EFFICACY

Social cognitive theory (Bandura, 1977, 1997) is a broad framework for understanding human learning and motivation. A salient concept in the framework is self-efficacy; defined as beliefs about one's capacity to organize and execute the actions required to produce a given level of attainment (Bandura, 1997). Efficacy beliefs are central mechanisms in human agency, the intentional pursuit of a course of action. Without a sense of efficacy to pursue actions, individuals and groups are unlikely to even initiate the actions. Thus the choices individuals and schools make, the plans and actions they initiate, are affected by the strength of their efficacy beliefs.

Research has consistently demonstrated the power of positive efficacy judgments in human learning, motivation, and achievement in such diverse areas as dieting, smoking cessation, sports performance, political participation, and academic achievement (Bandura, 1997; Goddard, Hoy,

& Woolfolk Hoy, 2004). Educational researchers have found links between student achievement and three kinds of efficacy beliefs—self-efficacy beliefs of students (Pajares, 1994, 1997), self-efficacy beliefs of teachers (Tschannen-Moran, Woolfolk Hoy, & Hoy, 1998), and teachers' collective efficacy beliefs about the school (Goddard, Hoy, & Woolfolk Hoy, 2000). Because we are interested in school properties amenable to change, our focus is on the collective efficacy of schools and student achievement.

Within an organization, perceived collective efficacy represents the judgments of the group about the performance capability of the social system as a whole (Bandura, 1997). Teachers not only have self-referent efficacy perceptions but also beliefs about the conjoint capability of the entire faculty. Such group-referent perceptions reflect the perceived collective efficacy of the school. In brief, perceived collective efficacy of a school is the judgment of the teachers that the faculty as a whole can organize and execute actions required to have a positive effect on students (Goddard, Hoy, & Woolfolk Hoy, 2004).

Bandura (1993) was first to demonstrate that teachers' beliefs in their collective efficacy contributed significantly to how well their schools perform academically, even after controlling for socioeconomic and other demographic characteristics. Elementary schools in which the faculty had a strong sense of collective efficacy flourished academically whereas those in which faculty had serious doubts about their collective efficacy achieved little progress or declined academically. There have been at least three other recent studies that support this conclusion.

Goddard, Hoy, and Woolfolk Hoy (2000) examined the role of collective efficacy in promoting school achievement in urban elementary schools. Building on Bandura's work, they tested the hypothesis that perceived collective efficacy would enhance student achievement in mathematics and reading. Using a multilevel model (HLM) to avoid the aggregation bias, misestimated standard errors, and heterogeneity of regression that may compromise the results of studies in which student characteristics are aggregated to the school level (Bryk & Raudenbush, 1992), Goddard et al. found that collective efficacy was significantly related to student achievement in urban elementary schools even controlling for SES, a result consistent with Bandura's earlier findings.

Building on this work, Hoy, Sweetland, and Smith (2002) developed a model of school achievement in high schools in which collective efficacy was the central variable. Controlling for both academic press and SES, collective efficacy was pivotal in explaining student achievement; in fact, in this study of a fairly representative sample of high schools, collective efficacy was more important than either socioeconomic status or academic press. Hoy et al. concluded that, "School norms that support academic achievement and collective efficacy are particularly important in motivating teachers and students to achieve … however, academic press is most potent when collective efficacy is strong" (p. 89). That is, academic press works through collective efficacy. Hoy et al. theorized further that when collective efficacy is high, a strong focus on academic pursuits not only directs behaviors of teachers, but also helps them persist in the face of difficulty and reinforces shared social norms of collective efficacy.

Finally, Goddard, LoGerfo, and Hoy (2004), using Bandura's social cognitive theory, developed and tested a more comprehensive theoretical model of perceived collective efficacy and student achievement. Using structural equation modeling, the results were consistent with earlier findings; even controlling for minority student enrollment, urbanicity, SES, school size, and earlier achievement, collective efficacy was critical in explaining student achievement in reading, writing, and social studies achievement.

The results of these four studies show that regardless of methodology—path analysis, structural equation modeling, or hierarchical linear modeling—and whether the schools are high schools or elementary, the results are consistent: collective efficacy is a key variable in explaining student achievement even controlling for socioeconomic status, previous achievement, and other demographic variables.

FACULTY TRUST IN PARENTS AND STUDENTS

A third school property that is related to student achievement, even after controlling for socioeconomic status, is faculty trust in parents and students. Trust exist when teachers can count on students to do their work and parents for their support. In other words, both students and parents are reliable. In this inquiry our analysis of trust in parents and students is at the organizational level, that is, faculty trust is a collective property of the school.

It may seem that trust in parents and trust in students should be two separate concepts; however, several factor analyses have demonstrated that these two aspects of trust cannot be separated (Hoy & Tschannen-Moran, 1999; Goddard, Tschannen-Moran, & Hoy, 2001). Moreover, Bryk and Schneider (2002) agree and make the theoretical argument that student-teacher trust in elementary school operates primarily through teacher-parent trust, a view consistent with Hoy and his colleagues.

Trust involves making oneself vulnerable to another in the belief that the other will act in ways that are not harmful, but instead are in the best interests of the trusting party. An extensive review of the literature (Tschannen-Moran & Hoy, 2000) revealed that trust is a general concept with at least five facets; benevolence, reliability, competence, honesty, and openness are the elements of trust most frequently examined in the trust literature (Hoy & Tschannen-Moran, 1999, 2003; Tschannen-Moran & Hoy, 2000).

Benevolence is likely the most common element of trust; it is the belief that those things one cares about will not be harmed (Baier, 1986; Cummings & Bromily, 1996). Benevolence is the "accepted vulnerability to another's possible but not expected ill will" (Baier, p. 236). When there is no trust in the good will and benevolence of parents or students, teachers become excessively concerned about both real and imagined problems. The teachers become vigilant rather than supportive or helpful.

Reliability is the extent to which behavior is predictable as well as beneficial to the other party (Butler & Cantrell, 1984; Hosmer, 1995). Consistent behavior is not enough; reliable behavior is both predictable and well intentioned. Again, if parents or students are seen as unreliable, teachers are less likely to invest effort in them and more likely to be suspicious of their words and actions.

Competence is ability to perform in accordance with appropriate standards. Good intentions are not enough (Baier, 1986; Butler & Cantrell, 1984; Mishra, 1996). Trust depends on tasks being carried out with skill and competence. For example, students or parents perceived as being incompetent are unlikely to elicit trust from the faculty because the students and parents are expected to fail.

Honesty is an individual's character, integrity, and truthfulness. Rotter (1967) defined trust as "the expectancy that the word, promise, verbal or written statement of another individual or group can be relied upon" (p. 651). Character, integrity, and truthfulness are shown when statements correspond to deeds. Truthful action neither distorts the truth nor shifts responsibility. Honesty and trust are inextricably part of one another (Baier, 1986; Cummings & Bromily, 1996). If parents or students are seen as dishonest, teachers cannot risk trusting in them.

Openness is a process in which relevant information is shared and often creates a vulnerability to another (Butler & Cantrell, 1984; Mishra, 1996). Openness shows a sense of confidence that neither the information nor the individual will be exploited. When students or parents are seen as guarded, they often provoke suspicion rather than trust.

Although it is theoretically possible that parents and students might be benevolent and not reliable, or competent and not benevolent, research has not found these patterns. In fact, all five facets of trust in schools vary together to form an integrated construct of faculty trust in schools, whether the schools are elementary (Hoy & Tschannen-Moran, 1999; Hoy & Tschannen-Moran, 2003) or secondary (Smith, Hoy, & Sweetland, 2001). Thus, our working definition: *Trust is an individual's or group's willingness to be vulnerable to another party based on the confidence that the latter party is benevolent, reliable, competent, honest, and open* (Hoy & Tschannen-Moran, 2003).

Cooperation and trust between teachers and students and between teachers and parents should set the stage for effective student learning, but only a few studies have examined this relationship. In one of the first studies of achievement and faculty trust in students and parents Goddard, Tschannen-Moran, and Hoy (2001) examined the role of such trust in promoting school achievement of urban elementary schools. Using a multilevel model (HLM), the researchers demonstrated a significant direct, positive relationship between faculty trust in students and parents and higher student achievement, even controlling for socioeconomic status. Like collective efficacy, faculty trust was an important organizational property able to overcome some of the disadvantages of low SES.

Later, Hoy (2002) examined the trust-achievement hypothesis in high schools and again found that faculty trust in parents and students was positively related to student achievement while controlling for socioeconomic factors. He theorized that trusting others is an important aspect of human learning because learning is often a cooperative process and distrust makes cooperation virtually impossible; hence, the importance of trust among students, teachers and parents. When students, teachers, and parents have common learning goals, then trust and cooperation are likely ingredients that improve teaching and learning.

Finally, Bryk and Schneider (2002) performed a 3-year longitudinal study in 12 Chicago elementary schools that were reorganizing to provide for greater involvement of parents and community leaders in neighborhood schools. Using survey and achievement data, HLM models, as well as in-depth interviews with teachers, principals, and parents, the researchers concluded that relational trust was a prime resource for school improvement. Trust and cooperation among students, teachers, and parents were critical factors that influenced regular student attendance, persistent learning in the face of difficulty, and faculty experimentation with new practices. In brief, trust among teachers, parents, and students produced schools that were more likely to demonstrate marked gains in student learning. In stark contrast, schools with weak trust relationships saw virtually no improvement in the reading and achievement scores of their students. Both the research of Bryk and Schneider and that of Hoy and his colleagues reinforce each other in the common conclusion that faculty trust of students and parents is an important school property to enhance student achievement.

Why are academic emphasis, collective efficacy, and trust consistently related to student achievement when controlling for SES whereas other school properties are not? Is there some latent construct that under girds these three properties? Are there some common theoretical bases for these properties? Are there other school properties that are amenable to change that can influence school achievement? We now turn to these and other related questions.

COMMON THEMES

Although academic emphasis, sense of efficacy, and faculty trust can be examined as individual variables, all three are collective properties as described and analyzed in this inquiry. Aggregated individual perceptions of the *group*, as opposed to the *individual*, assess these perceived properties as emergent organizational attributes, that is, the variables are emergent group-level attributes rather than simply the sum of teachers' perceived personal attributes (Bandura, 1986, 1997).

The studies that we have just reviewed suggest that academic emphasis, collective efficacy beliefs, and faculty trust shape the normative and behavioral environment of the school. Coleman (1985, 1987) explained that the development of norms gives group members some control over the actions of others, especially when such actions have consequences for the group. When teachers behave in ways that conflict with the shared beliefs of the group, the group will sanction their behavior; in fact, Coleman argued that the severity of the social sanctions is proportionate to the effect of norm breaking on the collective. For example, when a faculty is highly committed to academic performance, the normative and behavioral environment will press teachers to persist in their educational efforts to have students achieve academically. Likewise, a strong sense of collective efficacy in a school creates a powerful set of normative and behavioral influences on the school's culture that reinforce the self-efficacy beliefs of teachers. Moreover, the press for efficacious teacher behaviors will be accompanied by social sanctions for those who lack self-efficacy. Similar cases can be made for trust in parents and students and academic emphasis. When the faculty has strong norms that support teachers' trusting and working with parents, the group press will be for cooperation and collaboration with parents to help students succeed in school. From a sociocognitve perspective, the power of the school culture and its values and norms rest in large part on the social persuasion they exert on teachers in constraining certain actions and in restraining others.

Three collective properties—efficacy, trust, and academic emphasis—are not only similar in their development, character, and function, but also in their potent and positive influences on student achievement. The three concepts have so much in common that we turn next to the question of the general and theoretical nature of their commonalities. Specifically, we hypothesize that the three school properties define a more general underlying construct, which we call the academic optimism of the school.

ACADEMIC OPTIMISM: A THEORETICAL ANALYSIS

We theorize that the three collective properties of academic emphasis, efficacy, and trust work together in a unified fashion to create a positive academic environment we have named *academic optimism*. Individual optimism was defined by the anthropologist Lionel Tiger (1979) as: "a mood or attitude associated with an expectation about the social or material future—one the evaluator regards as socially desirable, to his advantage, or for his pleasure" (p. 18). This definition makes clear that optimism is in relation to a particular goal or outcome (Peterson, 2000). Other conceptions relate optimism to positive expectations for the future and to explanatory style or the individual's characteristic way of explaining the causes of negative outcomes and failures (Buchanan & Seligman, 1995). People who believe that bad outcomes are controllable have a greater sense of agency. Positive expectations and agency come together in a sense of hope that pathways can be identified to reach desired goals (Peterson, 2000; Snyder, Shorey, Cheavens, Pulvers, Adams, & Wiklund, 2002).

Many conceptions treat optimism as a cognitive characteristic—a goal or expectancy. But Peterson (2000) cautions that "Optimism is not simply cold cognition, and if we forget the emotional flavor that pervades optimism, we can make little sense of the fact that optimism is both motivated and motivating" (p. 45). Our conception of academic optimism includes both cognitive and affective dimensions and adds a behavioral element as well. Collective efficacy is a group belief or expectation and thus can be seen as *cognitive*. Faculty trust in parents and teachers is an *affective* response and academic emphasis represents the press for particular *behaviors* in the school workplace. Thus academic optimism is conceived as a latent variable with three basic properties—efficacy, trust, and academic emphasis. Collective efficacy reflects the thoughts and beliefs of the group; faculty trust adds an affective dimension, and academic emphasis captures the behavioral enactment of efficacy and trust. Academic optimism gives a rich picture of human agency because it provides an explanation of collective behavior in terms of cognitive, affective, and behavioral dimensions.

The relationships between the three major dimensions are graphically presented as a triadic set of interactions with each element functionally dependent on the others. We postulate reciprocal causality between each pair of elements as shown in Figure 6.1.

AE = Academic Emphasis
FT = Faculty Trust in Students and Parents
CE = Perceived Collective Efficacy of the Faculty.

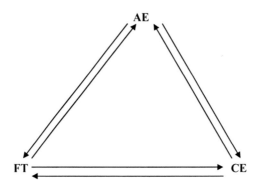

Figure 6.1.   The relationships between the three major collective properties in reciprocal causality with each other.

For example, faculty trust in parents and students supports a sense of collective efficacy, but collective efficacy enhances and reinforces the trust. Similarly, when the faculty trusts parents, teachers can set and insist on higher academic standards with confidence they will not be undermined by parents, and the focus on high academic standards in turn reinforces the faculty trust in parents and students. Finally, when the faculty as a whole believe they can organize and execute actions needed to have a positive effect on student achievement, they will emphasize academic achievement, and academic emphasis will in turn reinforce a strong sense of collective efficacy. In brief, all the elements of academic optimism are in transactional relationships with each other and interact to create a culture of academic optimism in the school workplace.

Why academic optimism? The term was chosen to reflect beliefs about control in schools. Since the Coleman report (1966), researchers and educators have been challenged to find ways to overcome the dele-terious consequences of low SES of students. A general pessimism gave way to cautious optimism with the work of Edmonds (1979) who found schools that apparently succeeded in spite of low SES. Subsequent research on effective schools was not as encouraging as the initial prom-ise, however, because it has proved exceedingly difficult to find school properties that make a difference in school achievement when controlling for SES. Our own research over the past 2 decades has led us to only three such school factors. The concept of academic optimism combines these three variables into a general latent construct.

Optimism is an appropriate overarching construct to unite efficacy, trust, and academic press because each concept contains a sense of the possible. Efficacy is the belief that the faculty can make a positive difference in student learning; teachers believe in themselves. Faculty trust in students and parents is the belief that teachers, parents, and students can cooperate to improve learning, that is, the faculty believes in its students. Academic emphasis is the enacted behavior prompted by these beliefs, that is, the focus is student success. Thus, a school with high academic optimism is a collectivity in which the faculty believes that *it can* make a difference, that *students can* learn, and academic performance *can be* achieved.

The final attraction to the term, academic optimism, is the implication that it can be learned; the pessimistic school can become optimistic. Academic optimism gains its name from our conviction that the properties of the construct all express optimism and are malleable. Administrators and teachers can be empowered; SES irretrievably traps neither them nor their students.

Table 6.1.   Comparison of State and Sample Demographic Information

School Demographic Information	State of Ohio	Sample of Schools in Study
Average school enrollment	374	436
Percentage of schools designated as urban	44%	36%
Percentage of schools designated as rural	33%	27%
Percentage of schools designated as suburban	23%	37%
Percentage of students participating in the federal free or reduce lunch program	34%	28%
Teaching staff	27 teachers	24 teachers
Teacher experience	13.28 years	13.14 years
Number	1,949 elementary schools	146 elementary schools

ACADEMIC OPTIMISM: AN EMPIRICAL ANALYSIS

We have made the theoretical case for academic optimism, but do empirical results support the theory? To answer that question, we turn to a sample of 145 elementary schools to confirm academic optimism as a latent construct composed of collective efficacy, faculty trust, and academic emphasis.

Sample

Nearly 3,400 teachers from 146 Ohio elementary schools in 33 of the 88 Ohio counties provided the data for this analysis. Demographic information is summarized in Table 6.1. The sample was fairly representative of Ohio elementary schools. According to the Ohio Department of Education, 44%, 33%, and 23% of all elementary schools are designated as urban, rural, and suburban, respectively. The current sample was comprised of 36% of urban schools, 27% of rural schools, and 37% of suburban schools. Although only 65% of Ohio elementary schools are configured as K–5 or K–6 buildings, about 90% of the study sample was K–5 or K–6. This discrepancy was due to missing data from one participating school. The teaching staff comparisons are similar. On average, an Ohio elementary school staffs 27 teachers with 13.28 years of teaching experience. The study's elementary schools, on average, have 24 teachers with 13.14 years of teaching experience. In brief, the sample is fairly typical of elementary schools in Ohio.

Data Collection

Data were collected from teachers during scheduled faculty meetings, which took place before or after the school day. The researcher administered the surveys to the teachers in each school. Participants were guaranteed anonymity and confidentially. School-level data describing socioeconomic status were provided by the Ohio Department of Education.

Measures

The three basic concepts of this study were collective efficacy, faculty trust in students and parents, and academic emphasis of schools. Each was assessed by valid and reliable measures. The analysis was simplified by doing a preliminary principal components analysis to select the four items from each measure with the strongest loadings. Then we checked the coefficients to insure high reliability.

Academic emphasis. The academic emphasis of a school is the extent to which the school focuses on intellectual activity and student achievement. The faculty presses students for high achievement and students work hard, are cooperative, and respect others who get high grades. The academic emphasis subscale of the Organizational Health Inventory (Hoy, Tarter, & Kottkamp, 1991; Hoy & Tarter, 1997; Hoy & Miskel, 2005) was used to tap the academic emphasis of the school. Previous research has demonstrated the reliability and construct validity of the subscale. The measure was a shortened version comprised of four Likert items scored on a 5-point scale; they are as follows:

AE1 Students respect others who get good grades.
AE2 Students try hard to improve on previous work.
AE3 Students are cooperative during classroom instruction.
AE3 Students neglect to complete homework (score reversed).

The reliability of the scale in this study was supported with an alpha coefficient of .85.

Collective efficacy. Perceived collective efficacy of a school is the judgment of the teachers that the faculty as a whole can organize and execute actions required to have a positive effect on students (Goddard, Hoy, & Woolfolk Hoy, 2000, 2004). The construct was measured using a shortened version of the 12-item collective efficacy scale (Goddard, Hoy, & Woolfolk Hoy, 2000). The items were scored on a 6-point Likert scale and made up of the following four questions:

CE1 These students come to school ready to learn.
CE2 Drug and alcohol abuse in the community make learning difficult for students here (score reversed).
CE3 Students here just aren't motivated to learn (score reversed).
CE4 Teachers here are confident they will be able to motivate their students.

Previous research has demonstrated the construct validity and reliability of the scale (Goddard, Hoy, & Woolfolk Hoy, 2000, 2004). The reliability of the subscale for the current sample was alpha = .92.

Faculty trust in students and parents. Recall that school trust is the faculty's willingness to be vulnerable to parents and students because they are confident in their good will, honesty, and openness. Faculty trust was measured by a shortened version of the Omnibus Trust Scale (Hoy &

Tschannen-Moran, 2003). The items were scored on a 6-point Likert scale and made up of the following four questions:

T1 Students in this school can be counted on to do their work.
T2 Teachers can count on parental support.
T3 Parents in this school are reliable in their commitment.
T4 Teachers in this school can trust their students.

The reliability and construct validity of the scale have been supported in several factor-analytic studies (Hoy & Tschannen-Moran, 2003). The alpha coefficient of reliability for the items in this study was .93.

Academic Optimism: A Confirmatory Factor Analysis

Factor-analytic techniques have been used extensively in education and psychology as a way of reducing a number of related variables to a smaller number of more general concepts. Principal-components analysis and principal-axis factor analysis are exploratory techniques often used to this end. More recently, with the advent of structural equation modeling, confirmatory factor-analytic procedures have emerged as a powerful way to test particular theoretical models *a priori*, that is, using deductive reasoning to hypothesize the theoretical structure beforehand and then testing the model in terms of its goodness-of-fit to the data. Exploratory factor analyses represent tools for theory building, whereas confirmatory factor analysis is a tool for theory testing (Bollen, 1989; Bryant & Yarnold, 1995).

Because our objective in this inquiry was to test the underlying theory of a new construct that we are calling academic optimism, we assessed our theory by doing a second-order factor analysis using LISREL. Our theoretical analysis discussed earlier led us to hypothesize that four specific observed measures for each of three concepts would identify the first-order factors of collective efficacy, faculty trust in students and parents, and academic emphasis. In addition, we postulated the existence of a second-order general school factor called academic optimism. These models are outlined in Figure 6.2.

The first- and second-order factor analyses were computed from the raw data collected as described in the methods above. The data were used as input to LISREL 8 (Joreskog & Sorbom, 1993). We specified the LISREL parameters in terms of an "all y-model" to test the first-order factors and structural model to test the second-order factor. Each item was constrained to load on one factor, following Sarason's (1984) recommendations. One item on each factor was constrained to equal 1 to set the metric

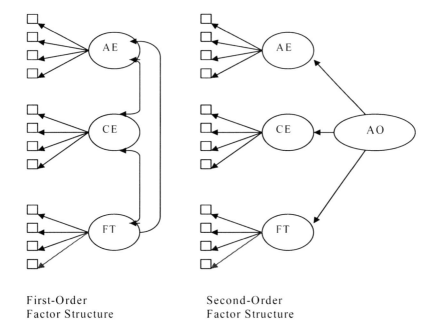

First-Order
Factor Structure

Second-Order
Factor Structure

Figure 6.2.   Hypothesized first- and second-order factor structure of Academic Optimism (AO) using Academic Emphasis (AE), Faculty Trust in Students and Parents (FT), and Collective Efficacy (CE).

for the factor. Factor covariances were left free to be estimated, but the measurement errors were not permitted to covary.

RESULTS

The confirmatory factor analysis supported the theory upon which this study was built. The Chi-square fit statistic was 62.20 ($p = .135$) and indicated a reasonably good fit of the data to the model. The root mean square residual (RMSER) was .04, and the goodness-of-fit index (GFI) was .93. Moreover, the norm fit index (NFI) was equal to .96. Because researchers (Benson & Bandelos, 1992; Bollen, 1989) have demonstrated that the GFI is influenced by sample size, we also used the comparative fit index (CFI). According to Bentler (1989), the CFI is not affected by sample size and a CFI of .99 for the current analysis suggested a good fit of data to model. All the Lambdas (factor loadings) are reported in standardized form for ease of comparison. The confirmatory factor analysis strongly supports the first- and second-order factors as predicted. The

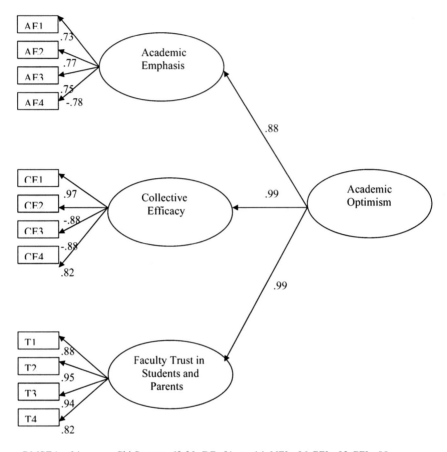

RMSEA=.04   Chi Square=62.20, DF=51, p=.14 NFI=.96 GFI=.93 CFI=.99

Figure 6.3.   Results of first and second-order confirmatory factor analysis.

results are summarized in Figure 6.3 (all coefficients are completely standardized).

DISCUSSION

The results of the analysis support our theory that the properties of academic emphasis, collective efficacy, and faculty trust in students and parents work together in a unifying fashion to form a general latent construct that we identified and called academic optimism. Recall that we postulated collective efficacy to be the cognitive aspect of academic optimism, the thinking and believing side; faculty trust in students and parents provided the affective side of the latent construct; whereas, academic emphasis tapped the behavioral side of the school, that is, the enactment of the cognitive and affective into action. Academic optimism provides a rich picture of human and social agency in its explanation of collective behavior.

The traditional view of achievement in schools operates on the assumption that success is a function of talent and motivation; talented students who are highly motivated are high achievers. Seligman (1998) suggests that there is a third factor of success—optimism—that matters as much as talent or motivation. Moreover, optimism can be learned; hence, optimism can be enhanced. Although learned optimism is an individual variable, academic optimism is a collective one. Nonetheless, we expect that many of the conclusions about individual learned optimism can be applied at the group level.

Seligman argues that learned optimism gets people over the wall of learned pessimism and not just as individuals but also as organizational members. Much as individuals can develop learned helplessness, organizations can be seduced by pervasive pessimism. The pessimistic view says, with a tired resignation, "These kids can't learn, and there is nothing I can do about it, so why worry about academic achievement?" This view is reinforcing, self-fulfilling, and defeating. Academic optimism, in stark contrast, views teachers as capable, students as willing, parents as supportive, and the task as achievable.

CONCLUSIONS

We have successfully demonstrated that academic emphasis, faculty trust, and collective efficacy form a general latent construct, which we call academic optimism. These three organizational variables have been consistently related to student achievement controlling for SES and other demographic variables. The construct draws on three different theories. Collective efficacy comes from Bandura's work (1997) in social cognitive theory; trust emerges as an important concept in Coleman's (1990) analysis of social interaction; academic emphasis evolves from Hoy and his colleagues' research on the organizational health of schools with its theoretical underpinnings from Parsons, Bales, and Shils (1953). Bringing these three streams of theory and research together gives a richer and yet more direct explanation of how schools enhance student learning.

Academic optimism combines two sets of critical beliefs and their enactment. Collective efficacy is the belief that the faculty has the capability to make a positive difference in student learning; teachers believe in themselves and their colleagues. Faculty trust in students and parents is the belief that students, parents, and teachers can rely on each other to improve learning; they believe students can learn. Academic emphasis is the behavioral enactment of these beliefs targeting student performance and achievement; teachers set high but achievable standards for learning. Given the strong relationships of each of the individual elements with student achievement and each other, it seems reasonable to assume that academic optimism of the school is closely linked to student achievement. The added benefit of knowing the composite elements of collective academic optimism suggests a wider set of strategies for improving optimism in the school.

Components of Academic Optimism

How can schools be led in a direction that builds efficacy, trust, and academic emphasis so that they pursue courses of action that will lead to student achievement? We suspect the general way to enhance the academic optimism of a school is to improve its component parts. Thus we consider how to build academic emphasis, collective efficacy, and trust and then look to the literature on optimism for additional ideas.

Academic Emphasis

The one goal that virtually everyone shares for schools is academic achievement of students. The reform and accountability movements have promoted a press toward the academic achievement of all students (No Child Left Behind). The focus of schooling is clear—it is an academic one. The challenge is to create school conditions in which teachers believe *they are up to the task and so are their students.* A push for academic achievement, however, in an environment where teachers do not feel efficacious is a recipe for frustration and stress.

Collective Efficacy

Because collective efficacy is grounded in social cognitive theory, we turn to Bandura's sources of efficacy for ideas about how to build collective efficacy in schools. The sources of self-efficacy are mastery experiences, vicarious experiences, social persuasion, and affective states, each of which conveys information that influences teacher perceptions about the school (Bandura, 1993, 1997; Goddard, Hoy, & Woolfolk Hoy, 2004; Pajares, 1997). For example, a school that responds to a decreasing graduation rate by implementing a program for at-risk students, which is effective in neighboring school, is engaged in a self-regulatory process informed by the vicarious learning of its members and, perhaps, the social persuasion of leaders. Collective efficacy can be improved by providing mastery experiences for teachers, modeling success, and persuading teachers to believe in themselves and their capabilities (Bandura, 1997; Goddard, Hoy, & Woolfolk Hoy, 2004).

Trust in Parents and Students

There is a body of research on family and community involvement in schools (cf. Epstein, 1989); however, there is little systematic research that addresses how to build authentic trust. It seems likely that faculty trust in students and parents can be promoted through useful interchanges, both formal and informal, between parents and teachers. Capitalizing on vicarious learning, for example, a school may respond to a lack of trust and community participation in school activities by emulating the practices and procedures of a lighthouse district known for its parental cooperation and involvement. But much more research is needed about what programs and factors support the development of teachers' trust in parents and students.

Such examples demonstrate that social cognitive theory can explain how changes in social perceptions influence what actions organizations choose to pursue. Collective perceptions about efficacy, academic emphasis, and trust shape the school's normative environment and can be developed through experiences that convey their value.

Fostering Optimism

The research on individual optimism provides some ideas about encouraging a culture of optimism in schools. Peterson (2000) suggests that optimism is thwarted by stress, so decreasing stress can support optimism. Appropriate participation in decisions that affect their lives (Hoy & Tarter, 2004) can help lower stress by giving teachers a legitimate sense of control and agency

Observational or vicarious learning—learning by observing the words and actions of others who serve as models—is another source of optimism. People are more likely to adopt the beliefs and imitate the actions of others who seem competent, powerful, prestigious, and who are seen as similar (Pintrich & Schunk, 2002). Thus teachers can serve as models for each other. What explanatory styles and attributions are used in school meetings and conversations to discuss student problems? Are problems seen as controllable or is there, "nothing we can do?" Particularly for novice teachers, vicarious learning in teachers' lounges and school hallways may encourage an optimistic approach to teaching or a sense of passive helplessness.

Snyder and his colleagues (Snyder, Cheavens, & Sympson, 1997; Snyder et al., 2002) have studied a concept that combines pathways thinking (there are several ways to reach our goal) with agentic thinking (we have the capabilities to initiate and continue actions along those pathways—changing if necessary). They call the concept, *hope*, and have found that individuals who are high on their measure of hope often work on shared goals. They enjoy interpersonal interactions: "high-hopers serve to make the group not only more productive but also, perhaps equally important, an interpersonally more enjoyable arena" (Snyder, Cheavens, & Sympson, 1997, p. 115). Thus a hopeful leader may be an important asset in building academic optimism in schools.

Our analysis is a promising clarification of the linkages within schools that influence student achievement. Although our data are drawn from elementary schools, we believe the findings are applicable to middle and secondary schools because the three elements of academic optimism have explained learning in those settings as well. Clearly, more research in a variety of school settings is necessary to build a comprehensive theory of academic optimism of schools.

The next step is to demonstrate that academic optimism is directly related to student achievement controlling for socioeconomic as well as other demographic characteristics at all school levels. We believe that academic optimism also exists at the individual level and the contributions of the individual and the organization need to be sorted out. Then, we need to discover the kind of interventions that produce higher academic optimism.

Here is our final observation. Academic optimism is especially attractive because it focuses on the potential of schools to overcome the drag of socioeconomic factors on student achievement. It is a social-psychological construct that is in part related to the positive psychology of Seligman and Csikszentmihalyi (2000), the social cognitive theory of Bandura (1997), Hoy and Tarter's (1997) research on school climate, and the social theory of Coleman (1990). There is a real use in focusing on potential with its strength and resilience rather than pathology with its attendant weakness and helplessness because optimism attempts to explain and nurture what is best in schools to facilitate student learning.

ACKNOWLEDGMENT

We thank Xiaodong Liu, the Ohio State University, for his excellent advice and guidance in structural equation modeling. Also, thanks to Dean Richard De Lisi of Rutgers University, who read the paper and made a number of useful suggestions.

REFERENCES

Alig-Mielcarek, J., & Hoy, W. K. (2005). Instructional leadership: Its nature, meaning, and influence. In W. K. Hoy & C. Miskel (Eds.), *Educational leadership and reform* (pp. 29-54). Greenwich, CT: Information Age.

Baier, A. C. (1986). Trust and antitrust. *Ethics, 96,* 231–260.

Bandura, A. (1977). Self-efficacy: Toward a unifying theory of behavioral change. *Psychological Review, 84,* 191–215.

Bandura, A. (1986). *Social foundations of thought and action.* Englewood Cliffs, NJ: Prentice-Hall.

Bandura, A. (1993). Perceived self-efficacy in cognitive development and functioning. *Educational Psychologist, 28,* 117–148.

Bandura, A. (1997). *Self-efficacy: The exercise of control.* New York: Freeman.

Benson, J., & Bandalos, D. L. (1992). Second-order confirmatory factor analysis of the reactions to test scale with cross-validation. *Multivariate Behavioral Research, 27,* 459–487.

Bentler, P. (1989). Comparative fit indices. *Psychological Bulletin, 107,* 238–246.

Bollen, K. A. (1989). *Structural equations with latent variables.* New York: Wiley.

Bryant, F. B., & Yarnold, P. R. (1995). Principal-component analysis and exploratory and confirmatory factor analysis. In L. G. Grimm & P. R. Yarnold (Eds.), *Reading and understanding multivariate statistics* (pp. 99–136). Washington, D.C.: American Psychological Association.

Bryk, A. S., & Raudenbush, S. W. (1992). *Hierarchical linear models:* Applications *and data analysis methods.* Newbury Park, CA: Sage.

Bryk, A. S., & Schneider, B. (2002). *Trust in schools*: A *core resource for improvement.* New York: Russell Sage Foundation.

Buchanan, G. M., & Seligman, M. E. P. (Eds.). (1995). *Explanatory style.* Hillsdale, NJ: Erlbaum.

Butler, J. K., & Cantrell, R. S. (1984). A behavioral decision theory approach to modeling dyadic trust in superiors and subordinates. *Psychological Reports, 55,* 81–105.

Coleman, J. S., Campbell, E. Q., Hobson, C. J., McPartland, J., Mood, A. M., Weinfeld, F. D., et al. (1966). *Equality of educational opportunity.* Washington, DC: U.S. Government Printing Office.

Coleman, J. S. (1985). Schools and the communities they serve. *Phi Delta Kappa, 66,* 527-532.

Coleman, J. S. (1987). Norms as social capital. In G. Radnitzky & P. Bernholz (Eds.), *Economic imperialism: The economic approach applied outside the field of economics* (pp. 133–155). New York: Paragon.

Coleman, J. S. (1990). *Foundations of social theory.* Cambridge, MA: Harvard University Press.

Cummings, L. L., & Bromily, P. (1996). The organizational trust inventory (OTI): Development and validation. In R. Kramer & T. Tyler (Eds.), *Trust in organization* (pp. 68–89). Thousand Oaks, CA: Sage.

Edmonds, R. (1979). Some schools work and more can. *Social Policy, 9,* 28–32.

Epstein, J. L. (1989). Family structure and student motivation. In R. E. Ames & C. Ames (Eds.), *Research on motivation in education: Goals and cognitions* (Vol. 3, pp. 259–295). New York: Academic Press.

Goddard, R. G., Hoy, W. K., & Woolfolk Hoy. A. (2000). Collective teacher efficacy: Its meaning, measure, and impact on student achievement. *American Educational Research Journal, 37*, 479–508.

Goddard, R. G., Hoy, W. K., & Woolfolk Hoy. A. (2004). Collective efficacy: Theoretical development, empirical evidence, and future directions. *Educational Researcher, 33*, 3–13.

Goddard, R. G., LoGerfo, L., & Hoy, W. K. (2004). High school accountability: The role of collective efficacy. *Educational Policy, 18*(30), 403–425.

Goddard, R. G., Sweetland, S. R., & Hoy, W. K. (2000). Academic emphasis of urban elementary schools and student achievement: A multi-level analysis. *Educational Administration Quarterly, 36*, 692–701.

Goddard, R. D., Tschannen-Moran, M., & Hoy, W. K. (2001). Teacher trust in students and parents: A multilevel examination of the distribution and effects of teacher trust in urban elementary schools. *Elementary School Journal, 102*, 3–17.

Hallinger, P., & Heck, R. (1996). Reassessing the principal's role in school effectiveness: A review of the empirical research, 1980–1995. *Educational Administration Quarterly, 32*(1), 5–44.

Hosmer, L.T. (1995). Trust: The connecting link between organizational theory and philosophical ethics. *Academy of Management Review, 20*(2), 379–403.

Hoy, W. K. (2002). Faculty trust: A key to student achievement. *Journal of School Public Relations, 23*(2), 88–103.

Hoy, W. K., & Hannum, J. (1997). Middle school climate: An empirical assessment of organizational health and student achievement. *Educational Administration Quarterly, 33*, 290–311.

Hoy, W. K., & Miskel, C. G. (2005). *Educational administration: Theory, research, and practice* (7th ed.). New York: McGraw–Hill.

Hoy, W. K., & Sabo, D. J. (1998). *Quality middle schools: Open and healthy*. Thousand Oaks, CA: Corwin.

Hoy, W. K., Sweetland, S. R., & Smith, P. A. (2002). Toward an organizational model of achievement in high schools: The significance of collective efficacy. *Educational Administration Quarterly, 38*, 77–93.

Hoy, W. K., & Tarter, C. J. (1997). *The road to open and healthy schools: A handbook for change* (2nd ed.) Thousand Oaks, CA: Corwin.

Hoy, W. K., & Tarter, C. J. (2004). *Administrators solving the problems of practice: Decision-making concepts, cases, and consequences*. Boston: Allyn & Bacon.

Hoy, W. K., Tarter, C. J., & Bliss, J. (1990). Organizational climate, school health, and effectiveness. *Educational Administration Quarterly, 26*, 260–279.

Hoy, W. K., Tarter, C. J., & Kottkamp, R. B. (1991). *Open schools/healthy schools: Measuring organizational climate*. Beverly Hills, CA: Sage.

Hoy, W. K., & Tschannen-Moran, M. (1999). Five faces of trust: An empirical confirmation in urban elementary schools. *Journal of School Leadership, 9*, 184–208.

Hoy, W. K., & Tschannen-Moran, M. (2003). The conceptualization and measurement of faculty trust in schools. In W. K. Hoy & C. Miskel (Eds.), *Studies in leading and organizing schools* (pp. 181-207). Greenwich, CT: Information Age.

Joreskog, K. G., & Sorbom, D. (1993). *LISREL 8.* Hillside, NJ: Erlbaum.

Mishra, A. K. (1996). Organizational responses to crisis: The centrality of trust. In R. Kramer & T. Tyler (Eds.), *Trust in organizations* (pp. 262–287). Thousand Oaks, CA: Sage.

Parsons, T., Bales, R. F., & Shils, E. A. (1953). *Working papers in the theory of action.* New York: Free Press.

Pajares, F. (1994). Role of self-efficacy and self-concept beliefs in mathematical problem-solving: A path analysis. *Journal of Educational Psychology, 86,* 193–203.

Pajares, F. (1997). Current directions in self-efficacy research. In M. L. Maehr & P. R. Pintrich (Eds.), *Advances in motivation and achievement* (pp. 1–49), Greenwich, CT: JAI Press.

Peterson, C. (2000). The future of optimism. *American Psychologist, 55,* 44–55.

Pintrich, P. R., & Schunk, D. H. (2002). *Motivation in education: Theory, research, and applications* (2nd ed.). Upper Saddle River, NJ: Merrill/Prentice-Hall.

Rotter, J. B. (1967). A new scale for the measurement of interpersonal trust. *Journal of Personality, 35,* 651–665.

Sarason, I. G. (1984). Stress, anxiety, and cognitive inference: Reaction to tests. *Journal of Personality and Social Psychology, 46,* 929–938.

Seligman, M. E. P. (1998). Positive social science. *APA Monitor, 29,*2–5.

Seligman, M. E. P., & Csikszentmihalyi, M. (2000). Positive psychology: An introduction. *American Psychologist, 55,* 5–14.

Smith, P. A., Hoy, W. K., & Sweetland, S.R. (2001), Organizational health of high schools and dimensions of faculty trust, *Journal of School Leadership, 11,* 135–151.

Snyder, C. R., Cheavens, J., & Sympson, S. C. (1997). Hope: An individual motive for social commerce. *Group Dynamics, 1,* 107–118.

Snyder, C. R., Shorey, H. S., Cheavens, J., Pulvers, K. M., Adams, V. H. III, & Wiklund, C. (2002). Hope and academic success in college. *Journal of Educational Psychology, 94,* 820–826.

Tiger, L. (1979). *Optimism: The biology of hope.* New York: Simon & Schuster.

Tschannen-Moran, M., Hoy, A. W., & Hoy, W. K. (1998). Teacher efficacy: Its meaning and measure. *Review of Educational Research, 68,* 202–248.

Tschannen-Moran, M, & Hoy, W. K. (2000). A multidisciplinary analysis of the nature, meaning, and measurement of trust. *Review of Educational Research, 70,* 547–593.

CHAPTER 7

TEACHER LEADERSHIP AND INSTRUCTIONAL IMPROVEMENT

Teachers' Perspectives

Melinda M. Mangin

Instructionally oriented teacher leadership roles—commonly known as coaches—aim at increasing students' academic achievement by first improving teachers' instruction through high quality professional development. This study explores the possible benefits and challenges of such teacher leadership by examining how 30 teachers from five school districts experienced the work of formal mathematics teacher leaders. Teachers reported that teacher leaders performed four primary activities: providing materials, assisting in the classroom, modeling lessons, and facilitating group sessions. These activities contributed differently and unequally to teachers' instructional improvement as indicated by their degree of alignment with the characteristics of effective professional development. Moreover, particular combinations of activities appeared more likely to produce changes in teaching practice.

Teacher leadership roles, commonly known as coaches or coordinators, have become an increasingly common strategy for school reform. These

Contemporary Issues in Educational Policy and School Outcomes, 159–192
Copyright © 2006 by Information Age Publishing
All rights of reproduction in any form reserved.

school-based positions are intended to increase students' academic achievement by first improving teachers' instructional acumen. In many instances, formal teacher leadership roles are connected to comprehensive school reform (CSR) models, which aim at systematically addressing school improvement via multiple pathways (Camburn, Rowan, & Taylor, 2003; Copland, 2003; Datnow & Castellano, 2001; Poglinco, Bach, Hovde, Rosenblum, Saunders, & Supovitz, 2003; Smylie, Wenzel, & Fendt, 2003). One outgrowth of this movement has been the implementation of similar teacher leadership roles in districts without CSR models.

Teacher leadership that focuses on instruction appears to be a logical pathway to building teaching capacity. Yet, research from previous teacher leadership initiatives—such as mentor, master, and lead teacher roles—indicates that formal teacher leaders face a number of challenges including role ambiguity, interpersonal tension, and conflict (Hart, 1990; Smylie & Denny, 1990). Such challenges may reduce teacher leaders' legitimacy, limit teachers' receptivity, and reduce effectiveness (Firestone & Bader, 1992). Moreover, recent research suggests that new instructionally-oriented teacher leaders may face some of the same problems experienced by their predecessors (Mangin, 2005). The extent to which these problems may impede the effectiveness of instructional teacher leadership remains unclear.

This study aims to increase our understanding of teacher leadership enactment and its relationship to teachers' instructional improvement. The questions guiding this investigation include:

- What kinds of interactions do teachers report having with teacher leaders?
- How do teachers perceive the quality of teacher leadership as a resource?
- What influence does teacher leadership have on teachers' instruction?

To explore these questions, interviews were conducted with 30 teachers, from five school districts, who worked with teacher leaders to improve their mathematics instruction. The findings have implications for the future design and development of teacher leadership roles.

TEACHER LEADERSHIP AS INSTRUCTIONAL REFORM

To better understand how teacher leaders contribute to instructional improvement, it is first helpful to understand how the teacher leadership role—as a mechanism for reform—is conceptualized. This section presents some of the research and theory used to support the creation and analysis of instructionally-oriented teacher leadership roles.

Instructional Leadership

The development of formal teacher leadership roles has been fueled by research on instructional leadership, which has traditionally focused on the role of principals (Firestone, 1996). This hierarchical view of instructional leadership has been extensively critiqued, prompting a move in the 1980s to recognize teachers as pivotal to instructional leadership (Cochran-Smith & Lytle, 1992; Lieberman, Saxl, & Miles, 1988; Smylie, 1994). In addition to being viewed as leaders in their own right, teachers are understood to have close connections to the classroom, positioning them as gatekeepers of instructional reform (Hart, 1995; Heller & Firestone, 1995). This perception of teachers as potential instructional leaders has increasingly led to the creation of new positions that formally expand instructional leadership responsibilities beyond the individual school principal (Camburn et al., 2003; Datnow & Castellano, 2001; Guiney, 2001; Neufeld & Roper, 2003; Poglinco et al., 2003; Smylie et al., 2003).

While formal teacher leadership roles have become almost commonplace, little is known about the practice of instructional teacher leadership (Smylie, Conley, & Marks, 2002). The extant research covers a broad range of formal leadership positions, making it difficult to draw conclusions across the body of work and leaving wide gaps in what we know about instructional teacher leadership (York-Barr & Duke, 2004). Previous research indicates that teachers need to have sufficient human capital, in the form of knowledge and skills, to be recognized as leaders by their peers (Spillane, Hallett, & Diamond, 2003). Moreover, recent studies indicate that instructional teacher leadership may be compromised by a lack of principal support (Camburn et al., 2003; Smylie et al., 2002), the school environment (Stoelinga, 2005), and limited classroom access (Mangin, 2005).

Professional Development

Support for teacher leadership roles has also been found in the literature on teachers' professional development. Like students, teachers need learning opportunities that are connected to real life situations, offer opportunities for hands-on practice, and involve them as a community of learners (Hawley & Valli, 1999; Hodges, 1996; Loucks-Horsley, 1995;

Loucks-Horsley, Hewson, Love, & Stiles, 1998; Richardson & Placier, 2001). Research on this kind of professional development suggests that the outcomes may include increased instructional capacity, changed teaching practice, and overall school reform (Chrispeels, 1997; Cohen & Hill, 2001). One way to promote high quality professional development may be through the creation of formal school-based teacher leadership roles (Smylie et al., 2003).

Teacher leadership roles may facilitate effective professional development when they attend to three main conditions:

Instructionally Oriented

High quality professional development builds teacher capacity and supports instructional change through activities that directly relate to instructional practice (Cohen & Hill, 2001). According to the literature, when professional development focuses on student performance it meets the learning needs of both educators and students (Hawley & Valli, 1999; Loucks-Horsley et al., 1998). Moreover, instructionally oriented professional development can help improve both teacher and student learning outcomes (Garet, Porter, Desimone, Birman, & Yoon, 2001).

Collaborative

Effective professional development emphasizes collaborative interaction between colleagues, giving teachers opportunities to share their knowledge and learn from others (Hawley & Valli, 1999; Loucks-Horsley, 1995). The benefits of collaboration are substantiated by research on professional development (Garet et al., 2001), teacher teaming (Crow & Pounder, 2000; Pounder, 1999) and professional communities (Bryk, Camburn, & Louis, 1999; Newmann & Wehlage, 1995). These studies conclude that teacher collaboration, marked by dialog, sharing, inquiry, and deprivatized practice, leads to enhanced teacher outcomes including collective responsibility and internal accountability (Louis & Kruse, 1995).

Context Specific

Effective professional development also occurs within the context of the school, contextualizing teacher learning within the collective needs of the school (Joyce & Showers, 1995; Little, 1993; Smylie, 1995) and fostering the direct transfer of learning to practice (Loucks-Horsley, 1995). Moreover, context specific professional development facilitates the instructional change process by enabling teachers to seek follow-up support from colleagues (Guskey, 1995; Hodges, 1996; Pink & Hyde, 1992).

Efforts by school districts to improve professional development have fueled the creation of formal teacher leadership roles (Camburn et al., 2003; Datnow & Castellano, 2001; Guiney, 2001; Neufeld & Roper, 2003;

Poglinco et al., 2003; Smylie et al., 2003). Unfortunately, evidence suggests that teachers may be ill-suited for leading their peers in professional development. The norms of autonomy and egalitarianism that characterize schools (Lortie, 1975), as well as teacher leaders' lack of positional power (Leithwood & Riehl, 2005) may diminish the teachers' legitimacy as leaders and limit their ability to exercise influence (Firestone & Bader, 1992). Moreover, research on mentor, master, and lead teacher roles indicates that formal teacher leaders face formidable challenges including role ambiguity, interpersonal tension, and conflict (Hart, 1990; Smylie & Denny, 1990). Whether instructional teacher leaders face similar challenges is unclear.

A THEORY OF ACTION

Although formal teacher leadership roles have grown increasingly common, few frameworks exist for analyzing or implementing such roles (York-Barr & Duke, 2004). This study uses the literature outlined above to illustrate one possible framework (see Figure 7.1), which serves as a theoretical map as well as a theory of action for teacher leadership practice.

In this theoretical depiction, teacher leadership practice is situated within multiple contexts: the district's history, social relations and tensions, cultural norms, available resources, curriculum, the role design, organizational structures and contractual factors. The teacher leader operates within these contexts, interacting with the classroom teacher about issues related to mathematics instruction through the medium of professional development activities. Thus, the teacher leader serves as an instructional resource helping teachers build knowledge and skills. The content of the interaction includes instructional topics such as curriculum standards, instructional strategies, assessment strategies, and subject matter knowledge. The process of interaction is characterized by increased dialog, inquiry, resource sharing, and deprivatized practice. An intermittent line between classroom teachers symbolizes teacher leadership's collaborative potential.

In theory, the possible outcomes of instructional teacher leadership include new knowledge and beliefs, instructional improvement, student learning, collective improvement, professional communities, and internal accountability. The likelihood of these outcomes depends on the extent to which teacher leadership practice reflects theory. We know that contextual factors can unpredictably influence and alter the implementation of policies, programs, or theories (Berman & McLaughlin, 1977; Sabatier & Mazmanian, 1979). Moreover, this theory of instructional teacher leadership presupposes that teachers' professional development goals align with

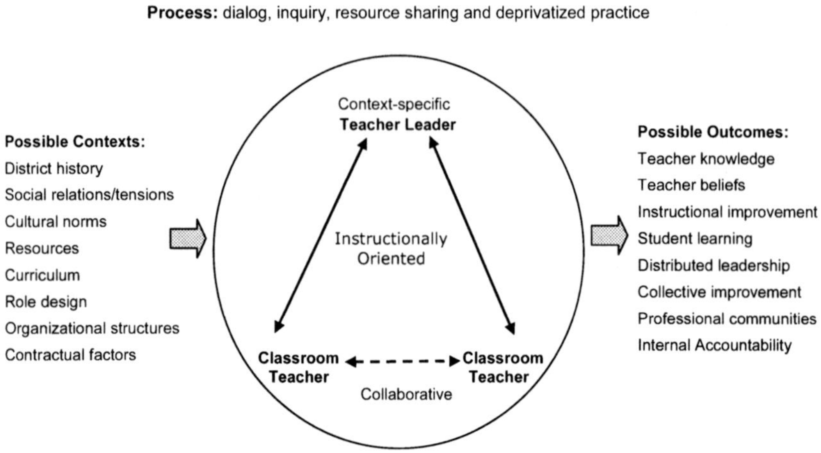

Process: dialog, inquiry, resource sharing and deprivatized practice

Figure 7.1.   Conceptual framework and theory of action.

those of the district—an assumption that is not supported by research (Firestone, Mangin, Martinez, & Polovsky, 2005). Thus, teacher leaders face the challenge of balancing teachers' preferences with what we know about effective professional development.

Distributed Leadership

The term *distributed leadership* refers to the scholarship of James Spillane and his colleagues (Spillane, Halverson, & Diamond, 2001) who define it as a conceptual frame that can facilitate comprehensive understandings of leadership. Drawing on activity theory and distributed cognition, they call for an investigation of leadership activity, which they describe as the interaction between leaders, followers, and situation. The distributed perspective "argues for the development of rich theoretical knowledge based on studies of practice that are context-sensitive and task-specific" (Spillane, Halverson, & Diamond, 2004, p. 29). In brief, a distributed perspective posits that, (a) school leadership is composed of both macrofunctions and microtasks; (b) leadership tasks are mediated by people and situations; (c) leadership is constituted through social interactions and interdependencies; (d) leadership practice and the contexts in which it occurs are mutually influential to the extent that they are constitutive of one another. Thus, a distributed perspective of leadership seeks to understand "the *how* and *why* of leadership activity" (p. 27).

The distributed perspective conceives leadership as a naturally occurring phenomenon—a fundamental part of interaction—and not the exclusive domain of formal leadership roles. Yet, Smylie et al (2003) notes a paradox in this situation, arguing that the creation of leadership roles for teachers may generate interaction. On this basis, formal positions such as instructional teacher leaders offer ripe examples of the kind of interaction that distributed leadership theory aims to explore. Thus, this study examines the interaction between teachers and formal teacher leaders and documents the micro tasks involved in providing instructional leadership.

METHODS

This study used a comparative case study methodology (Creswell, 1998) to explore teachers' interactions with elementary-level math teacher leaders[1]—teachers released from teaching responsibilities to assist colleagues with math-related professional development to improve mathematics instruction. Data were collected in 2003–04 from 30 elementary school teachers from five school districts in New Jersey. The data reported here are from a larger study that included interviews and observations with 63 participants including 12 teacher leaders, 15 principals, and 6 district-level curriculum supervisors in addition to teachers.

Sampling

Districts were sampled purposefully to maximize variation in teacher leadership design (Miles & Huberman, 1994) despite having similar instructional improvement aims (see Table 7.1). Four of the five districts were low socioeconomic status districts according to New Jersey's publicly available "report card." The districts were relatively small, ranging from 2,200 to 7,500 students, reflecting the average district size for the state (see Table 7.2).

Participant selection conformed to the recommendations of Miles and Huberman (1994). Selection began with a representative sample of 12 full-time, math teacher leaders drawn from the five districts. Those teacher leaders worked in a total of 21 schools. Principals from 15 schools were recruited to participate in the study. Principals and teacher leaders assisted in selecting a sample of 30 teachers. This sample included two teachers from each of the 15 participating schools. Pairs of teachers were sampled purposively to capture varying perspectives (Creswell, 1998). Thus, one teacher was more receptive to the work of the math teacher leader and one was more resistant. Moreover, the researcher asked that the teachers not represent extremes but, merely diverging viewpoints. Teachers' status—resistant or receptive—was not revealed to the researcher.

Data Collection

The data reported here come from audiotaped interviews with the 30 elementary school teachers. The semistructured interview protocol was piloted with a teacher from a nonparticipating district to ensure the appropriateness of the interview questions (LeCompte & Goetz, 1982). The open-ended questions focused on the kinds of interactions occurring between teachers and teacher leaders as well as the teachers' perceptions of the intent and the outcomes of the teacher leader role (see Appendix A).

Data Organization, Analysis, Interpretation

The procedures used for data analysis included deductive and inductive reasoning (Miles & Huberman, 1994) and incorporated strategies such as memoing and using data matrices (Patton, 2001). A computer software program aided the process of data organization and reduction (Creswell, 1998). The broad themes captured in reflective and analytic memos were revised as new data was assimilated and themes emerged. Moreover, the analysis aimed at identifying patterns and discontinuities across respondents and contexts (Creswell & Miller, 2000). Data interpretation focused on relationships between contexts, teacher leadership practices, and instructional impact.

Study Limitations

The sampling strategy for teachers, which aimed at capturing variation in receptivity, *precludes* generalizability to the larger study population (LeCompte & Goetz, 1982). For that reason, this study does not lend itself to making statements about the overall receptivity of teachers in any given district or the study population in general. On the contrary, it was expected that the teachers who were sampled would be composed of roughly 50% more receptive teachers and 50% more resistant teachers. These proportions are in no way reflective of actual ratios of receptive and resistant teachers. Instead, this sampling strategy provides greater under-

Table 7.1.   Characteristics of Teacher Leadership by District

Characteristics	Districts				
	A	B	C	D	E
Number of math teacher leaders	11	2	2	2**	3
Number of elementary schools	10	2	8	4	4
Number of schools per teacher leader	1*	1	8	3	1***
Subjects covered	Math	Math	Math Social studies Lang. arts	Math	Math
Year position created	Fall 2001	Fall 2002	Fall 2000; Redesigned Fall 2002	Fall 2000; Fall 2002 ****	Fall 2002

*One large school has two math teacher leaders.
**Third position added March 2003; not included in study.
***Two smallest K-2 schools shared by one math teacher leader.
****Second position added in 2002.

**Table 7.2.   Demographic Characteristics of
Participating Districts, 2001-02**

Characteristics	Districts				
	A	B	C	D	E
District Factor Group	B	C/D	B	G/H	B
Total enrollment	7,526	2,202	5,898	6,052	3,332
% White	1	41	37	31	85
% Black	71	45	37	44	6
% Hispanic	28	10	22	11	7
% passing rate on high school proficiency test	29.4	42	47.4	59	63.9**
% of students on free or reduced lunch	64	50	45	27	35
Ratio of 9th to 12th grade enrollment	1.79:1	*	1.33:1	1.64:1	1.40:1
% high school attendance	90.5	90.4	92.8	87.2	93.2

*No 12th grade class.
**The high school, unlike the elementary schools, enrolled students from surrounding townships that were better off socioeconomically. This difference is reflected in the higher graduation rates.

standing of the range of teachers' interactions and perceptions with regard to teacher leadership roles.

This paper privileges teachers' perceptions of teacher leadership. Triangulating teachers' perceptions with teacher leaders' reports and with observations revealed differing and sometimes conflicting accounts of teacher leadership enactment. These legitimate differences occurred for two primary reasons: teacher leaders may not enact their reported intentions and teachers may not know the scope of activities performed by the teacher leader.[2] This paper seeks to understand teacher leadership from the perspective of the teacher, while acknowledging the legitimacy of all participants' viewpoints.

TEACHER LEADERSHIP ACTIVITIES

Classroom teachers reported that teacher leaders performed a range of activities that varied across districts, across schools, and by teacher leader. Despite this variation, each district exhibited trends and patterns in the kinds of leadership activities that were most prevalent. To discern these trends, teachers were asked to report on their interaction with the teacher leader and, to the best of their knowledge, their colleagues' interaction. The results indicated four primary kinds of teacher leadership activities. Each is described here drawing examples from districts that reported a high incidence (see Table 7.3).[3]

Providing Materials

The provision of materials generally occurred in combination with other leadership activities such as modeling or grade-level meetings. Although all of the participating teachers received some kind of classroom materials, the examples presented here are drawn from Districts D and E, where providing materials was a predominant teacher leadership activity.

In District D, the provision of materials occurred primarily in the form of instructional packets designed to strengthen teachers' content knowledge. The packets, or binders, that teachers received included math games, word problems, and sample test questions, modeled after the state standardized test. These constructivist materials were meant to supplement the more traditional math textbook. In District E, the teacher leaders' approach to materials provision was focused more on the organization and dissemination of classroom supplies such as posters, place mats, overhead transparencies, manipulatives and, to a lesser

Table 7.3. Teachers' Reports of Leadership Activities by District

Activity			Districts		
	A	B	C	D	E
Provide materials				X	X
Assist in classroom		X	X		X
Model lessons		X		X	X
Facilitate group sessions	X			X	

degree, assessment rubrics and pacing schedules. Along with the supplies, teacher leaders also provided advice about how to use the materials and how to avoid unforeseen challenges they might encounter in presenting a new lesson.

According to the teachers, the provision of materials had a number of benefits, including saving teachers' time and energy. As one District E teacher explained, "She cuts out a lot of the legwork that we would have to do." Not only did materials provision help teachers implement constructivist math curriculum, it also provided teachers with new instructional ideas. A teacher from District D reported, "They give us these photocopies of really good problems on money, shopping, discounts, graphing, on loads of things." Thus, providing materials introduced teachers to new and useful instructional information, saving teachers time and energy.

Teachers from both districts reported drawbacks to teacher leadership that focused on providing materials. Foremost, teachers indicated that they didn't always need additional materials, citing an overabundance of math texts, binders, and packets. Teachers who expressed this viewpoint indicated infrequent use of the materials that they received.

Classroom Assistance

Another activity that teacher leaders performed was to assist teachers the classroom. Teacher leaders from three school districts—B, C, and E—commonly relied on this mode of leadership. Across these three districts, two distinct means of providing classroom assistance were reported: auxiliary help and coteaching. The examples used here come from Districts B and E where classroom assistance was most strongly reported.

Auxiliary help was described by teachers from Districts B and E as being "an extra pair of hands" in the classroom. Teacher leaders typically provided auxiliary help when the lesson involved grouping students into learning centers or an extensive use of manipulatives. In such instances, the math teacher leader provides auxiliary help so that the students would be better monitored and assisted.

A coteaching approach, which occurred primarily in District B (and with one District E teacher leader), involved the teacher and teacher leader sharing responsibility for planning and leading the lesson. A common format was for the teacher leader to prepare a "problem of the day" or an introductory activity that she would use to start the math lesson. Then, the classroom teacher would continue with the day's main lesson. Using this format, neither teacher became the sole leader. Both felt free to interject into the other teacher's section of the lesson. Coteaching was reported primarily in District B, where teacher leaders targeted subsets of teachers with whom they worked regularly.

Teachers reported a number of benefits from receiving classroom assistance. Foremost, auxiliary assistance helped the lesson run smoothly and enabled methodologies that were otherwise considered too challenging to implement. A teacher from District E received help with math labs explaining, "It's very difficult for me to get around to every single group and assess where they're at ... so a lot of times she'll come in and sit down with other groups" Classroom assistance also introduced teachers to new instructional strategies. One teacher from District B who received weekly assistance from the teacher leader explained, "it was almost like she was doing a demonstration lesson for me because she was teaching in a way that I had never thought of. I learned so much from her just doing that." Thus, although formal modeling was not involved, the teacher leader's assistance with centers introduced her to new ways of teaching.

The primary drawback associated with classroom assistance was the difficulty of coordinating schedules and making sure that the teacher leader would be available on the right day and appropriate time. This challenge was especially pronounced when trying to coordinate a coteaching experience. For example, one District E teacher remarked that she would be unlikely to seek assistance with student learning centers "because that requires a lot of planning and we don't really have that much time with her to plan. And sometimes it's just easier to do it yourself." Thus, the added work of planning and organizing a visit from the teacher leader was sometimes more than teachers were willing to do.

Modeling Lessons

Teachers from Districts B and D reported that teacher leaders commonly modeled lessons or materials. Within these two districts, modeling took two different forms.

In District B, modeling was generally an extension of auxiliary class-room assistance, marked by increased instances of coteaching and opportunities for teachers to observe instructional methods. Frequently, this kind of interaction was organized so that the teacher leader spent part of the lesson modeling a new concept while the teacher assumed the role of learner. Thus, modeling allowed teacher leaders to introduce new ideas while simultaneously offering extra instructional assistance.

Modeling in District D focused more exclusively on demonstrating an entire lesson and the teacher would sit with the students and participate in the lesson as a learner. Teacher leaders provided a series of model lessons that focused on learning a particular skill, mathematical concept, or manipulative. The sessions were organized to expose grade specific teachers to the same lesson. In addition, the sessions occurred in tandem with grade level meetings, enabling teachers to discuss what they had learned.

Teachers who experienced these kinds of modeling activities reported benefits for students. For example, one District D teacher indicated that the teacher leader helped liven up the class and captured the students' attention. Aside from short term benefits for students, teachers also reported long-term benefits with regard to students' enthusiasm about math. Another District D teacher shared this story: "There was a game that I was very interested in called 24 … and the math trainer got me the game! And she came in and she modeled it and demonstrated—played it with the children—and it was great! The kids loved it and then we played it all year long." These kinds of student-oriented benefits were reported by all of the teachers who experienced modeling.

In addition to student benefits, teachers reported learning new and valuable information as a result of increased access to instructional resources. One District B teacher indicated that her interactions with the teacher leader resulted in "fabulous ideas," prompting her to exclaim, "Oh! I never thought of that! I think that's really awesome!" Other teachers gave specific examples of what they had learned. For instance, one District D teacher explained,

> I thought it was very interesting that [the teacher trainer] allowed them time to play [with the Cuisenaire Rods]. I've never allowed them to really play, to become familiar with it. So that was a new concept for me—they have to get used to feeling and touching and making comparisons.

This kind of teacher learning appears to reflect the instructional improvement aims of teacher leadership.

Given teachers' overall positive reports of modeling, it is not surprising that only two teachers, both from District D, indicated drawbacks to modeling. One, a veteran teacher, cited a lack of need due to her 37 years of experience. The second teacher expressed concern that modeling offered only isolated benefits, rather than an extended instructional impact: "They come in and they do a subject-specific lesson, which is nice for that day but you can't do it again." For these two teachers, model lessons provided limited benefits, prompting them to question the utility of modeling.

Despite these drawbacks, teachers most frequently cited modeling as their preferred leadership activity and teachers from all five districts expressed a desire for more opportunities to watch model lessons. For example, in District C where teachers' opportunities to interact with the teacher leader were extremely limited, one teacher with 30 years of experience explained,

> If they made themselves available, even if it was just once a month—even to teachers who have been here for a while—and conducted a hands-on game for math or something different that I don't do with the class. That would be a good experience for the children and for me because that way I could learn more—have more ideas of what I can do in the room. I would like that but I don't know if they have time.

Many teachers indicated the time-intensive nature of modeling, a factor that makes modeling especially difficult for teacher leaders who work across large numbers of teachers or schools.

Facilitate Group Sessions

The fourth kind of teacher leadership activity reported by teachers was group sessions, which generally took the form of grade-level meetings. Teachers from four of the five districts reported that grade-level meetings occurred to some degree, although the amount of time provided and utilized varied by district and school. In Districts B and E, grade-level meetings occurred irregularly and without a clear instructional improvement aim, sometimes for as briefly as 10 or 15 minutes. In contrast, teacher leaders in Districts A and D systematically planned and led grade-level meetings, although the organization and delivery of these meetings differed for each district.

In District A, grade-level meetings were the primary form of contact between the teachers and teacher leaders. All classroom teachers participated in weekly grade-level meetings that would alternate topics: literacy 1 week and mathematics the next. The meetings were facilitated by the teacher leader who would plan and lead the session. Occasionally, math and literacy might be combined or two grade levels might meet to discuss articulation of subject matter across grades. These 80 minute, mandatory sessions were closely monitored by the principals who kept track of attendance and content. Topics might include analysis of students' test scores; instructional goal setting; pacing; student assessment including the use of rubrics, portfolios, and anecdotal notes; or general challenges that teachers faced in implementing the district's rigorous constructivist curriculum.

Unlike District A, the majority of teachers in District D did not have regularly scheduled grade-level meetings, yet, they were a common means of interaction. Grade-level meetings would typically take place during a half-day training session, an after school professional development event, or during release time when the principal would hire substitute teachers to cover classes. For each grade level, the teacher leader would organize two or three group sessions per year. These sessions would be complimented by follow-up model lessons and the provision of related materials for teachers' use.

Although both Districts A and D had designed and implemented a formal system of grade-level meetings, teachers from District D were more likely to indicate benefits, reporting that grade-level meetings gave them a chance to share ideas and strategies and receive helpful advice. One teacher reported, "We'll all sit there and we have manipulatives and hands-on materials and we learn ideas and new things.... I find that there's other ways of [teaching] that I've never thought of" In addition to learning useful information, teachers indicated that grade-level meetings gave them a sense of camaraderie, particularly in districts where teachers expressed frustration with a new math curriculum. For example, District E teachers indicated that their grade-level meetings, which occurred infrequently, gave them a chance to "vent" frustrations and helped them feel less isolated.

Despite the instructional benefits reported by teachers from District D, teachers from other districts indicated a number of drawbacks, especially the amount of time required to participate and overall resistance to "give-up" limited planning time. In the words of one District E teacher, "[If] you're forced to get together then it becomes a complaining session on why we're here.... I'm not gonna spend 45 minutes of my time talking about what they didn't like." Thus, although grade-level meetings might provide a context for teachers to express frustration and offer support, they did not guarantee constructive conversation.

Similar problems were noted by teachers from District A who reported that grade-level meetings frequently became a forum for complaining about the constructivist math curriculum, which teachers described as difficult to implement and widely disliked by the elementary teachers. One teacher shared,

To be honest with you, we argue—it's just an argument, it's a non-stop battle. And it's not the math coordinator's fault, it's just ... we complain about the book because we don't feel that we should have done this book.... The kids have a hard time with it.

Although this teacher indicated that teachers' complaining was not the teacher leader's "fault," she later suggested that the teacher leader provided insufficient instructional support. "She should have to go to all the classrooms to model. I just think if I was [sic] in that position, I wouldn't really feel comfortable telling people what to do if I'm not actually doing it" This was a common complaint in District A where teachers viewed grade-level meetings as a forum for making directives without providing classroom support.

IMPACT: DISTRICT BY DISTRICT

This section considers how teacher leadership activities were combined and enacted in each district. Three aspects are addressed: a) the interactional context, b) teachers' reports of overall quality of teacher leadership and, c) teachers' perceptions of its influence on instruction and changes they would make to increase influence.

District A

Context

Unlike the other districts, District A had implemented a literacy coordinator role several years prior in conjunction with the America's Choice comprehensive school reform model. The math teacher leader role was designed to mirror the literacy position in its instructional intent and teacher focus. This set the stage for the implementation of a new and challenging constructivist math program. Ironically, teachers grew to dislike the new program, reportedly because of its unrealistic expectations, unfriendly teachers' manual, lack of alignment with the state test, and failure to address traditional math facts. Teachers frequently spoke of the teacher leaders as working to ensure implementation of the math program, sometimes conflating the teacher leadership role with the math program. Eventually, the teachers' discontent, combined with parental concern, prompted District A to adopt a more moderate constructivist math program shortly after completion of this study.

Within this contentious context, teachers reported that their primary means of interacting with math teacher leaders was through bimonthly grade-level meetings. These sessions covered topics such incorporating new manipulatives in the classroom, analyzing students' test data, working together on assessment rubrics, studying the state mathematics standards, reviewing lesson pacing and cross-grade alignment of instruction, setting instructional goals, and incorporating literacy into the math curriculum. According to teachers, although modeling had been a significant activity in previous years it was now limited to casual drop-ins or to newly hired teachers.

Quality

Four of the six teachers reported aspects that made the teacher leadership position a good resource. Foremost, all four teachers indicated that the teacher leader was knowledgeable about math and/or the math program. One teacher remarked, "They really know their stuff. And what I like about them is that if there's something that they don't know, they don't make it up just to give you an answer. They'll say, 'let us get back to you' ... and nine times out of ten, they do." Such comments indicate that teachers generally saw the teacher leadership role as a useful resource for improving teaching.

In addition to positive comments, another four teachers (three of whom also made positive remarks) indicated aspects that made the position a poor resource. For example,

> Everyone's intentions are good but in reality the position ... has not really been that meaningful. [The math coordinator] just gives me the heads up in terms of what I should have in place for a walk-through, what I need for an assessment. But in terms of literally helping work with these children, it's almost non-existent.

According to this teacher, the position focused on "window dressing" in preparation for critical site visits from administrators. A teacher from another school expressed a similar desire for classroom assistance saying, "Our coordinator provides a lot of training.... But as far as in-class support, we don't see a lot of that."

Influence

Teachers from District A indicated varying levels of influence on their instruction. Two teachers reported a positive impact, saying it helped them become comfortable with the math program and implement it more effectively. Another teacher indicated that the program had influenced him, but not necessarily in the way he wanted:

> In terms of me becoming more formatted with [the math program].... I would say yes, the math coordinator acclimated me to how to keep records

and how I am to observe the students. But in terms of how I interacted with [students] … and got the lessons to become more meaningful, no.

In addition, three other teachers reported that the position had not influenced them, two of whom had advanced math training and a deep understanding of the curriculum. The third teacher who reported no impact was a kindergarten teacher who expressed a disinterest in math and an overall reticence to change her instruction.

Five of the six teachers indicated that they would change the teacher leader position. Of those five, three commented on the work of a particular teacher leader, suggesting that she was unsupportive, overly critical, and inefficient. As a result, these teachers thought the position should be more closely monitored and that "there should be more accountability." Two of the teachers reported that teacher leaders' work should be aimed at providing classroom assistance. In the words of one teacher, "[The teacher leader] could be a real help to the classroom teacher and it's very simple—all I need is someone else in there helping me with these lessons." This viewpoint was compounded by the fact that, the previous year, the district had cut Instructional Support Teachers (IST), who would have provided this kind of support to teachers. In addition, two other teachers wanted changes to the distribution of the positions. One indicated that a single teacher leader was insufficient and the other reported that her school, which housed two math teacher leaders, only needed one.

District B

Context

A number of contextual factors influenced teacher leadership enactment in District B. Foremost, the district only had two elementary schools and the principal of each school had autonomy in executing the teacher leader role. As a result, the principal at School 1 instructed the teacher leader work part time with students, especially in the months prior to the state standardized test. The teacher leader spent the rest of her time working with a targeted group of fourth and first grade teachers. At School 2, three different principals supervised the teacher leader the year that data were collected for this study. These included an out-going principal, an interim principal, and then a new principal. This shifting leadership dynamic afforded high levels of autonomy to the teacher leader, who organized her schedule to see as many teachers as possible on a rotating basis. One contextual component shared by the two schools was that each teacher leaders piloted a different constructivist math program with one of their school's fourth grade teachers. At the end of the school year, one of these math programs was selected for district-wide adoption.

Teachers from District B reported that the primary forms of teacher leader interaction were classroom assistance and modeling, which generally occurred with a coteaching approach (described above). At School 1, interaction was typically limited to the targeted teachers and occurred frequently—once a week for the two first grade teachers and every day for the three fourth grade teachers. As a result, teachers and the teacher leader developed close professional relationships. At School 2, similar interactions occurred daily in the two math pilot classrooms (a first and a fourth grade) and then less frequently with the rest of the faculty. The teacher leader reported interacting with 22 teachers on average each week, leaving only a handful of teachers with whom she had no interaction. Because the teacher leader worked with so many teachers, she seldom planned activities, serving more as an assistant offering advice or ideas throughout the lesson.

Quality

All four District B teachers indicated that teacher leadership was a good resource. In School 1, teachers cited the teacher leader's level of expertise and her easy-going personality. Teachers also indicated that the math specialist was accessible and provided incentives for them to contact her. One teacher explained, "She's always [saying] 'come on out.' And a lot of times she'll have candies, she has a lot of good ideas, and she makes you feel welcome." Similar sentiments were expressed by the teachers at School 2 with one remarking, "She was approachable, she sympathized, she validated [my work], she was creative, and she tried everything to make it work and to help you out." In fact, only two teachers reported aspects that made the position a poor resource, including a need for greater interaction with more teachers and a desire for common planning periods.

Influence

In District B, all four teachers indicated being positively influenced by the teacher leader. As one teacher described:

> I think a big impact on me was seeing math as a daily life skill.... Also, that math can be fun. You can teach skills and still do it through games. That there's different ways to teach math. It's not one way only. I think that has been a big impact on me—it's not the dreaded math.

Teachers also reported receiving reassurance, validation, confidence, and inspiration as a result of teacher leadership. These reports were likely influenced by the high level of interaction the teachers had with teacher leaders. Three of the four participating teachers taught targeted grades, two of whom interacted daily with the teacher leader and one who interacted weekly. The fourth teacher was part of the general faculty at School 2.

Despite the positive impact cited by all four District B teachers, three of the four teachers also reported changes that would make the position more influential. A teacher from School 1 recommended removing the student-oriented component of the position to facilitate more interaction with the teachers and a teacher from School 2 suggested more "teacher contact time." The third teacher indicated that more formal modeling would be useful to both students and teachers explaining, "You can learn and get some strategies for yourself.... For her to come in and do this awesome lesson—even if she does the same lesson in each fourth grade—that would be nice."

District C

Context

In District C, the design of the teacher leadership position severely compromised its enactment. Unlike the other districts in this study, the teacher leaders from District C were responsible for three subject areas: mathematics, literacy, and social studies. The two teacher leaders were also spread across eight schools, greatly limiting the time they spent at any one school. As a result, only two of the four teachers reported significant interaction with the teacher leaders and those interactions were limited to a few times a year.

One of the two teachers who reported virtually no interaction explained, "They just pop in about twice a month ... they ask if there's anything I need or help with anything and my answer is 'no.' And that's it." Of the two teachers who reported interaction, one indicated that she had a long-term relationship with the teacher leader, who had supervised her student teaching experience. This teacher reported receiving help with classroom projects, such as a Build-a-Bear art activity, and interacting through report card and scheduling committees. The other teacher who reported interaction indicated that she had received advice related to instruction including help with writing activities and information about a Jeopardy-like game she used to teach literacy and social studies.

Quality

When describing the quality of teacher leadership, all the teachers from District C had something positive to say, describing the teacher leaders as having a broad perspective on the district, making themselves available, and as a valuable resource to new teachers. According to one teacher,

> If anything ever came up and I didn't know where else to go to find out what I needed to do to improve something, [the teacher leader] is always there.... So I think she's a great resource if you need anything.

At the same time, all four teachers also indicated that the position's quality was diminished by the number of schools they covered. Thus, although the teachers saw the role as a potential resource, the distribution of teacher leaders across schools and (presumably) across subject matter limited its quality.

Influence

Given teachers' low levels of interaction with the teacher leader, it is unsurprising that only one District C teacher—the one with a long-standing relationship—indicated that the role had influenced her teaching practice. According to her, the teacher leader influenced teachers' work by serving as an advocate for teachers and speaking on their behalf in meetings. The other three teachers indicated that the teacher leadership position did not affect them. When asked about a possible impact on the school district in general, the teachers reported having too little interaction to make a judgment.

Regarding the kinds of changes teachers would make to the teacher leadership position, three of the four teachers offered suggestions. One teacher suggested to,

> Have the teacher and the helping teachers understand the roles of [one another].... I think we need to communicate more with them and let them know what's going on in the classrooms because just in this school alone they're seeing 40 classrooms.

This point was underscored by another teacher who responded that she could not comment on possible changes to the position because, "I don't know what their responsibilities are, so I have no idea." Another teacher, with 30 years of experience, suggested that it would be useful to both students and teachers if the teacher leaders provided model lessons on a monthly basis, presenting new topics and strategies that teachers typically don't teach.

District D

Context

The two teachers leaders in District D, who were spread across four schools, developed a systematic process of interaction, focusing their efforts on the upper elementary grades—levels 3, 4, 5, and 6. First, they arranged a grade-level meeting where they would discuss a specific mathematic topic, such as algebra or discrete math. Second, teacher leaders would follow up with a model lesson to demonstrate the concept within the context of the each teacher's classroom. Third, they would offer a packet of supplemental materials for the teacher to use. And finally, teacher leaders would make themselves available to answer questions or conduct additional model lessons. Occasionally, the teacher leader might also convene a follow-up grade-level meeting to discuss teachers' progress and concerns.

This systematic design provided similar levels of interaction across teachers, with all but one of the eight teachers indicating that they had attended two grade level meetings and observed two model lessons. In addition, all the teachers reported receiving numerous packets of math problems. Three teachers indicated that they had sought additional opportunities to interact with the teacher leader.

Quality

Regarding teacher leadership quality, all eight District D teachers cited components that made the role a good resource. These included the teacher leaders' math expertise, access to resources, openness and responsiveness, and experience as former teachers. One teacher explained the value of teacher leadership saying:

> The administrators are geared toward the building and administration ... and they might not have a good grasp on what goes on in a classroom. Whereas, I think these teacher trainers have been teaching for a long time and they can talk to a teacher on a teacher level.... I go to [colleagues] a lot when I have questions about management and other issues [but] I'm a little bit shy about talking to them about how to really teach a class.

Such comments indicate the positive influence of teacher leaders' work on teachers.

In addition to positive assessments, teachers identified aspects that made the position a poor resource, including the infrequency of visits, lack of administrative pressure to interact, and ineffective training. For example, five of the eight teachers indicated a desire for greater interaction; two reported the position should have greater authority to demand instructional change; and one teacher requested "more effective training, more hands-on training." This mix of comments suggests a generally positive view of teacher leadership, with teachers calling for more interaction with a greater emphasis on changed practice.

Influence

In District D, teachers reported a positive influence as well as room for improvement. Four teachers indicated that the teacher leader had influenced their teaching practice. To explain how his instruction had changed one teacher said,

> I do a lot more open-ended [questions] … having [students] explain how they got their answer, why their answer is correct or, if they made a mistake, why is your answer incorrect? What did you do wrong? Where did you make your mistake? What could you have done differently?

Two other teachers said the impact had been minimal—nothing they couldn't have done themselves. The final two teachers—a veteran and a novice—viewed teacher leadership as a good resource but said they were personally uninterested in the position, preferring to work alone.

In light of these generally positive reports, it is not surprising that District D teachers wanted increased teacher leader availability. In total, seven of the eight teachers thought teacher leaders were spread too thinly and suggested that each school should have its own teacher leader. As one teacher said,

> [The teacher leader] is one person in a sea of numerous teachers in this district. When you think about all the elementary schools we have here and all the different grades in each school, I would think that's pretty overwhelming for one person.

Only one teacher expressed concerns that the position might be too expensive and suggested reducing it to part-time. Four teachers indicated they would like to see changes in the type of assistance they received. For example, one wanted more "drop bys" and three suggested making the role more authoritarian with mandated observations, expectations for change, and greater respect for the stature of the position. Finally, one teacher thought teacher leaders should focus more on assisting students, rather than teachers.

District E

Context

Teacher leadership enactment in District E varied due to two factors: differences in position distribution and principal supervision. Regarding distribution, two of the three teacher leaders worked at upper-level elementary schools that served students in Grades 3–6. The third teacher leader worked in two small, lower-level elementary schools with students in Grades 1 and 2. Although the teacher leaders worked with similar numbers of teachers, their respective principals exerted differing levels of influence over the position. At School 1, an upper elementary, the principal asked the teacher leader to order and distribute supplies, manage a recycling program, offer three after-school programs, and serve as a resource person for science. At School 2, another upper elementary, the teacher leader and principal experienced personality conflicts that partially paralyzed the teacher leader's efforts in accessing classroom teachers. The third teacher leader worked with one principal (School 3) who requested that she perform managerial duties and another principal (School 4) who supported her role as an instructional resource.

Although contextual variations led to some differences in enactment, all three teacher leaders focused primarily on providing materials and assisting in the classroom. Seven of the eight participating teachers received materials and another seven reported receiving classroom assistance. In addition, one teacher from School 2 and three of the four teachers from the lower elementary schools experienced model lessons.

Quality

Six of the eight teachers described the teacher leadership position as a good resource, with two teachers citing availability and four individual teachers citing the teacher leader's supportive personality, ability to share information across schools, access to materials, and assistance with pacing and assessment. For example, a teacher from School 4 explained how the teacher leader helped her with materials: "I ask her [for assistance] when I know a complicated lesson is coming up with materials like cereal and stuff—so that we don't have to go and buy it." Similarly, a teacher from School 3 reported receiving student assessment materials from the teacher leader, which she described as useful.

Conversely, three of the eight teachers reported aspects of the teacher leadership role that made it a poor resource, including inaccessibility, a focus on nonmath-related tasks, an ambiguous job description, and general ineffectiveness. One teacher from School 2, who declined to be tape-recorded, indicated that the teacher leader performed tasks that teachers could easily do, such as making posters and distributing materials. She also indicated that the teacher leader's "hands were tied" by the lack of a specific job description and a personality conflict with the principal, which kept her from being more active. A teacher from School 1 expressed similar concerns, reporting that the teacher leader frequently performed duties un-related to math or teacher leadership. "I don't know if that's the best use of our money" she reflected, raising questions about teacher leadership quality and the use of resources.

Influence

Half of the eight District E teachers reported being influenced by the teacher leadership position. Two teachers, a veteran and a novice, felt more confident about their math teaching and another said she received practical advice about the math program. One teacher said she was more willing to seek help, explaining "Before, it wasn't available so I did without." Similarly, another teacher reported engaging in greater collaboration with her colleagues as they learned about the new math program together with the teacher leader. She explained, "It's been everybody working together. Even though she is the lead person it's everybody working together." For all four of these teachers, the teacher leadership role influenced their understanding and/or their approach to teaching math.

Three District E teachers reported changes they might make to the teacher leadership position although none of these suggestions was expressed strongly. For example, two teachers wanted more interaction— with one teacher preferring the interaction to focus on students. Another teacher indicated a preference for teacher leaders to be hired from within the existing faculty, noting that it can take time for teachers to "warm up to a new person."

DISCUSSION

These case studies provide information about the kinds of microtasks that teacher leaders perform and how teachers experience those tasks. Examining teacher leadership task enactment provides a more thorough understanding of how the social and the situational mediate leadership (Spillane et al., 2004).

Teachers identified four primary teacher leadership activities and reported their perceptions of the quality of those activities, their influence on teaching practice, and the kinds of changes teachers would make to teacher leadership enactment. Teachers reported a general willingness to work with teacher leaders provided that interactions were useful to their practice. In fact, teachers repeatedly indicated an appreciation for teacher leadership that was nonthreatening, saved time, provided new information, and facilitated complex instruction. Also, teachers preferred leadership activities that occurred within the context of their classroom and provided them with instructional support, such as classroom assistance and model lessons. Yet, teachers' preferences do not always align with what researchers know about effective professional development (Firestone et al., 2005); rather, the four activities contribute differently and unequally to instructional improvement.

Assessment of Activities

To better understand how teacher leadership contributes to instructional improvement, I assess the four activities on the basis of three evidence-based characteristics of effective professional development: (a) instructionally oriented, providing opportunities for capacity building and support change; (b) collaborative, with processes that include dialog, sharing, inquiry, and deprivatized practice; (c) context specific, enabling teachers to transfer new knowledge to the classroom (Hawley & Valli, 1999). Teacher leadership activities that embody these characteristics would be more likely to result in enhanced instructional outcomes. Conversely, the absence of these characteristics would make instructional improvement less likely.

Materials

The provision of materials saved teachers time and energy, but they doubted its value, questioning whether the teacher leaders' expertise was being well utilized. Moreover, some teachers indicated that they already had materials, suggesting that the role was unnecessary. The provision of materials such as rubrics, textbooks, manipulatives, and so forth … appears to be only minimally associated with the characteristics of effective professional development. Although materials may appear to be instructionally oriented, there is no guarantee that the materials will be utilized correctly—if at all. Furthermore, materials provision presents almost no opportunity for collective improvement. Given that materials provision has few of the characteristics of effective professional development, it appears to offer low potential for improving teachers' instruction. Yet, teachers might argue that they need appropriate materials before they can make progress toward improving instruction.

These findings raise questions about teacher leadership strategies that focus on nonthreatening behavior, leading teacher leaders to provide nonintrusive assistance such as providing materials. Paradoxically, teacher leaders provide nonintrusive assistance as a means of gaining teachers' trust and confidence and as a first step toward gaining entry to their classroom (Mangin, 2005). Nevertheless, such actions, although appreciated for their time saving benefits, may actually lead teachers to question the value of such positions, wondering whether there might be more efficient and productive means of spending school budget dollars. Thus, schools and districts would be wise to invest in other mechanisms that would reduce the need for teacher leaders to utilize such strategies.

Assistance

Whereas teachers doubted the value of materials provision, teachers had high praise for classroom assistance, indicating that it enabled them to conduct complex lessons that might not have otherwise been possible. Teachers also indicated that assistance helped lessons run smoothly and, when classroom assistance was akin to modeling, it provided opportunities for classroom teachers to observe the teacher leader and gain new instructional insights. In its most basic form—auxiliary help—classroom assistance appears to be limited in its potential to improve instruction. Although the teacher leader may assist with aspects of instruction, it appears unlikely that her assistance will prompt changes in instruction or increase teachers' capacity when the teacher leader's primary role is to be an extra pair of hands.

At the same time, the teacher leader's presence may enable the teacher to present especially complex or challenging lessons that otherwise might have been disregarded. Thus, assistance could potentially lead to changed practice. However, observations suggested that most classroom assistance served a managerial function rather than promoting instructional change. This raises important questions about the feasibility of successfully implementing constructivist math programs without sufficient managerial assistance for classroom teachers. Finally, although classroom assistance presented little, if any, chance for collaborative processes, it may be a first step to deprivatized practice.

Modeling

As discussed earlier, teachers cited modeling as a preferred activity, describing it as a highly useful. Besides being informative, teachers saw modeling as nonthreatening and time-saving. Modeling was also a change of pace, giving students an opportunity to see a new instructional approach and creating greater enthusiasm for math. Only a couple teachers indicated that model lessons had nothing new to offer and were unnecessary.

Regarding its potential to improve instruction, modeling presented teachers with an opportunity to build their capacity by watching experienced teachers present new mathematical concepts and instructional strategies. Moreover, this instructionally oriented professional development took place within the context of the classroom, enabling the teachers to make direct connections to their own classrooms and students. Where modeling fell short was in the area of collaborative instructional improvement. At best, modeling is a two-way interaction, although it may be characterized by dialog, sharing, and inquiry. Nevertheless, modeling lacks the kind of teacher collaboration described as most likely to promote instructional improvement. Moreover, modeling is a time intensive activity for teacher leaders, raising the question of whether or not such one-on-one kinds of interactions are an efficient use of teacher leaders' time.

Group Sessions

The last teacher leadership activity, facilitating group sessions, received mixed reviews from teachers, particularly when there was little collaborative time built into teachers' schedules and when teachers' interpreted the intent as delivering directives rather than offering assistance. Nevertheless, some teachers, particularly in District D, found group sessions useful, indicating that they provided an opportunity to share ideas and strategies, to develop camaraderie and to vent frustrations. In other instances, group sessions were described as gripe sessions, or a forum for complaining.

Viewed in light of instructional improvement aims, group sessions, appeared to be most closely aligned with the characteristics of effective professional development. Group sessions, or grade level meetings, offered high potential for instructionally oriented teacher collaboration. In theory, such sessions might enable teachers to discuss instructional concerns, share strategies, and engage in reflective inquiry, all within the context of their school setting and with teachers working in similar situations. Yet, such group sessions were not guaranteed. Instead of collaboration, the session could be managed in a top-down manner, characterized more by directives rather than discussion. Similarly, the content of group sessions may not retain an instructional focus. These findings indicate a need for a clearly delineated protocol for conducting group sessions, enabling them to be productive for both teachers and teacher leaders.

Implications

Applying principles of effective professional development to assess teacher leadership activity generates new insights into how teacher leadership practice links to instructional improvement. This new information can be used by districts to help them better design and implement teacher leadership positions.

For the districts in this study, teacher leadership activities appeared to evolve over time and along a kind of continuum. One end of the continuum includes activities that demand less instructional change (e.g. provision of materials) and at the other end are activities that demand greater change from teachers (e.g. group sessions). Teacher leaders' activities appeared to progress over time in accord with teachers' increased level of comfort. Thus, as teachers grow accustomed to notions of teacher leadership and changed practice, they may become more receptive to activities that demand greater change. For example, Districts A and D, which had the highest incidence of group sessions, were also the two districts that had implemented teacher leadership roles for the longest period of time.[4] The idea that teacher leadership evolves over time to reflect increasingly effective professional development activities raises the concern that some districts may not retain teacher leadership positions long enough to permit for this progression.

Another implication is that combinations of teacher leadership activities may be more likely to lead to instructional improvement than any single activity. As discussed, each of the teacher leadership activities by itself had limitations. For example, in District A, where grade-level meetings predominated, teachers expressed resistance and called for greater support in their classrooms, saying that group sessions were too time intensive for too few returns. Conversely, in District D, where grade-level meetings were combined with comparable numbers of model sessions and material support, teachers indicated a more positive reaction and greater instructional change. Thus, combining activities in ways that foster teacher receptivity but also begin to urge change may have the greatest instructional impact. For teacher leaders this means striking a balance between teachers' preferred activities and activities that align with instructional improvement.

The findings from this study also lend support to distributed perspectives of leadership enactment, underscoring the notion of leadership as constituted by and constitutive of social interaction (Spillane et al., 2004). The intended theory of action was altered in the process of enactment. In part, this finding corroborates research on policy and program implementation (Berman & McLaughlin, 1977; Sabatier & Mazmanian, 1979). At the same time, it suggests the inevitability of modifying theory, rather than the notion that, by considering all contextual variables we can somehow eliminate distortions. Instead, we should anticipate that theory will be altered in practice, study those negotiations and modifications, and incorporate them into our understanding of how leadership is enacted.

CONCLUSION

These findings have important implications for how scholars think about leadership and how educators plan for change. Moreover, understanding how teachers experience teacher leadership and its influence on their practice provides important insights for the design of future instructional teacher leadership roles. Teachers have legitimate concerns about the kinds of activities that teacher leaders perform and how they influence teachers' practice. Similarly, schools and districts have reasonable concerns about the effective and efficient use of finite resources. Understanding the connections between theory and practice, and between leadership and instruction may improve the implementation of teacher leadership roles and the instructional outcomes they aim to achieve.

NOTES

1. The term *math teacher leader* is inclusive of five titles that were used in the sample districts: specialist, helper, lead teacher, coordinator, and trainer.
2. What teacher leaders said they do, what they were observed doing, and what teachers experienced were not always the same. For example, teacher leaders were observed in fewer group sessions than reported by the teacher leaders themselves. Similarly, teachers were not always cognizant of teacher leader-led afterschool workshops, parent activities, or time spent planning. The examples cited here are not all inclusive.
3. In District C, where two teacher leaders were spread across eight schools and three subjects, patterns in leadership activities were almost indistinguishable. Therefore, District C is not used as an exemplar for any of the four activities.
4. Although the teacher leadership roles in District C had been in place for the same amount of time, they were originally central office positions. It was not until 2 years later that the roles were reconfigured to reflect the design studied here.

APPENDIX A

Interview Protocol: Classroom Teacher

Describe my project: I am interested in your work with the math coordinator, the kinds of interactions that you have and the extent to which you work together. My questions are about the math coordinator position, not the performance of the individual. The interview lasts approximately one hour and is intended to be noninvasive and confidential. You may chose not to respond to any question, and to stop the tape recorder or the interview at any time.

1. When did you first learn about the math coordinator position? How was it introduced to the faculty? What was your initial reaction? How did you think the position might impact the school? Did you think it would impact you directly?

2. Is there a particular math curriculum or program that you are required to teach? What are its goals and objectives? How is it related to the WSR program (if applicable)?

3. What is the role of the math coordinator? What kinds of activities does she/he do?

4. Do you rely on the math coordinator as a resource? Why or why not? Please give an example. What about the math coordinator makes him/her a good resource? What about the math coordinator makes him/her a poor resource?

5. What kind of interactions do you have with the math coordinator? How frequently do you interact—monthly, daily, never? Are they formal/informal sessions? Where do they take place? Who initiates the sessions? What would you say is the purpose of those interactions?

6. Are there particular goals or issues that either you or the math coordinator has for this year? How were those goals determined? What are some of the activities that you do that support those goals?

7. How is it decided that the math coordinator will—(model, lead group mtg, assist, etc.). Are the sessions required? How does the topic or subject matter get decided upon? Does the principal/supervisor have a hand in what takes place? Are you required to incorporate any suggestions the math coordinator might make?

8. What do other teachers think about the math coordinator position? As far as you can tell, how well do the math coordinator and the principal get along?

9. Has the creation of the math coordinator position had an impact on you? How so? Is that the kind of impact that you think was intended? Have you seen the kinds of improvement or change that you had expected? Why or why not? Would you like to have more or fewer opportunities to work together? Are there changes that you would make to the position?

Is there anything you'd like to add about your work with the math coordinator?

REFERENCES

Berman, P., & McLaughlin, M. (1977). *Federal programs supporting educational change, VII: Factors affecting implementation and continuation*. Santa Monica, CA: Rand.

Bryk, A., Camburn, E., & Louis, K. S. (1999). Professional community in Chicago elementary schools: Facilitating factors and organizational consequences. *Educational Administration Quarterly, 35*(Supplement), 751–781.

Camburn, E., Rowan, B., & Taylor, J. E. (2003). Distributed leadership in schools: The case of elementary schools adopting comprehensive school reform models. *Educational Evaluation and Policy Analysis, 25*, 347–373.

Chrispeels, J. H. (1997). Educational policy implementation in a shifting political climate: The California experience. *American Educational Research Journal, 34*(3), 453–481.

Cochran-Smith, M., & Lytle, S. L. (1992). *Inside/outside: Teacher research and knowledge.* New York: Teachers College Press.

Cohen, D. K., & Hill, H. C. (2001). *Learning policy: When state education reform works.* New Haven, CT: Yale University Press.

Copland, M. (2003). Leadership of inquiry: Building and sustaining capacity for school improvement. *Educational Evaluation and Policy Analysis, 25*(4), 375–395.

Creswell, J. W. (1998). *Qualitative inquiry and research design: Choosing among five traditions.* Thousand Oaks, CA: Sage.

Creswell, J. W., & Miller, D. L. (2000). Determining validity in qualitative inquiry. *Theory into Practice, 39*(3), 124–130.

Crow, G. M., & Pounder, D. G. (2000). Interdisciplinary teacher teams: Context, design, and process. *Educational Administration Quarterly, 36*(2), 216–254.

Datnow, A., & Castellano, M. E. (2001). Managing and guiding school reform: Leadership in Success For All schools. *Educational Administration Quarterly, 37*(2), 219–249.

Firestone, W. A. (1996). Leadership roles or functions? In K. Leithwood, J. Chapman, D. Corson, P. Hallinger, & A. W. Hart (Eds.), *International handbook of educational leadership and administration* (Vol. 2, pp. 395–418). Dordrecht, The Netherlands: Kluwer.

Firestone, W. A., & Bader, B. D. (1992). *Redesigning teaching: Professionalism or bureaucracy?* Albany, NY: SUNY.

Firestone, W. A., Mangin, M. M., Martinez, M. C., & Polovsky, T. (2005). Content and coherence in district professional development: Three case studies. *Educational Administration Quarterly, 41*(3), 413–448.

Garet, M. S., Porter, A. C., Desimone, L., Birman, B. F., & Yoon, K. S. (2001). What makes professional development effective? Results from a national sample of teachers. *American Educational Research Journal, 38*(4), 915–945.

Guiney, E. (2001). Coaching isn't just for athletes: The role of teacher leaders. *Phi Delta Kappan, 82*(10), 740–743.

Guskey, T. R. (1995). Professional development in education: In search of the optimal mix. In T. R. Guskey & M. Huberman (Eds.), *Professional development in education: New paradigms and practices* (pp. 114–131). New York: Teachers College Press.

Hart, A. W. (1990). Impacts of the school social unit on teacher authority during work redesign. *American Educational Research Journal, 27*(3), 503–532.

Hart, A. W. (1995). Reconceiving school leadership: Emergent views. *Elementary School Journal, 96*(1), 9–28.

Hawley, W. D., & Valli, L. (1999). The essentials of effective professional development. In L. Darling-Hammond & G. Sykes (Eds.), *Teaching as the learning profession: Handbook of policy and practice* (pp. 127–150). San Francisco: Jossey-Bass.

Heller, M. F., & Firestone, W. A. (1995). Who's in charge here? Sources of leadership for change in eight schools. *The Elementary School Journal, 96*(1), 65–86.

Hodges, H. L. B. (1996). Using research to inform practice in urban schools: Ten key strategies for success. *Educational Policy, 10*(2), 223–252.

Joyce, B., & Showers, B. (1995). *Student achievement through staff development: Fundamentals of school renewal*. White Plains, NY: Longman.

LeCompte, M. D., & Goetz, J. P. (1982). Problems of reliability and validity in ethnographic research. *Review of Educational Research, 52*(1), 31–60.

Leithwood, K., & Riehl, C. (2005). What do we already know about school leadership? In W. Firestone & C. Riehl (Eds.), *A new agenda for research on educational leadership* (pp. 12-27). New York: Teachers College Press.

Lieberman, A., Saxl, E. R., & Miles, M. B. (1988). Teacher leadership: Ideology and practice. In A. Lieberman (Ed.), *Building a professional culture in schools* (pp. 148–166). New York: Teachers College Press.

Little, J. W. (1993). Teachers' professional development in a climate of education reform. *Educational Evaluation and Policy Analysis, 15*(2), 129–151.

Lortie, D. (1975). *Schoolteacher: A sociological analysis*. Chicago: University of Chicago Press.

Loucks-Horsley, S. (1995). Professional development and the learner centered school. *Theory into Practice, 34*(4), 265–271.

Loucks-Horsley, S., Hewson, P. W., Love, N., & Stiles, K. E. (1998). *Designing professional development for teachers of science and mathematics*. Thousand Oaks CA: Corwin Press.

Louis, K. S., & Kruse, S. D. (1995). *Professionalism and community: Perspectives on reforming urban schools*. Thousand Oaks, CA: Corwin Press.

Mangin, M. M. (2005). Distributed leadership and the culture of schools: Teacher leaders' strategies for gaining access to classrooms. *Journal of School Leadership, 15*(4), 460–488.

Miles, M. B., & Huberman, A. M. (1994). *Qualitative data analysis: An expanded sourcebook*. Thousand Oaks, CA: Sage.

Neufeld, B., & Roper, D. (2003). *Coaching: A strategy for developing instructional capacity*. Colorado: The Aspen Institute Program on Education.

Newmann, F., & Wehlage, G. (1995). *Successful school restructuring*. Madison, WI: Center on Organization and Restructuring of Schools.

Patton, M. Q. (2001). *Qualitative evaluation and research methods*. Newbury Park, CA: Sage.

Pink, W. T., & Hyde, A. A. (Eds.). (1992). *Effective staff development for school change*. Norwood, NJ: Ablex.

Poglinco, S. M., Bach, A. J., Hovde, K., Rosenblum, S., Saunders, M., & Supovitz, J. A. (2003). *The heart of the matter: The coaching model in America's choice schools*. Philadelphia: CPRE.

Pounder, D. G. (1999). Teacher teams: Exploring job characteristics and work related outcomes of work group enhancement. *Educational Administration Quarterly, 35*(3), 317–348.

Richardson, V., & Placier, P. (2001). Teacher change. In V. Richardson (Ed.), *Handbook of research on teaching* (4th ed., pp. 905–947). New York: Macmillan.

Sabatier, P., & Mazmanian, D. (1979). The conditions of effective implementation: A guide to accomplishing policy objectives. *Policy Analysis, 5*(5), 481–504.

Smylie, M. (1995). Teacher learning in the workplace: Implications for school reform. In T. R. Guskey & M. Huberman (Eds.), *Professional development in education: New paradigms and practices* (pp. 92–113). New York: Teachers College Press.

Smylie, M., & Denny, J. W. (1990). Teacher leadership: Tensions and ambiguities in organizational perspective. *Educational Administration Quarterly, 26*(3), 235–259.

Smylie, M. A. (1994). Redesigning teachers' work: Connections to the classroom. In L. Darling-Hammond (Ed.), *Review of research in education, 20* (pp. 129–177). Washington DC: American Educational Research Association.

Smylie, M. A., Conley, S., & Marks, H. M. (2002). Exploring new approaches to teacher leadership for school improvement. In J. Murphy (Ed.), *The educational leadership challenge: Redefining leadership for the 21st century; 101st yearbook of the National Society for the Study of Education* (Vol. 101, pt. 1, pp. 162–188). Chicago: University of Chicago Press.

Smylie, M. A., Wenzel, S. A., & Fendt, C. R. (2003). The Chicago Annenberg challenge: Lessons on leadership for school development. In J. Murphy & A. Datnow (Eds.), *Leadership lessons from comprehensive school reforms* (pp. 135–158). Thousand Oaks, CA: Corwin.

Spillane, J., Halverson, R., & Diamond, J. B. (2001). Investigating school leadership practice: A distributed perspective. *Educational Researcher, 30*(3), 23–28.

Spillane, J., Halverson, R., & Diamond, J. B. (2004). Towards a theory of leadership practice: A distributed perspective. *Journal of Curriculum Studies, 36*(1), 3–34.

Spillane, J. P., Hallett, T., & Diamond, J. B. (2003). Forms of capital and the construction of leadership: Instructional leadership in urban elementary schools. *Sociology of Education, 76*(1), 1–17.

Stoelinga, S. R. (2005). *"Stretching" leadership models over distributed leadership conceptions.* Paper presented at the annual meeting of the American Educational Research Association, Montreal, Canada.

York-Barr, J., & Duke, K. (2004). What do we know about teacher leadership? Findings from two decades of scholarship. *Review of Educational Research, 74*(3), 255–316.

CHAPTER 8

RESEARCH INTO PRACTICE

A Case Study of How *Success for All* Builds Knowledge for School Improvement

Amanda Datnow and Vicki Park

The purpose of this chapter is to examine the linkage between research and practice in one instance of educational reform. We use Success for All (SFA), a research-based, whole-school reform model that focuses on reading, as a case in point. Drawing on Cochran-Smith and Lytle's (1999) framework for relating knowledge and practice, we discuss the forms of knowledge Success for All draws on in its work. In general, we find that there is considerable "formal" research knowledge—or knowledge-for-practice—informing SFA. However, while there is a reliance on rigorous, traditional, quantitative research methods in informing model development, there is also a commitment to learn from teacher practice—and to support teachers' reflection on their own practice. We also find that the federal policy context has both enabled and constrained SFA—and more recently, become part of the "knowledge" of what constitutes SFA. Implications for further research and theory building are discussed.

Contemporary Issues in Educational Policy and School Outcomes, 193–213

INTRODUCTION

The purpose of this chapter is to examine linkages between research and practice in educational reform by examining how Success for All (SFA) builds knowledge for school improvement. Success for All is a research-based, whole-school reform model that organizes resources to focus on prevention and early intervention to ensure that students succeed in reading throughout the elementary grades (Slavin, Madden, Dolan, & Wasik, 1996). Originally developed by Robert Slavin, Nancy Madden, and a team at Johns Hopkins University, the program is currently based at the Success for All Foundation (SFAF) in Baltimore. First implemented in one school in 1987, the model itself was an outgrowth of a series of research and development projects that date to the mid-1970s. Over the past 15 years, the number of schools implementing SFA has grown substantially, with approximately 1,300 elementary schools currently implementing the program. SFA is one of the most popular whole-school reform models in the United States. Most SFA elementary schools receive Title I funds and serve large numbers of low-income and minority students. In addition to working with these elementary schools, the SFA Foundation works with a smaller number of preschools and middle schools.

Success for All focuses primarily on reading. Major components of SFA include a 90-minute reading period every day, the regrouping of students into smaller, homogeneous groups for reading instruction, quarterly assessments, cooperative learning, and one-to-one tutoring. The Success for All reading curriculum is comprised of an Early Learning program for prekindergarten and kindergarten students; Reading Roots, a beginning reading program; and Reading Wings, its upper-elementary counterpart. There are both English and Spanish versions of the program

Success for All takes an aggressive approach to changing teaching and learning. As a result, the program is highly specified and comprehensive with respect to implementation guidelines and materials for students and teachers. Almost all materials for students are provided, including reading booklets for the primary grades, materials to accompany various textbook series and novels for the upper grades, as well as activity sheets and assessments for all grade levels. Teachers are expected to follow SFA lesson plans closely, which involve an active pacing of activities during the 90-minute reading period (Madden, Livingston, & Cummings, 1998).

The SFA Foundation requires that the majority of a school's teaching staff votes to adopt the program before they will provide the materials and technical assistance. The SFA program also asks that schools employ a full-time SFA facilitator, organize a Solutions Team to help support families, and organize biweekly meetings among Roots and Wings teachers. The principal of an SFA school is responsible for ensuring staff motivation and commitment for the program, as well as adequate resources. The role of the SFA facilitator is to ensure the quality of the day-to-day implementation of the program by supporting teachers, monitoring the progress of all students, and managing assessments and regrouping efficiently (Madden et al., 1998). Implementation of the program is supported through ongoing professional development from SFA trainers and through local and national networks of SFA schools (Slavin et al., 1996).

SFA is founded on the belief that instructional strategies delivered to schools should be based on rigorous evidence of effectiveness. Since its inception in schools, Success for All has been the subject of over 50 rigorous quantitative research studies and several in-depth qualitative studies (Slavin, 2005). Quasi-experimental studies of student achievement effects have typically found that, particularly when implemented with fidelity, SFA yields positive achievement outcomes (see Borman, Hewes, Overman, & Brown, 2003). A recent large randomized study has also found positive effects favoring SFA (Borman, Slavin, Cheung, Chamberlain, Madden, & Chambers, 2005; Slavin, Madden, Cheung, Chamberlain, Chambers, & Borman, 2005). A qualitative study of Success for All found that students' engagement in reading was high, classroom instruction during reading was more effective (in comparison to academic subjects other than reading), and teachers acquired new, valuable skills for teaching reading (Datnow & Castellano, 2000a). This study of SFA also revealed most teachers supported the continuation of SFA in their schools because of its positive effects on students; however, some felt that SFA constrained their autonomy in the classroom (Datnow & Castellano, 2000b).

Thus, there is a great deal of "formal" research knowledge on the effects of SFA, and evidence that this research knowledge informs the program and its continual development (Slavin, 2005). There is also an inherent assumption in the program, by virtue of its specification, that knowledge for school improvement can in fact be created by external groups and transported across contexts. But what about the knowledge and practice of teachers in SFA schools? How do they help to inform the reform model? What other forms of knowledge are drawn on and how? Finally, how does the policy context surrounding SFA influence knowledge construction and research-practice linkages? This chapter will address these questions by focusing on (1) the forms of knowledge (e.g., researcher, practitioner, trainer) employed in SFA; (2) the process by which various forms of knowledge work together in SFA; (3) how the policy context influences knowledge development in SFA. By examining these questions, we hope to illuminate research-practice linkages in one instance of educational reform in the United States.

CONCEPTUAL FRAMEWORK

Understanding the relationship between research knowledge and teacher practice is fundamental for making sense of Success for All, as it is a reform model that explicitly tries to change teaching practice. Hatch and White (2002) concisely articulate two central issues about knowledge for school improvement that relate to this chapter. First, there is the problem of how to capture knowledge so that schools can implement it. Second, there is a critical question of how the local knowledge of educators and the knowledge developed by researchers or others outside schools relate to each other. Hatch and White (2002, p. 120, citing Lehming & Kane, 1981), refer to the following definition of knowledge: "[K]nowledge consists of information and understandings derived from research, practice, or both; it is empirically or socially validated; and it can reside in ideas, theories, explanations, advice, programs, materials, or technologies." This definition captures the notion that the knowledge of school improvement resides with both practitioners and researchers; but it does not specify where it might *best* reside, or what the combination of researcher and practitioner knowledge might look like.

Cochran-Smith and Lytle (1999) attempt to tackle these questions with respect to teacher learning. They examine several prominent conceptions of teacher learning which relate knowledge and practice. Each of these conceptions is grounded in a different set of assumptions about how to go about improving teacher practice. First, they describe *knowledge-for-practice* as university-based researchers generating what is commonly referred to as formal knowledge and theory for teachers to use in order to improve their practice. Widely referred by educators as "the knowledge base," teachers typically access this type of knowledge through preservice and inservice training. Thus, the *knowledge-for-practice* orientation perceives teachers as consumers of knowledge and assumes that knowledge for teaching can be tested through rigorous methods and codified. However, as Shulman (1987) pointed out in a chapter that helped to shape teacher education reform in the subsequent decade (Cochran-Smith & Lytle, 1999), there are multiple and varied sources for the teaching knowledge base. In addition to formal educational scholarship, sources for knowledge of teaching might also include: knowledge of content; knowledge of educational materials, processes, and structures; and finally, teachers' wisdom of practice (Shulman, 1987).

Along these lines, the *knowledge-in-practice* perspective described by Cochran-Smith and Lytle (1999) assumes that knowledge resides in the practice of expert teachers, rather than in researchers. The emphasis is placed on knowledge that is embedded in teachers' practice and derived from reflections or narratives about their practice. The assumption is that teaching is a spontaneous activity that is constructed in response to the particulars of each classroom context. According to this perspective, knowledge for teaching resides with teachers, particularly expert teachers, not with outsiders.

Cochran-Smith and Lytle's (1999), third conception of teacher learning, *knowledge-of-practice*, eschews the divide between formal and practical knowledge inherent in the other two perspectives. The authors argue against the formal knowledge-practical knowledge distinction on the grounds that it reifies power and status differentials between university-generated knowledge and teacher-generated knowledge, ultimately separating teachers from researchers. Instead, the knowledge-of-practice perspective argues that teachers learn best when they interrogate their own practice through action research and work within inquiry-based communities of practice. Such inquiry activities should involve teachers across the professional life span. "The goal is not to do research or to produce 'findings,' as it is often the case for university researchers. Rather, the goal is understanding, articulating, and ultimately altering practice and social relationships in order to bring about change in classrooms, schools, districts, and professional programs" (p. 224).

On the face, it would seem that Success for All might fit the knowledge-for-practice conception of teacher learning. However, as we will attempt to demonstrate through our data, while SFA begins with this as its starting point, it is not the end point. Rather, teacher knowledge is incorporated much more than expected, blurring the traditional boundaries between formal and practical knowledge, but not in the same way that Cochran-Smith and Lytle (1999) propose. Before we discuss our findings on these matters, we briefly describe the methodology for the study.

METHODOLOGY

The primary method of this study is case study analysis, with Success for All itself as "the case." The case study of SFA is nested within a set of 11 case studies on initiatives that reconceptualize and reorganize the role of research vis-à-vis practice. The broader study is being led by Mary Kay Stein at the University of Pittsburgh and Cynthia Coburn at UC Berkeley. Case study methods enable us to examine SFA in real life contexts and allow us to present the perspectives of those actually implementing or working with the program (Yin, 2002). Our research methods are qualitative and involve multiple sources of data including interviews, focus groups, observations, and a review of relevant documents.

Because we are interested gathering various sources of knowledge, our study has focused on the SFA Foundation and two SFA schools. In keeping with the tenets of case study research, the sites and participants were chosen purposefully to address our research questions. From SFAF, we have interviewed Robert Slavin and Nancy Madden, cofounders of Success for All and researchers at Johns Hopkins University. We have also interviewed several other SFAF staff including three SFA trainers, the director of training for SFAF, an area manager, an implementation officer, and an individual in charge of policy. Each of these interviews lasted 1 hour or more.

We also gathered qualitative data during site visits to two SFA schools. The schools were recommended to us by an SFA area manager on the basis that they had been implementing SFA for several years and were in the state of California (for practical reasons). School A has been implementing SFA for 5 years and School B has been implementing SFA for 6 years. School B recently became a charter school. Both of the schools are Title I schools, serving large numbers of low-income students. The majority of the students in both schools are Hispanic. Both are large schools serving more than 1,000 students each. The schools are located in different school districts, one in a very large urban district and one in a midsize district.

Our data collection at each school has involved interviews, focus groups, and classroom observations. At both schools, we conducted interviews with the school principal. At School A, we also interviewed the SFA facilitator. At School B, we interviewed the assistant principal who oversees SFA and also several lead teachers who serve as SFA facilitators. Because the school is so large, they have individuals at each grade level helping to facilitate SFA, rather than just one facilitator. At School A, we conducted a focus group with four regular classroom teachers from different grade levels. At School B, we also interviewed several teachers from various grade levels. All interviews were tape-recorded and have been transcribed verbatim. In both schools, we observed classroom instruction in numerous classrooms during the SFA 90-minute reading period. We also took field notes during classroom observations.

Our qualitative data analysis activities have included coding the interview transcripts based on the research questions guiding this study. Interviews were coded with the aid of qualitative data analysis software called HyperResearch. Our review of documents has included reports that details SFA's history (Slavin, 2005; Slavin & Madden, 1998) and documents describing the schools. For the purposes of confidentiality, pseudonyms are used for all school, person, and place names. However, we are unable to keep the identities of Robert Slavin and Nancy Madden confidential, given that they are the leaders and founders of SFAF.

FINDINGS

Tools for Construction: Forms of Knowledge in Success for All

The Role of Research in SFA

Our first aim in this study was to determine the forms of knowledge that comprise SFA. As mentioned above, the primary forms of knowledge that the Success for All design team drew on at the beginning of its work were rigorous quasi-experimental research studies and comprehensive reviews of existing research. That is, components of the program (e.g., cooperative learning) were investigated through reviews of existing research and then tested in school settings before becoming part of SFA. Slavin (2005) states: "Success for All was intended to be an example of what education reform would be like if it were based on evidence and then continually evaluated itself to progressively improve" (p. 4). In other words, the program was created with the belief that if teachers' used practices that were supported by research findings, their teaching would be more effective. Consequently, program components of SFA have been subject to research-based trials and great care appears to have been taken in ensuring that each component is supported by data.

Slavin (2005) further explains:

> Since it was first conceived, Success for All has been designed as a means of creating conditions in which teachers would use the results of rigorous research everyday. Each of the major components of the program was designed to operationalize practices known from research to increase the achievement of students at risk. At the outset, and again as the program developed, SFA researchers have carried out reviews of research in many areas relevant to practice to inform us about effective strategies. (p. 4)

The educators we spoke with were quite aware of the way research functioned in SFA and they were impressed by the research base behind it. However, when asked whether the strong research base affected the choice to adopt SFA, one principal said, "I'd like to say it did, but probably not.... I looked more at the program and how it worked.... It was more based on my background knowledge as a teacher." However, the research base on SFA did help to engage the teachers' support. As one teacher in School A said, "It really showed that we weren't just paying a lot of money for something that looked good but didn't have any effect on students. The research ... really showed significant gains with a population like ours." These comments validated Slavin's statement to us that achievement "outcome research" was what practitioners wanted. Slavin felt it was the responsibility of SFAF to provide them with "well done, matched control [studies] ... and now randomized experiments to evaluate the program."

Educators were highly cognizant of the role of research in the continual development of SFA. When new program components were introduced, educators attributed changes in part to advances in research. An SFA school facilitator explained the research link:

> And they've done a good job of every time there's a new component, like they've brought in clarification, they've brought in summarization, the questioning strategy piece, targeted Treasure Hunts, anything that's new in the research, they've been really good with us and they.... Okay, we're going to get this trainer; she's going to a do a whole training on this.

When trainings on new components occurred, teachers and administrators were made aware of the research supporting the changes. The teachers we spoke at one school with seemed to understand the theory informing the new practices. One teacher shared, "What I learned was that the reason for [the new component], based upon the research they did, was to really help the students to understand the meaning of the vocabulary words better in a specific story." This statement was echoed by others in the school.

The Role of Practitioner Knowledge in SFA

Educators also believed that changes in the program were also based on observations of their practice and lessons learned from their own experiences with SFA. One facilitator explained:

> The first year when they were changing [the program], we were there and we had questions that we asked, and the next thing we knew they were waiting a year to come out with it. And you know, it was like some of the stuff possibly was related to questions that we brought up.

Interestingly, while still maintaining a heavy reliance on "rigorous research," or what Cochran-Smith and Lytle (1999) term *knowledge for practice*, what counts as knowledge seems to have broadened since the program's inception. Slavin (2005) states, "As the program developed, we continued to focus on using research to learn from the teachers and principals implementing it and, most importantly, to learn how program implementation, variations, and conditions affect student outcomes (p. 4). As Slavin's comments reveal, the development of SFA appears to rely more on the knowledge of educators implementing the program. Thus, while more traditional research efforts continue, there are also efforts to gather educators' insights and incorporate them into the model. These processes are described in the next section.

The Success for All Foundation's broadening of the types of knowledge it draws upon is reflected in their change in policy regarding fidelity to implementation. Whereas in the past, SFAF had a strong focus on fidelity to the model, they now allow some adaptations to the model if they are aimed towards improving student outcomes and meeting the individual school's goals. This shift in stance towards fidelity to implementation allowed the schools greater freedom in making adaptations that were geared towards student outcomes. As one principal observed, "They're comfortable with any changes that we have made that we've needed support it.... Our point trainer has been very good about coming out and looking at it with us, analyzing the data with us, and saying, "Yeah, that's probably a good change. Have you thought of this?"

The principal and facilitator at one school explained the shift regarding fidelity:

> SFA has changed too along with us. They've loosened up a lot. When they first started it was very "you follow this routine, you get it done in this amount of time." And with their research they have found that it doesn't really matter if your knees are touching and you're facing each other in partner reading.

Program fidelity is still expected on a number of key dimensions (e.g., the reading curriculum, cross grade grouping, full time facilitator). However, SFAF's measure of the quality of implementation differs as it now provides space for innovative practices arising from the needs of specific schools. The theory appears to be that program consistency should serve program effectiveness rather than consistency for its own sake. SFAF calls their new approach "goal-focused implementation." An SFAF area manager explained that, "it's very heavy data-based and we build on strengths. There's a whole cycle we look at, looking at your goal, looking at your data, what's keeping you from getting to your goal, looking at strengths, looking at the actual implementation, looking at what else you may have going on and the modifications that need to occur." Educators we spoke with confirmed her description of this process.

This shift from a focus on pure fidelity—which was heavily based on feedback received from schools—and to one focused on schools' needs appears to have substantially changed the relationship between the SFAF staff and the educators in the schools they work with. Previously, SFA trainers were seen as "SFA police" focused on visible details of implementation (e.g., Are the Word Walls posted in the classrooms?), but now they are seen as valuable sources of instructional support. Another change is that whereas in the past, trainers would meet only with administrators or with whole staffs to share the results of their "implementation checks," they now meet one-on-one with teachers to help them improve their practice.

Overall, as a result of this change, the relationship between educators and the SFAF appears to be more collaborative rather than evaluative. An SFA facilitator explained how the relationship between trainers and teachers had become one characterized by support:

> When we first started ... they would come in and watch the teachers, "are you following the schedule? Are you doing Adventures in Writing on Day 3?"... And they've lightened up on it. Now they come in and they are looking and listening to the kids and seeing, "okay, what's the conversation the kids are having? Are they using the strategies?"... Not so much, "here's a schedule." And I think it has been beneficial for the teachers and for them. It let's teachers have some flexibility.... But I think they are more focused on what the student outcomes are and supporting teachers so that those kids have those outcomes.

A teacher reiterated: "They trust our judgment that we are doing the program, that we are following the components, and if we add something, if we lengthen it, if we shorten something, if I do it on the wrong day, it's not taking away from the overall comprehension of the program." "They encourage quality over quantity," said another teacher. An SFAF area manager confirmed, "If you can do meaningful sentences this way and still get the same outcome, then all the more power to you, but it really takes an understanding and an acceptance of what the rationale is behind the activity."

As the director of the Training Institute at SFAF reinforced, the manner in which the SFAF works with school has "morphed over time to being more and more a partnership model, and less and less an expert kind of model." She goes on to add, "We certainly have some expertise to share and facilitation, but there's more and more emphasis on our trainers having consultative skills, in addition to the expertise in the curricular areas."

In summary, knowledge *for* practice (Cochran-Smith & Lytle, 1999) was the foundation for the initial development of SFA. Research knowledge remains highly valued by SFAF and is also seen as important by the educators in SFA schools. At the same time, practitioner knowledge about implementing SFA is also an integral part of efforts to further refine the program, as is trainer knowledge (discussed more later). The shift to "goal-focused" rather than simply fidelity-focused implementation is a significant exemplar of a change in the program that is the result of the valuing of local knowledge.

Scaffolding Knowledge: The Process of Knowledge Use and Development in SFA

In this section, we describe the process by which knowledge is created, shared, and reshaped in the continual development of SFA. We attempt to explain how various forms of knowledge work together.

The Processes of Formal Versus Informal Research

Regarding *knowledge-for-practice*, there are formal efforts to evaluate schools' achievement outcomes associated with SFA implementation, and these help to inform the model's development. Formal research efforts are typically federally or privately-funded studies conducted by SFAF researchers or external parties. Typically, these studies have employed quasi-experimental design research methods, and increasingly, randomized studies of SFA are being conducted. One of the schools we visited, School B, was involved in two research studies related to SFA.

New SFA components are also piloted using quasi-experimental methods. Often the pilot studies are part of formal research projects being conducted by Foundation staff. About the pilots, the principal of School B said, "We'll try them because in the long run, who is it going to help? It's going to help the kids.... So yeah, we might be the guinea pig, but that's okay, we get perks too." This school was piloting a new video teaching tool for phonics and a computer-assisted tutoring program. Thus far, they had found these technological advances to be very beneficial for the students and well received by teachers. However, being part of a pilot and the rigors of experimental research had some unexpected consequences. The use of materials was restricted to designated classes since classes serving as control groups were prohibited from utilizing the pilot resources. This created a moral dilemma for one administrator at the school who felt all students should benefit.

In general, the entire culture of SFA is one that revolves around the continuous use of student achievement data as the basis for decision making, both at the school and Foundation levels. Schools are expected to conduct their own informal research on their practice with SFA by collecting and analyzing student data. At each school, educators examine the 8-week and quarterly assessments of their students' progress and make changes in practice accordingly. A teacher explained: "We have ongoing data collection.... If we see, oh my gosh, half of my kids aren't really getting this, then even within the program they give us reteaching lessons." SFAF also gathers data on schools' assessments and analyzes these data when making a decision about a change in the program. Slavin noted that, "We're making modifications or additions all the time. There's never been a year when we haven't come out with new stuff, but we're also constantly revising the old stuff."

In addition to these quantitative and somewhat more formal research efforts, there is continual "informal" research which involves a frequent dialogue between school educators, trainers, other SFA Foundation staff, and the SFA directors. The topics of these discussions might range from implementation issues, successes or problems with particular program components, and the degree to which SFA was helping meet schools' goals. The process is such that trainers gather information about how the program is working when they visit local schools, and they share this knowledge with other foundation staff on a regular basis. At one school we visited, the principal, teachers, and SFA facilitator all mentioned taking part regularly in this type of dialogue. A teacher observed:

> It's kind of like formal versus informal research, because some of the component meetings we have with our trainers... We sit down and she asks us questions, 'are you comfortable? Do you need more training? What do you like? What don't you like?' And so she's kind of doing informal research, you know.

Slavin also spoke about formal and informal research: "And so we have a whole system of formal research with an overlay of research that is more internal ... and that never leads to publications, but it's internal and leads to both changes at the local level and changes ultimately in the overall program." He added: "A large part of what we think we're doing in the world is continuously learning from the schools and learning from our own experiences, and other things going, to provide the best stuff we know how to provide."

Along these lines, there are additional, relatively new efforts at gathering information—or knowledge—from educators about their experiences with SFA. First, SFA trainers can be available on speaker phone to address questions and gather feedback during teachers' monthly "teacher learning community" meetings that occur in each school. Teachers also engage in discussion about their practice at biweekly meetings at each school site. Second, phone interviews with educators in particular schools take place, particularly when the foundation staff is interested in finding out how a new component of SFA is working. A teacher explained:

> We've been on conference calls to Maryland in the past, just talking. They want to know how the questioning is going.... So they are listening to us, and they want to know.... So you feel like they are going into classrooms, talking to teachers to find out what is working and what is not. So I really feel like the research is coming from us.

As the last sentence implies, the teachers we interviewed very much felt as though they were an integral part of the continual development of the SFA model. On a separate note, School A was featured in new training videos for SFA, an experience which was very validating for the teachers. One principal said, "SFA has really given us a lot of recognition. They made us an implementation visit school the first year we were in business.... They did a bunch of training videos here on summarization and clarification, so you know, when we went to the SFA conference and they're using *our* people in all of the trainings."

While the schools saw themselves as continually learning about SFA, the Foundation also turned to the schools to learn as well. Focus groups among teachers are held at the annual SFA conferences. One teacher explained, "At the conference [they are] really good at asking, what's working, what's not working..." This was an opportunity for teachers in SFA schools to reflect on their practice, hence some evidence of knowledge in practice (albeit practice initially defined by the SFA model, which is different from what Cochran-Smith & Lytle (1999) describe).

Training and Trainers in the Process of Knowledge Development

The constant blend between research and practice was a regular part of the ongoing SFA training, both for teachers and for school leaders. One principal explained:

> We also have the Leadership Academy where [a lead SFAF trainer] is coming out and meeting with our schools in a couple of the districts around here, where we get together and talk about what's happening in the different schools, what are you doing, what are we doing, plus she's [the trainer] bringing in research and stuff.

Undoubtedly, SFAF has more interaction with some schools than others, depending on their maturity in program implementation and on the number of days that schools contract with SFAF for training. Continuing implementation sites can contract for as few as two days of training (the minimum) to as many as they need. There are approximately 150 SFA trainers across the country who work with anywhere from 5-20 schools each, depending on the number of contracted days per school. "Every school is assigned a point trainer and sometimes even a copoint, and that's their first line of communication" explained a SFAF staff member. The two schools in this study were mature implementation sites but continued to invest considerable amounts of time and resources in ongoing training.

Overall, the ongoing training was seen by educators as an integral part of building their own knowledge for school improvement. One SFA facilitator we interviewed believed that they received support based on their self-identified areas of need, rather than generic support: "When [our trainer] comes in to sit with [the principal], she asks us, 'what are the needs of your school? What training do you want from us? What support?' So it's not just them dictating what support it's going to be." This statement by a principal gives insight into the level of collaboration between SFAF trainers and educators in her school: "I think we have always felt a give and take and that we are accepted as peers and colleagues ... that they are interested in what we say and that there's a response to that." At the same time, teachers and administrators at one SFA school also said that they feel free to say no to some recommendations made by SFAF trainers: "They can suggest, but we don't feel it's [in the best interests of] our children, then we don't have to do it." This comment suggests a tension between knowledge for practice and knowledge in practice. Educators might disregard trainers' suggestions depending on what they perceive as in the best interests of their students.

In any event, face-to-face interactions between schools and trainers provided a mechanism by which schools were able to address needs specific to their local context. Trainer-school relationships were central bridges between the program developed by SFAF and the actual implementation. Trainers, in addition to codified tools, made abstract concepts such as reading strategies more concrete and also provided models and examples.

The relationships between the schools and trainers were also indicative of the depth of engagement with program implementation. A positive, trusting relationship seems to facilitate a deeper level of engagement with SFA components as well as allowing for continuous feedback between the two parties. Cofounder Nancy Madden described trainers as, "really expert teachers ... who just had real strong concepts about teaching and could communicate that to other teachers, have the respect of other teachers and could really work will all of them to be really good coaches." Madden's comments indicate that trainers have not only acquired deep knowledge about curriculum and instructional delivery but also have interpersonal knowledge that enables them to communicate effectively with various participants. This appreciation for interpersonal knowledge was expressed by both schools participating in our study. Teachers and principals also felt that the trainers were well matched to their schools in terms of expertise and background. As one administrator explained, "They're like a perfect match for our school. The people, their personalities, their backgrounds in bilingual [education] you know, for ELD [English Language Development]."

The role of SFA trainers in the development of the "knowledge" of the model is also important. Annual conferences are held for trainers where they convene to share strategies for working with schools and discuss successful and unsuccessful program adaptations they have observed. During these conferences, trainers also engage in discussion about current research that is related to SFA, but not on SFA per se. For example, we heard that Foundation staff might refer to new research on strategies for teaching English language learners. Trainers then use this research when they are meeting with school educators to help them understand why particular program components are necessary.

Understanding how SFAF is structured with respect to the training and support of schools is important to making sense of the process of how knowledge flows within the organization. Described by one staff member as "vaguely hierarchical," many of the people we interviewed from SFAF had difficulty remembering their titles since they were taking on multiple tasks and roles. Slavin and Madden are copresidents of the Foundation, and they are also affiliated with Johns Hopkins University. SFAF employs approximately 220 employees, including 150 regionally-based trainers, some of whom work in offices and others who work out of their homes. As we alluded to earlier, SFAF recruits trainers from schools, usually former SFA teachers and facilitators, who have expert knowledge in how the model works in a particular local context. Overseeing the trainers are 15 area managers, who also deal with district relations and respond to trainers questions regarding school adaptations of SFA. Area managers are supported by a team of expansion and outreach staff. Two "implementation officers" oversee the area managers and outreach personnel. There are also business and production staffs. While some staff members are located at the foundation office in Baltimore, others are spread around the country. Meanwhile, knowledge is shared among SFAF staff on a continual basis. An SFAF staff member explained: "Headquarters is headquarters, where we regroup every so often. And then everybody else is just kind of spread out, so we communicate by phone and email."

About the process of communication between schools and Foundation staff, a SFAF area manager explained:

> It usually goes point trainer, me, and then whoever needs to be contacted within the foundation … we have several different people for each component or skills area, technology, ELD, whatever it is.… And that's one thing we let teachers know, you know, schools know, we have this huge foundation behind us, you know, if I can't get you the answer, there's somebody back there that designed this that can tell you exactly why it is the way it is.

As this statement implies, the Foundation was seen—at least by this trainer as a storehouse of knowledge that could be accessed as needed.

In sum, when we examine the processes by which SFA draws on various forms of knowledge in program development, we find evidence of both formal and informal research efforts. In general, formal research efforts were described as quantitative studies of student outcomes connected with implementation of SFA as a whole or particular components of SFA. Informal research that takes place in SFA may best be described as knowledge-of-practice, as it involves SFAF learning from the knowledge of school educators implementing the program. There are instances in which these informal research efforts cause teachers to reflect on their practice with SFA. There are also structures within the program (e.g., biweekly meetings among Roots and Wings teachers at each site) that are intended to enable reflective dialogue and the sharing of strategies among teachers in each school. At the same time, it is important to note the practice that teachers are reflecting on has been defined, at least initially, by SFAF. And, inquiry and reflection are clearly not the building blocks or primary processes of the SFA model (as contrasted with the Coalition of Essential Schools, for example), but they do play a part in the model's continual development.

The Policy Contexts Shaping Development in SFA

It is important to consider the role of the broader policy context in relation to SFA, as it has been instrumental in shaping how the reform model and the processes within SFAF have changed over the past few years. As we will argue, the policy context has both enabled and constrained SFA—and more recently, become part of the "knowledge" of what constitutes SFA.

In the 1990s, the federal policy context advantaged SFA, leading to a significant growth in the number of schools adopting the model. First, SFA received a boost from the 1994 change in Title I laws allowing the use of funds for school-wide reform projects. In 1997, the passage of the Comprehensive School Reform Demonstration (CSR) program in U.S. Congress in 1997 spurred further expansion of SFA. CSR, also known as the Obey-Porter initiative, allocated federal funds to schools for the adoption of "research-based" school reform models, such as SFA.

In the period of 1995-1998, the total number of schools using SFA quadrupled, having sextupled in the 3 years prior (Slavin & Madden, 1998). During this period, the number of SFA schools grew so significantly that developers felt they could no longer efficiently support schools from their original location at Johns Hopkins University. The decision was then made to launch the Success for All Foundation (SFAF), a nonprofit organization (Slavin & Madden, 1998). At the same time, SFAF added layers of organizational complexity and morphed into the structure described in the previous section.

Whereas the federal polices of the 1990s appear to have advantaged SFA, recent federal policies have generally been constraining. In particular, policies accompanying the No Child Left Behind (NCLB) Act of 2002 have, ironically (given their emphasis on research-based practices) led to numerous challenges. However, these challenges have led to some important, well-received changes within the SFA model and in how SFAF works with schools. Whereas in the past, SFAF was looked to primarily for instructional support for reading, now SFAF serves a support role in helping schools meet accountability demands.

First, the policy changes at the federal and state levels have been so numerous and significant in the past few years that the SFA Foundation has appointed a person in charge of keeping up with federal and state policies. An SFAF staff person we interviewed called this person the "Policy Master," though that is not her official title. One of her main responsibilities is to help SFA schools and districts make sense of the Adequate Yearly Progress (AYP) accountability mechanism in NCLB and to help them set goals accordingly. The area manager mentioned that she often knew about policy changes from the "Policy Master" well before her schools did. She herself also spent time in meetings and hearings at the state department of education so that she could keep abreast of state policy changes.

The advent of NCLB has meant that trainers now serve as policy mediators, helping schools gain the knowledge to meet state and federal mandates. An area manager explained the shift in how trainers interface with schools:

> Five or six years ago, it was like, "yeah, it looks good, you're asking the right kinds of questions, maybe you should try this." It's much more global now, and it's all about aligning.... We're very aligned to No Child Left Behind, we bring them the information, we help them interpret what it really means, "this is what the federal law is saying, let's look at what California is saying, and see where you fit." Like the last year and a half, really, it was mostly training full staff and even district folks on what No Child Left Behind really was about because the districts could not keep up with it very well. They just didn't have the time or the funds or whatever.

Trainers helped schools understand how they can meet NCLB mandates, apparently providing them with knowledge that their districts did not. As one school administrator explained, "If we move those 124 [students in terms of achievement] then we're going to make Safe Harbor [with NCLB]. Well, we never knew this. None of the principals around here knew this. The district never told them that. And we found this out through SFA."

Trainers also work with educators to help them use SFA to meet state curriculum standards. This process is very localized, based on individual school needs. As one principal explained, "When [our trainer] has come out, she has met with grade levels and we have done an item analysis by question, by standard … okay, what parts of SFA can address this standard and where" SFAF has also recently developed benchmark SFA assessments that schools can use five times a year. These benchmark assessments are linked to state assessments. While obviously reflecting a change in response to the policy climate, this change was also made very much in response to educators' requests, who wanted assessments that related better to what they were being measured on by their states. Slavin explained: "That was based very much on the comments from practitioners."

Another recent challenge for the SFA Foundation has been the Reading First Initiative, a federal policy regarding reading instruction that is part of NCLB. Educators applying for Reading First grants have typically been unsuccessful when including SFA as part of their proposals. Slavin explained, "We've had a real disaster with Reading First, which everybody in America, everybody in the education world, believes is being enormously beneficial to us … that it's talking about research-based practice. But, in fact, it has been extremely damaging," as it favors traditional basal readers. This is again ironic, as Reading First purports to support scientifically-based practice.

Coinciding with Reading First, the reading text adoption in the state of California has constrained SFA, as it only allows for the adoption of one of two reading series (Houghton Mifflin and Open Court) which educators have interpreted as excluding SFA as an option. In fact, SFA can be adapted for use with both of these reading series, but most educators and policymakers are aware of this. Simultaneously, districts are moving towards curricular uniformity and coherence, posing additional challenges for SFA, which Slavin described as having grown up "in the era of site-based management." That is, as districts have moved towards mandating literacy programs across entire districts, this has sometimes meant the demise of SFA (Datnow, 2005). One school in our study, located in a large urban district that has mandated the Open Court reading program, actually converted to a charter school in order to have the freedom to continue with SFA. They use Open Court texts with SFA strategies.

In response to the numerous changes in the policy climate, SFAF now allows schools to purchase some components, such as the Early Learning program, "a la carte," rather than adopting the whole comprehensive school reform model now referred to internally as "Classic SFA." One might call this "unbundling" SFA. As an area manager for SFAF explained, "We have a whole new approach to schools because of No Child Left Behind."

In summary, as a result of the changes in federal policy, the SFA model itself has changed. In other words, policy knowledge has become part of the reform. SFAF has changed the way it works with schools. SFA trainers are now serving as policy mediators or policy knowledge brokers with respect to NCLB guidelines. This appears to have increased the level of collaboration and community between trainers and educators, as educators now see trainers as allies in their quest to meet accountability demands. At the same time, SFAF has also found ways to work more flexibly with schools, particularly with respect to implementing the whole model versus particular components.

CONCLUSION

Our goal in this chapter was to explore research-practice linkages in educational reform by examining how Success for All builds knowledge for school improvement. In particular, we were interested in finding out *whose* knowledge is taken up in the continual development of SFA and *how*. In order to address these questions, we drew on qualitative data gathered in a case study of SFA and we analyzed the data, at least in part, using categories from Cochran-Smith and Lytle's (1999) framework for understanding teacher learning. Although their framework was not necessarily intended for the purpose of unpacking a school reform model, we have found it useful for our analysis.

Essentially, the continual development of SFA is a story of how developers, trainers, researchers, and practitioners work together. There is considerable "formal" research knowledge—or knowledge-for-practice—informing the program and its continual development. However, while there is a reliance on rigorous, quantitative research methods in informing model development, there is also a very strong commitment to learn from teacher practice—and to support teachers' reflection on their own practice (though we have a less data to support this latter finding). Thus, reflecting on Cochran-Smith and Lytle's (1999) framework, we can conclude that we saw at least two conceptions of teaching learning when we examine SFA, knowledge-for-practice and knowledge-in-practice (but defined a bit differently).

Albeit, lessons from teachers' practice are not the starting point for this reform (i.e., it is not a model that relies on organic invention or on teacher action research), it is a model that seeks a constant interplay between teachers' practice and research. The knowledge of SFA trainers, many of whom were former SFA teachers, is also integral to the continual development of the model and its implementation strategies. Additional data gathering is needed to determine the roles of other SFAF staff, including the original founders, in the continual development of the model.

This chapter has also revealed how the broader policy context has shaped the development of the model and the ways in which SFAF works with schools. In essence, strategies for meeting accountability demands at state and federal levels have become part of the "knowledge" of SFA. Thus far, it appears that SFAF is mostly assisting schools in understanding the policies, rather than vice versa, contrary to the model of knowledge-exchange that we see with respect to the model as a whole. However, it appears that the expert policy knowledge that SFA trainers are bringing to schools may be helping to build collaborative relationships between SFAF staff and practitioners.

This chapter yields important implications for research and theory in educational administration. First, our hope is that the findings of our study will spur further research on research-practice linkages with respect to other examples of educational reform. We believe it is important to unpack how various educational reforms and reform designers conceptualize the linkages between research and practice, particularly given the current emphasis on "scientifically-based" educational research. Second, we believe there is a need for theory building with respect to research-practice linkages in education. New frameworks are needed for understanding the complex ways in which research and practice interest and the contributions of educational reform to that process. Finally, as an education community, we need to continue to search for ways for educational research to influence practice, and we must approach this problem broadly, rather than narrowly as current policy frameworks might suggest.

ACKNOWLEDGMENTS

An earlier version of this chapter was presented at the Annual Meeting of the American Educational Research Association, April 12, 2005, in Montreal. The research reported herein was supported by grants from the MacArthur and Spencer Foundations to the Learning Research and Development Center (LRDC) of the University of Pittsburgh. However, any opinions expressed are the authors' own and do not represent the policies or positions of the funders. We wish to thank the participants of this study from the Success for All Foundation and in schools who gave graciously of their time for our research.

REFERENCES

Borman, G. D., Hewes, G., Overman, L. T., & Brown, S. (2003). Comprehensive school reform and student achievement: A meta-analysis. *Review of Educational Research, 73*(2), 125-230.

Borman, G. D., Slavin, R. E., Cheung, A., Chamberlain, A., Madden, N., & Chambers, B. (2005). Success for All: First-year results from the national randomized field trial. *Educational Evaluation and Policy Analysis, 27*, 1-22.

Cochran-Smith, M., & Lytle, S. (1999). Relationships of knowledge and practice: Teacher learning in communities. *Review of Research in Education, 24*, 249-305.

Datnow, A. (2005). The sustainability of comprehensive school reform in changing district and state contexts. *Educational Administration Quarterly, 41*(1), 121-153.

Datnow, A., & Castellano, M. (2000a). *An "inside look" at Success for All: A qualitative study of implementation and teaching and learning* (Report No. 45). Baltimore, MD: Center for Research on the Education of Students Placed at Risk, Johns Hopkins University.

Datnow, A., & Castellano, M. (2000b). Teachers' responses to Success for All: How beliefs, experiences, and adaptations shape implementation. *American Educational Research Journal, 37*(3), 775-799.

Hatch, T., & White, N. (2002). The raw materials of reform: Rethinking the knowledge of school improvement. *Journal of Educational Change, 3*(2), 117-134.

Lehming, R., & Kane, M. (Eds.). (1981). *Improving schools: Using what we know.* Beverly Hills, CA: Sage.

Madden, N., Livingston, M., & Cummings, N. (1998). *Success for All, Roots and Wings principal's and facilitator's manual.* Baltimore, MD: Johns Hopkins University.

Shulman, L. (1987). Knowledge and teaching: Foundations of the new reform. *Harvard Educational Review, 57*(1), 1-22.

Slavin, R. E (2005, February). *Research in, research out: The role of research in the development of Success for All.* Baltimore, MD: Johns Hopkins University.

Slavin, R. E., & Madden, N. A. (1998). *Disseminating Success for All: Lessons for policy and practice.* Revised technical report. Baltimore, MD: Center for Research on the Education of Students Placed At Risk, Johns Hopkins University.

Slavin, R. E., Madden, N. A., Dolan, L., & Wasik, B. A. (1996). *Every child, every school: Success for All.* Thousand Oaks, CA: Corwin.

Slavin, R. E, Madden, N., Cheung, A., Chamberlain, A., Chambers, B., & Borman, G. D. (2005). *A randomized evaluation of Success for All: Second-year outcomes.* Draft. Baltimore: Johns Hopkins University.

Yin, R. (2002). *Case study research* (3rd ed.). Thousand Oaks, CA: Sage.

CHAPTER 9

AN ENDURING TENSION

Kindergarten Education
in an Era of Accountability

Jennifer Lin Russell

Since the institutionalization of kindergartens in public elementary schools in the early nineteenth century, what and how to teach kindergarten students has been an enduring tension. This exploratory interview-based study of 17 kindergarten teachers in California addresses the ways in which teachers perceive that standards-based accountability policy influences what and how they teach. Teachers report that rising external control over their curricular and instructional choices pushes kindergarten curriculum and instruction toward standardized academic content aimed at preparing students for the primary grades. The findings have implications for understanding the mechanisms through which accountability policy affects teachers work and raises questions for further research about how these mechanisms play out in the classroom.

Since the institutionalization of kindergarten classes in public elementary schools in the early nineteenth century, what and how to teach kindergarten students has been a contested issue. The original kindergarten model

Contemporary Issues in Educational Policy and School Outcomes, 215–240
Copyright © 2006 by Information Age Publishing

215

was decidedly nonacademic, child centered, and grounded in the natural development of children. Yet, once housed in elementary schools, kindergarten teachers confronted pressure to conform to the didactic, academic primary school model. Due to efforts of early childhood advocacy groups, as well as the structural looseness of elementary schools (Bidwell, 1965; Weick, 1976) and norms of teacher autonomy (Little, 1990; Lortie, 1975) many kindergarten teachers maintained a child-centered, developmental focus throughout the twentieth century. Now, another wave of educational reform seeks to introduce higher standards into public schools and raise the academic performance of all students. Consequently, this chapter explores how standards-based accountability policy contributes to the enduring tension over what and how much kindergartners should learn.

In this chapter, I examine teachers' perceptions of changes in kindergarten education which coincide with California state accountability policy. The chapter is situated within a larger body of research examining the relationship between standards-based accountability policy and teachers' work. Yet the chapter embarks on unexplored territory in that it examines the effect of accountability policy on teachers' practice in an untested elementary grade, which has historically been loosely connected to the other primary grades. By extending the examination to a grade which is not directly subject to the state's main accountability mechanism—standardized testing—the study provides insight into the various mechanisms through which accountability policy influences teachers' work. Doing so suggests a potential for more wide ranging impacts of these policies than typically emphasized. Specifically, I argue that accountability policies, imposed by school districts in response to state accountability policy, have a direct influence on kindergarten teaching and contribute to profound changes in kindergarten education. The chapter draws on a larger study of California elementary school teachers' experiences with standards-based accountability policy, providing preliminary evidence of change in teachers' practice through the voices of teachers. While the study does not directly examine teachers' practice, it illuminates potential changes and lays the groundwork for future study of kindergarten teachers' work. Therefore, the chapter explores the question: what effect has state and local standards-based accountability policy had on the enduring tension to define the character of kindergarten education?

The chapter proceeds with the following organization. First, a brief history of kindergartens and relevant literature on teachers' responses to accountability and curriculum policy is presented. After outlining the study's methodology, the chapter presents findings related to kindergarten teachers' perceptions of changes in their practice due to the imposition of accountability polices at the state and district level. Through teachers' perceptions of change, the chapter explores the mechanisms through which change occurs in the absence of direct accountability for test results. The chapter concludes with a discussion of the contributions and limitations of the study, and presents directions for future research evoked by the findings.

PREVIOUS RESEARCH

The analysis and findings presented in this chapter are grounded in previous research and analysis of the history of kindergartens and the relationship between educational policy and teachers' practice. Kindergarten's unique history contributes to its institutional position—structurally disconnected from the other elementary grades—affording teachers a degree of autonomy and independence. However, conceptions of appropriate kindergarten content and kindergarten's connection to the primary grades are contested. Review of more general literature addressing the relationship between educational policy and teachers' practice reveals that curriculum policy, such as state content standards, influence teaching. However, this work has not fully investigated the addition of accountability mechanisms implemented in recent years. Research on the specific role of accountability policy has tended to focus on the impact of high stakes standardized testing and thus provides little insight into the impact of accountability policy on teachers' practice in untested grades such as kindergarten.

Kindergarten's Unique Institutional History

Kindergarten originated as a distinctive educational form independent from public elementary schools. After being incorporated into elementary schools at the turn of the century, they were influenced by their new institutional contexts, but also retained considerable autonomy and distinction. In this section I argue that over time, a tension emerged over whether kindergarten curriculum and instruction should focus on academic skills and preparation for first grade or retain its traditional developmental, child centered model. This tension continues to influence teachers' construction of their practice in kindergarten classrooms today.

Review of historical literature suggests that the original kindergarten model: accepted children's spontaneous and natural activity such as free play; focused on social development over academic skills; and respected the individual learning trajectory of each child (Beatty, 1989). As kindergartens were gradually pulled into public elementary schools, they were influenced by their new organizational context. For example, kindergarten teachers were required to obtain training and certification similar to elementary school teachers and were increasingly viewed by principals as a way to prepare students for the academic demands of first grade (Cuban, 1992; Lazerson, 1971). However, by and large, kindergartens retained their distinctive educational approach—specifically a developmental perspective emphasizing education of the whole child—despite their institutionalization in public elementary schools (Weber, 1969). In addition, kindergartens often remained structurally disconnected from their schools located on separated floors/wings, often with their own playgrounds or recess periods, and following different schedules, all of which lead to distinct work demands for kindergarten teachers.

In one of the only comprehensive analyses of the evolution of kindergarten education throughout the twentieth century, historian Kristin Dombkowski (2001) argues that Americans disagree over the content and quality of kindergarten education. She describes a tension persisting, throughout the twentieth century, between the traditional nonacademic or "developmental" kindergarten model and pressure to assimilate kindergartens to the academic goals and didactic methods of primary schooling. Pressure from policymakers and parents sought to push kindergarten toward more academic content. Representing the interests of taxpayers, policymakers sought to justify the expense of kindergartens by linking them directly to student preparation for academic training. Parents pushed for a more academic kindergarten in order to jump start their children's individual achievement. Yet, these efforts faced opposition from advocacy and professional groups seeking to maintain a nonacademic, developmental focus grounding their objection to an academic kindergarten in research on child development and maturation theory. Ultimately, the debate over competing conceptions of appropriate kindergarten teaching has remained unresolved. This study examines whether contemporary changes in the policy context and possibly the organizational structure of schools will contribute to the debate over what and how much children should be expected to learn in kindergarten.

Policy and Practice Relationships

This study is framed by empirical work related to the intersection between educational policy and teachers' practice. A growing body of research documents the effects of state accountability systems, and high stakes testing in particular, on elementary school curricula, teachers' work, and student learning. This research confirms that testing leads elementary school teachers to increase the time spent teaching tested subjects, and to decrease the time spent teaching nontested subjects such as science and social studies (Jones, Jones, Hardin, Chapman, Yarbrough, & Davis, 1999; Stecher & Barron, 1999). In addition, teachers report increased time spent teaching directly to tests (Smith, Edelsky, Draper, Rottenberg, & Cherland, 1991; Whitford & Jones, 2000). Teachers find high stakes testing stressful and voice concerns that testing negatively affects their students (Kubow & Debard, 2000). Most of this research focuses on the role of high stakes testing in influencing teachers' practice. Yet, the degree to which these effects extend to the kindergarten level is unclear because kindergartners in California are not required by the state to take standardized tests used for accountability purposes and therefore, kindergarten teachers are not directly held accountable by the state for improving student outcomes. This chapter extends upon the literature on standards-based accountability policy and its impact on teachers' work by exploring its effects on a nontested grade with historically low interdependence with the elementary grades.

More generally, educational research has explored the relationship between curriculum policy and teachers' practice. Drawing on their study of high school teachers subject to varying curriculum control policies in the 1980s, Archbald and Porter (1994) conclude that teachers subject to strong curriculum controls were more likely to modify their teaching practice in line with policy mandates than teachers subject to weak controls. Yet, other research in the 1980s and 1990s emphasized that curriculum policies penetrate classroom boundaries, but suggests that teachers play an active role in mediating policy, constructing their teaching practice from both external influences as well as their preexisting knowledge, beliefs and practices (Coburn, 2004; Cohen & Ball, 1990; Spillane, 1999). Drawing on data collected in the 1990s, Ingersoll (2003) concludes that teachers have considerable control over the instructional domain of their work, but Ingersoll's assessment of control may overemphasize teacher discretion over curriculum and instruction, because it was collected before the height of the accountability movement. Therefore, while empirical evidence suggests that teachers play an active role in mediating external policy demands, it has not yet fully explored more overt curriculum policy controls spawned by state and district accountability policy. The ways in which teachers are held accountable for implementing state curriculum policy may influence their responses to policy and ultimately reduce the range of responses exhibited. Therefore, this chapter extends previous analyses to examine the impact of local educational policy on kindergarten teachers' curriculum and instruction.

METHODS

Data Collection

To study the relationship between standards-based accountability policies and educators' changing conceptions of kindergarten education, I drew on interview data from a larger qualitative study of educators' experiences with accountability policy in California. During the 2002-2003 school year, Policy Analysis for California Education (PACE) conducted an interview-based study to investigate educators' perceptions of the impact of accountability policy on their practice (Woody, Buttles, Kafka, Park, & Russell, 2004). The goal of the project was to better understand how local educators experience state-led reforms, and ultimately to inform the efforts of policymakers to improve the California accountability system.

The projects' research team[1] conducted semistructured individual interviews and focus groups with teachers and administrators in eight elementary schools within four districts throughout the state. Two of the school districts were in urban communities, one was in a surburban community, and the other in a rural community. The districts and the eight schools (2 per district) were selected to represent diverse student populations, community characteristics, and performance on the state's Academic Performance Index in the 2001-2002 school year (see Figure 9.1).

Teachers of students in kindergarten, second and fourth grade in each school were recruited for interviews. All kindergarten teachers—except for one teacher who declined to participate in the study—were inter-

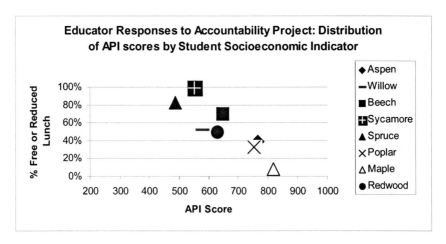

Figure 9.1.   Distribution of sample schools' API scores plotted against percent of students qualifying for free or reduced price lunches.

Table 9.1. Background Data for Sample Teachers

Teacher (School)	Age	Years of Teaching	District Context
Ms. Dove (Aspen)	59	36	Tech Valley / Suburban
Ms. Dudek (Aspen)	40s	17	Tech Valley / Suburban
Ms. Berman (Beech)	64	46	South City / Urban
Ms. Kapuscinski (Beech)	37	11	South City / Urban
Ms. Chang (Maple)	50s	27	North City / Urban
Ms. Diab (Maple)	40	18	North City / Urban
Ms. Kosmos (Maple)	53	8	North City / Urban
Ms. Smith (Maple)	34	10	North City / Urban
Ms. Garcia (Poplar)	32	8	Central Plains / Rural
Ms. Romero (Poplar)	43	17	Central Plains / Rural
Ms. Giordano (Redwood)	75	40	North City / Urban
Ms. Huntington (Redwood)	57	36	North City / Urban
Ms. Jordan (Sycamore)	54	20	South City / Urban
Ms. Robinson (Sycamore)	50s	23	South City / Urban
Ms. Villanueva (Sycamore)	24	3	South City / Urban
Ms. Edwards (Willow)	40s	22	Tech Valley / Suburban
Ms. Menendez (Willow)	60	22	Tech Valley / Suburban
Ms. Peterson (Willow)	50s	7	Tech Valley / Suburban
Ms. Ward (Willow)	55	31+	Tech Valley / Suburban

viewed in the eight schools. This produced a total of 21 interviews, including two teachers at Spruce Elementary[2] who taught combination kindergarten and first grade classes. Table 9.1 presents demographic data for the sample kindergarten teachers. Interviews followed a semistructured protocol covering the following broad topics: teacher experience and background, school context, school reform efforts, equity, professionalism, and policy recommendations. Interview questions asked teachers to briefly describe their professional backgrounds and their school as context for their work. The bulk of the interviews asked teachers to describe significant reforms facing their school in recent years and specifically probed for teachers' knowledge of, attitudes toward, and experiences with the state system of accountability. The interviews concluded with questions regarding teachers' beliefs about the ability of the accountability system to address inequities in student achievement, and the system's impact on their professional commitment and satisfaction.

Analysis

During preliminary analysis, the PACE research team realized that accountability policy was having an unexpected impact on kindergarten teachers. Examining kindergarten teacher interviews revealed that some kindergarten teachers were struggling to accommodate increased testing requirements and feeling pressure to modify their teaching practice to meet accountability demands. These demands were causing teachers to experience tension between state and district mandates and what they believed to be appropriate teaching for their students. Kindergarten teachers' passionate responses to accountability issues and references to changes in their practice due to accountability were unexpected given that kindergarten teachers are not held accountable for student performance under the state system. Therefore, the analysis I pursued resulting in this chapter emerged directly from our time in schools and was not an anticipated focus of the study. In fact, kindergarten teachers were originally included in the design of the study to represent a contrasting case of a grade not subject to accountability policy, rather than teachers deeply impacted by accountability policy. As a result, I pursued an independent line of analysis to address the following exploratory research question: how is externally imposed accountability policy in California influencing kindergarten teachers' work?[3]

In order to examine kindergarten teachers' experiences with accountability policy, I performed a series of passes through the kindergarten interviews. Initially, I used Nvivo qualitative data analysis software to code segments of interviews documenting descriptions of changes in practice which were directly linked to components of state or district accountability policy. Review of the coded passages revealed key themes including descriptions of: change in practice; change in teaching content; links between kindergarten and first grade; increased testing and test preparation; and changes in pedagogy. I counted the prevalence of each theme across all interviews to check for representativeness. Counts are included throughout the following narrative in order to account for the scope of the themes presented. Finally, I returned to the coded passages in order to more fully account for teachers' descriptions of change in practice, coding for the mechanisms that compelled teachers to make changes in their practice.

Limitations

The larger PACE study was designed and interviews broadly framed to allow these discoveries about kindergarten to emerge from our time in schools. However, because the data were not directly collected with this line of inquiry in mind, they present some limitations. While the interviews explored teachers' experiences with state and district accountability policy in general, the focus was not specifically on kindergarten teaching.

A few interviews focused more on teachers' accounts of how their school was responding to accountability policy rather than on the changes experienced in their classrooms. In addition, there is a fair amount of asymmetry in the data. Six different researchers conducted the interviews. While all roughly followed the same interview protocol, different areas are emphasized and probed in each interview. Finally, I eliminated two potential cases—both kindergarten teachers from one school in the Central Plains district—because they taught kindergarten and first grade combination classes. For purposes of the larger study, these cases were relevant but did not fit my particular focus on kindergarten teachers. Eliminating these teachers left only one school in the Central Plains district represented in the sample. Before turning to the findings, the next section provides brief background information about California's accountability system.

ACCOUNTABILITY POLICY IN CALIFORNIA

Study data were collected at the very early stages of implementation of the No Child Left Behind Act and consequently the study primarily reports on teachers' experiences with the California state system of accountability. This system, mandated by the Public Schools Accountability Act (PSAA) of 1999, represented the culmination of more than a decade of policymaking in California aimed at systemic educational reform. Despite a history of frustrated and short lived attempts to establish a statewide system of content standards and assessments in the late 1980s and early 1990s, California resumed its efforts to create a statewide system in 1995 with the passage of the California Assessment and Academic Achievement Act (AB 265). This legislation resulted in the adoption of content standards in English/language arts and mathematics in 1997, followed by science in 1998. The State Board of Education required districts to align their local standards with the new state standards and to ensure that local standards were at least as rigorous as those adopted by the state. In 1999, California legislators and Governor Gray Davis passed their version of a high stakes incentives-based accountability system, PSAA. The law called for all schools to be publicly ranked based on a performance index linked to student test scores, with schools facing serious consequences for poor performance and eligibility for rewards for demonstrating progress. Originally, a school's Academic Performance Index (API) was solely based on results from an off-the-shelf, norm referenced, standardized test (SAT-9, Stanford Achievement Test published by Harcourt Brace). At the time data were collected for this study, the API also included student performance on a standards-based assessment in mathematics and English/language arts: the California Standards Test. Students in California are tested every spring in Grades 2 through 11.

The state requires that local school districts use content standards to guide curriculum and instruction in kindergarten classrooms, outlining standards in English/language arts, mathematics, science, social studies/ history, and visual and performing arts (dance, music, theatre and visual arts). However, kindergarten students are not included in the state testing program, and therefore their performance does not contribute to their schools' API ranking. Given that kindergarten teachers are not held accountable for outcomes in the same way that teachers are in tested grades, it was a surprise to find teachers reporting pressure to change their teaching practice in response to state accountability policy.

FINDINGS

Findings are presented in two sections. The first details the specific changes in kindergarten teaching described by teachers. The second accounts for changes in teaching practice in the absence of high stakes testing for kindergartners.

Teachers Describe Changes in Kindergarten Teaching

Despite their diverse teaching contexts, the vast majority of the sample teachers (17 out of 19) spoke of recent changes in the nature of kindergarten teaching without being directly asked about such changes. It is not clear whether the other two teachers were experiencing similar changes because the topic simply may not have come up in their interviews. For example, one of these two teachers spoke very little about her teaching practice. Formerly a principal, Ms. Jordan at Sycamore Elementary had recently been "demoted" to classroom teacher; she directed the bulk of her comments to issues outside her classroom. Examination of the responses of teachers who did describe changes in their instructional practice revealed that their descriptions fall into three broad categories: changes in kindergarten curriculum, connections between kindergarten and the primary grades; and increased testing/assessment. The following findings sections focus on the responses of the 17 teachers who spoke of change in their practice.

Changes in Kindergarten Curriculum

Teachers describe changes in kindergarten curriculum on two dimensions: (1) changes in the content or subjects covered in the curriculum such as an emphasis on academic skills; and (2) changes in student performance standards, specifically an expectation that all students will master the standardized curriculum. This changed orientation toward kindergarten teaching and learning stands in stark contrast to traditional expectations regarding kindergarten curriculum content and student performance. Ms. Edwards at Willow Elementary explained,

> They [kindergartens] used to be, "okay, we will do graham crackers and milk. We will do singing. We will do a lot of socialization." ... [now] the emphasis is not socialization skills. The emphasis is on academics. These little kids are required to read and write in English by the end of the year. (para. 161)

Like Ms. Edwards, other teachers described the kindergarten curriculum of the past as emphasizing exposure to academic content (rather than student mastery of content), inclusion of both academic and social skills, and differential expectations for student performance based on the individual developmental trajectories of students.

References to changes in curriculum content are present in 12 out of 17 interviews that speak of change in practice. Seven out of these 12 teachers use the words "more academic" to describe the change in what is taught in kindergarten. For example, Ms. Garcia at Poplar Elementary described this change saying,

> I guess I haven't been in this business really long, but there seems to be a real switch from, at least in kindergarten, from doing more kinds of social, arts, and crafts and things like that, to more of a push to academics, meeting particular standards to get them ready for first grade. (para. 491)

Another teacher, Ms. Dudek at Aspen Elementary said,

> First of all, I think that the goals that I have for the children now are quite different than what my heart tells me they should be doing and my years of practice coming with it, that I should be doing. So that I am doing much more paperwork and academic work and less of the types of things that I think really, really work for little kids. (para. 305)

Ms. Garcia's comments highlight a change in kindergarten, initiated by content standards, from a focus on social and creative activities to preparation for first grade. Like many other teachers in the sample, Ms. Dudek goes a step further and illuminates a tension between the academic work she is told to teach and what her professional experience indicates she should be teaching.

While only 7 out of 17 teachers used the words "more academic" to describe a change in their practice, 16 out of 17 teachers describe their current focus in the classroom as teaching traditional academic subjects such as language arts and math. Teachers spoke with the greatest frequency about teaching reading. Fourteen out of 17 teachers spoke of a change in the expectation that they should teach reading in kindergarten. For example, Ms. Robinson at Sycamore Elementary remarked,

> So yeah, that is a shift. Because now the push is to read. Make sure these children can read. And so we do as much as we possibly can to make sure that they read. Ten years ago we had a principal that would not allow pencils in kindergarten. It was not appropriate. Children were not really supposed to be writing. So it has changed a good deal. (para. 314)

Ms. Robinson emphasizes the dramatic nature of change in kindergarten teaching describing how 10 years ago kindergartners at her school were not permitted to do written work, but are now expected to be reading. In this comment she draws attention to both a change in curriculum content, but also in expectations for student performance. Not only are teachers expected to teach reading, but all students are expected to be reading by the time they leave kindergarten. This may seem like a subtle distinction, but it represents a new direction for kindergarten education. Frequent comments throughout the interviews emphasize student readiness suggesting that in the past students were exposed to reading instruction with the understanding that students would begin reading when developmentally ready. Now teachers describe feeling pressure to ensure that all students meet a standardized level of performance. This change was described by Ms. Dove at Aspen Elementary who said,

> There's a lot more reading instruction now than there used to be. And we always had a number of children who were ready to learn to read by the end of kindergarten, and we handled that. But now, it's expected that all children reach that level. And so, um, so that's very, you know, there's a push towards that now where it didn't used to be a push; it was kind of a wonderful thing that just unfolds. It's expected and I feel that many children face failure too. (para. 310)

Three of the teachers quoted above use similar language in describing changes in curriculum content and student performance standards. Ms. Garcia spoke of a "push to academics" and Ms. Robinson refers to a "push to read," both indicating the pressure the teachers feel to meet present kindergarten standards. In the last passage, Ms. Dove also emphasizes a change in standards for student performance regarding reading. Echoing Ms. Garcia and Ms. Robinson, she uses the language of a "push" to get students reading, and contrasts today's expectations with a natural developmental process.

Other references to change in content identified the emphasis on language arts, and sometimes mathematics curriculum, as leaving little time for other areas of the curriculum. This pattern corresponds with comments made by upper grades teachers in the larger study who said that they now emphasize the subjects included on the state's accountability tests (language arts and math) at the expense of other subjects (Woody et al., 2004). When asked about the most pressing issues facing her classroom, Ms. Berman, a kindergarten teacher at Beech Elementary said,

> That's not being able to teach the other subjects. Not having enough music. Not having time to do as much art as we used to. Um, as much interaction, dramatic play, children playing together, block play. We are just not able to do that anymore. And it has taken a lot of the fun out of the kindergarten experience, for the teachers and the parents and the children. That is the basic thing. (para. 117)

Mrs. Dudek at Aspen expressed a similar sentiment saying:

> One of my main concerns about children now is the lack of age appropriate activities for kindergartners. I come from a philosophy where I really think that children should do more physical, you know more physically involved activities rather than the present push to learning reading, writing. (para. 29)

Other teachers spoke of the inability to have choice time: a traditional activity when students chose activities from various stations. Still others mentioned limited time for other academic subjects such as science and social studies. Overall, comments about the narrowing of the curriculum to emphasize tested subjects have become common place in studies of teachers' work in the context of accountability policy, but are surprising given that kindergarten students are not subject to state testing.

In summary, the majority of teachers in the study describe significant changes in the content of what is taught in kindergarten and expectations for kindergarten student performance. Teachers describe kindergarten curriculum and instruction focused on academic skill development, particularly reading, which precludes time for fine arts, play, and other traditional academic subjects such as science and social studies. In reference particularly to reading, teachers stress that students are now expected to meet a standardized level of reading proficiency. Teacher reports of changes in their practice reflect the imposition of curriculum standards that define a set level of performance for all students by the end of kindergarten. However, the narrowing of the curriculum to focus on reading, language arts, and to some extent mathematics cannot be explained by the standards which also include science, social studies and fine arts. The mechanisms through which teachers feel pressure to emphasize tested subjects are addressed in subsequent sections.

Kindergarten Increasingly Connected To Primary Grades

Another prevalent change—noted by teachers across schools—was a tighter link between kindergartens and the first and second grades. Six out of the 17 teachers said they now feel like they are teaching first grade instead of kindergarten. This view was evident in comments such as those made by Ms. Romero at Poplar who said, "The standards from first grade have been pushed on kindergarten now, and we're supposed to teach them to read in kindergarten now" (para. 208). Since Ms. Romero and the five other teachers who spoke of kindergarten becoming more like first grade were formerly first grade teachers, they have at least some basis for this comparison.

Most of the teachers' comments which compare the kindergarten standards with what was once first or second grade curriculum surpass neutral description. Ms. Hutchinson at Redwood Elementary problematizes this change referring to higher standards that students are not ready to reach:

> And so when you ask me how it is different. Well, the kids are developmentally in the same place where they were, but the expectation is for them to be doing academic work that is first grade work. And for some of these kids, you are stepping over all of their developmental foundation things. To teach them something that they are not ready for. (para. 53)

As argued in the previous section, Ms. Hutchinson's comments also emphasize a contradiction between the new performance standards for kindergarten students and students' readiness or developmental trajectories.

Ms. Menendez at Willow Elementary describes another connection between kindergarten and the primary grades at her school saying:

> In kindergarten we don't have the SAT-9 (state test). *But* we do get the information from the other grades. So we can sort of lay the foundation for the next grade. We do that a lot here so that when we look at the standards, we know that we are *required* to meet so many standards so that they can build up *upon* those standards in first-grade and second-grade. (para. 500, emphasis original)

This comment indicates that kindergarten teachers in some schools are working directly with state test data to plan instruction, in order to prepare students for academic demands and testing in the primary grades. In this way, state testing may be having an impact on kindergarten curriculum and instruction despite the fact that students are not included in the testing program.

In sum, these comments suggest two ways in which kindergartens are now more interdependent with the primary grades. First, content previously covered in first grade has moved down to kindergarten. In addition, kindergarten teachers may be using standards and test results from first and second grade as a guide for the standards of performance their students must meet in the future. These comments, about greater interdependence between kindergarten and the primary grades, provide preliminary evidence to support a change in the characteristically loose structure of elementary schools, in that kindergarten teachers are increasingly connected with content from the primary grades.

Increased Testing for Kindergartners

The fact that the vast majority of teachers spoke of increased testing requirements for kindergartners was somewhat surprising considering the fact that kindergartners are not subject to state accountability tests. However, districts have responded to state demands for increased test scores by mandating more frequent progress tests that extend down to kindergarten. In fact, 13 out of 17 teachers spoke of increased testing demands in kindergarten, without being directly asked about testing for their students. In addition, the format of testing changed from past observational screening measures that required teachers to observe and document student developmental milestones such as following verbal directions to include written tests of basic skills with response formats such as students circling answers or filling in bubbles: formats that simulate standardized test formats.

Despite the fact that testing is not mandated by the state for kindergartners, school districts are imposing their own testing requirements for younger students. And in many ways, district mandated testing has a more significant impact on teachers' work because it is required at multiple points throughout the year. Kindergarten teachers in the South City school district reported being required to administer the following tests: a district entrance assessment, the CELDT (a test of English proficiency), math assessments twice a year, and reading/language arts assessments six times each year. It is not surprising that teachers in this district made comments such as those by Ms. Villanueva from Sycamore Elementary:

> There's so much testing that it boggles you down and it, there definitely needs to be less testing. But I think the testing does need to take place in order for you to say okay, well this is the area that I need to improve on and it gives you a little bit of, you know you need to evaluate yourself and say okay, now, what is that I can do to help in that area. But just with so much

testing it just, it boggles you down, it's gotten to the point where its, its really ridiculous. Really ridiculous. (para. 318)

Teachers such as Ms. Villanueva expressed support for assessments that provide feedback on student performance, yet objected to the sheer magnitude of tests they must administer.

Teachers described increased testing as having a significant effect on their practice. Ms. Dudek at Aspen Elementary explained, "you spend a lot of your time testing and less of your time teaching" (para. 289). Other teachers explained how they must administer tests individually or in small groups to their young students, which exacerbates the time spent testing and away from other instructional activities. In addition, 6 out of 17 teachers said they also engage in test preparation activities in kindergarten. For example, Ms. Smith at Maple Elementary said,

> It generally does [affect my practice] because we end up teaching children how to take tests, and because you have time constraints and you have to get this information for the tests, you may not give them opportunities to explore, opportunities to work at their pace, you know? And um, it's just kind of get them the information quickly; let's not worry about mastery, let's not worry about understanding, just get them the information. So that definitely guides, you know, what you do in the classroom. (para. 276)

Similar to the passages presented in the previous section that describe a push to get all students to read despite their developmental readiness, Ms Smith's comments reflect her inability to let students work at their own pace due to pressure to prepare for upcoming tests. She also highlights a tension expressed by upper grade teachers in the larger study that given limited time and a large amount of content covered on tests, teachers are forced to emphasize content coverage at the expense of student mastery (Woody et al., 2004).

Some teachers supported increased testing because of the feedback that it provides on student progress and the consistency in curriculum coverage testing promotes across classrooms. However, even supporters of increased testing articulated the need to carefully monitor the impact of testing on teaching and learning. For example, Ms. Peterson at Willow Elementary remarked,

> So, you know, I think the assessments are good, I think it's good that we've got these tests. I think it's good that we're all working towards a common goal. I think it's important that we're going to come out with you know, a quality product at the end of the 12 years of California education, hopefully, 16 but I think we need to look at some of these [changes], what are the implications of that? What does this really mean in terms of what we're doing in the classroom? (para. 242)

Ms. Peterson's comments echo those of other teachers who argued that testing both leaves less time for teaching and other classroom activities, and also shapes the content of classroom activities in encouraging explicit test preparation. As shown in the next section, testing is one of several ways in which kindergarten teachers in this study reported less discretion over their work.

In sum, teachers describe several significant changes in kindergarten teaching. Kindergarten curriculum is now focused on academic skill development and particularly reading. Standards for student performance promote a benchmark level of student proficiency at the end of the kindergarten year. Kindergartens increasingly resemble and are connected to first grade. In addition, teachers must administer a variety of district mandated assessments. Moreover, teachers connect changes with elements of the state and district accountability systems such as content standards and assessments.

Change Results from Greater External Control

As outlined in the beginning of this chapter, kindergartens have historically retained considerable autonomy from their elementary school contexts. Yet, teachers interviewed in this study describe external pressure to change their teaching practice in recent years. The fact that teachers attribute changes in their practices to external sources is evidenced in part by the recurrent language of a "push" or "pressure" to focus on academic skills. In fact, all 17 teachers spoke of rising external direction over their work. And while research on teachers in tested grades highlights teachers' perceptions of eroding control over their work in the context of state-led reforms, kindergarten teachers are only subject to state content standards and are not directly held accountable by the state for student progress in mastering the standards. Therefore, the question remains how is accountability policy having the profound impacts on kindergarten curriculum and instruction reported by teachers in the previous section? The previous discussion alludes to several mechanisms by which accountability is affecting teachers work. More academic content is introduced by curriculum standards. District testing takes times away from other instructional activities. Yet, the following discussion will raise, and begin to answer, further questions such as, why do teachers report complying with curriculum standards especially when many teachers criticize these changes for not being developmentally appropriate for students? Ultimately, I argue that the logic of standards-based accountability movement has become so pervasive, that district policymaking extends state policy to include even very young children in their accountability systems.

Content Standards Give Direction and Focus

Teachers expressed complex views regarding the external direction provided by state curriculum standards. Six teachers out of 17 applauded the standards for providing greater direction over what they teach. Ms. Garcia at Poplar Elementary said,

> They're [my goals for students] a lot more clear. And I see a purpose in them. You know, what I'm doing in class activities, there's always a purpose to it. And of course, if you're working you want to make sure you're heading somewhere. (para. 260)

Ms. Robinson at Sycamore Elementary recalled "floundering" as a new teacher because she did not have curriculum standards to follow, and thought the standards would help beginning teachers know what to teach. Other teachers said having standards makes their work, particularly planning instructional activities, easier. Teachers also identified benefits of the standards for student learning, such that standards make it more likely that teachers are working toward common curricular goals. For example, Ms. Ward at Willow Elementary argued that teachers previously taught what ever they wanted leaving students with holes in their knowledge, but content standards now ensure that goals for students are consistent.

However, seven teachers expressed concerns that the content of the standards was not developmentally appropriate for kindergartners. This group did not object to the concept of having curriculum standards, and in fact several of the same teachers supported the direction and consistency provided by standards. They objected to inclusion of content in standards that they believed was not developmentally appropriate for kindergarten students. For example, Ms. Peterson at Willow Elementary described kindergarten standards that she believes do not follow principles of child development such as telling time and writing in different styles. These comments echo those of teachers earlier in the chapter who compare the content of kindergarten standards to what was previously taught in first or second grade. With many teachers objecting to changes in kindergarten teaching imposed on them by the state or district accountability mandates, why are teachers not simply buffering unwanted external influences on their practice?

Districts Impose Overt Control Mechanisms

Across schools and districts, teachers described more overt control mechanisms such as highly structured curriculum programs, pacing plans, and district compliance monitoring which they distinguish from the curriculum standards. For example, when asked how the system of accountability affected her sense of what it means to be a teacher, Ms. Smith at Maple Elementary replied,

> It's affected my teaching because of flexibility and just not being able to go where the children want to go. If we're on a topic, you might get really excited about a topic. "Let's explore this topic more," whereas "This isn't the lesson. We have to get through this by this date," type of stuff. We have to cover this and we have to cover that. Even though you can still pull the skills that they need out, you can still meet the standards if you are allowed to do that. But you're really not allowed to meet the standards by different vehicles, or like vehicles of your choice. You have to use these particular vehicles through standards. So it's limiting. (para. 340)

Similar to the comments of teachers in the previous section, Ms. Smith emphasizes the pressure to cover curriculum content imposed by the standards. Her references to covering lessons by particular dates, also highlights an increasingly prevalent practice among school districts: the specification of pacing plans which outline a schedule that teachers must follow for covering curriculum standards. Ms. Smith goes on to say later in her interview that she is also constrained in the way that she teaches standards by having to follow the Open Court reading/language arts curriculum and to report periodically to the district which Open Court lessons she is currently teaching.

In four of the seven schools, the method of reading instruction changed dramatically in recent years due to the district's adoption of the Open Court curriculum. As part of its systemic reform policies, California mandated that school districts select from two approved reading programs for elementary grades (Open Court and Houghton Mifflin) in order to receive state textbook funding. Therefore, it is not surprising that four of the seven districts adopted Open Court. But what is notable is the way districts chose to implement the curriculum program. The two districts that had mandated use of Open Court at the time of our study—North City and South City—also issued pacing plans, which tell teachers "to be at a certain place at a certain time" (Ms. Giordano, Redwood Elementary, para. 214). In references to Open Court, Ms. Diab at Maple said,

> My schedule of teaching definitely changed last year when we started the Open Court reading. I am spending a lot more time doing whole group instruction where I have a certain lesson I have to get through everyday and meet a certain timeframe for these lessons and assessments. And activities have to be completed so I have to spend a lot more time with the language arts program doing whole group instruction. And in that sense I am spending a little less time on things like social studies and science and even math. You know because I mean an hour and fifteen minutes out of my day is all language arts. (para. 141)

Common to other teachers of Open Court reading in the study, Ms. Diab highlights the amount of time taken up by reading instruction in her classroom in order to implement the curriculum program, which takes time away from other activities. Both the North and South City districts mandated a particular amount of time that teachers must spend on Open Court instruction. In addition, Ms. Diab emphasizes that Open Court not only influences the content of the curriculum but also her pedagogy. Due to the fact that it is a teacher centered curriculum, Open Court dictates that teachers spend the majority of their reading instructional time engaged in whole group, direct instruction.

In fact there were many references to teachers receiving direction over how to teach through mandated curriculum packages (e.g. Open Court) and district created curriculum pacing plans. For example, Ms. Kosmos at Beech Elementary said, "I am a big supporter of Open Court, my problem with it is that it is 90 minutes (each day), and of that 90 minutes, 75 is spent on our carpet. I have 15 minutes where I get to work with them in an independent work time where I can pull them back into group and I don't feel like that is enough time" (para. 117). So despite her general support for the Open Court curriculum, Ms. Kosmos feels constrained by the expectation she will spend the majority of the time engaged in whole class, direct instruction. In addition, her reference to 90 minutes is a district requirement that teachers spend 90 minutes of their time with students directly teaching the Open Court curriculum. At Beech Elementary, kindergarten students attend school for 3 hours each day. Thus half of the time teachers spend with students is mandated to be spent teaching a highly structured reading program.

Teachers described a variety of ways in which they were held accountable for compliance with external mandates dictating what and how to teach. Teachers must submit student scores on progress tests and other forms of documentation such as standards-based report cards to the district. In addition, district officials in two districts directly monitor classroom activities through what teachers call "Open Court police" or curriculum consultants who monitor the implementation of Open Court curriculum in North City, and "Learning Walks" in South City when principals and district officials visit classrooms looking for standards-based instruction and student ability to articulate the standard they are learning. Ms. Huntington at Redwood Elementary described feeling like she was being monitored to ensure her use of the Open Court curriculum:

I think maybe it has affected me negatively. I always think that somebody is breathing down my neck. And so if I deviate, and again I will go back to Open Court because that is a real anchor here. Um, you know, if I say, we are going to plant some seeds today and put Open Court on the shelf. I kind of look over my shoulder to see if anybody heard me say to the kids that that is what we are doing. Or if we stay outside for 10 more minutes of recess then maybe I should. Or if I read this book instead of what the Open Court is telling me to do. I think it is a discomfort. It certainly is not, it has not been anything that has enhanced my teaching or driven it in a positive way. (para. 169)

It is understandable that Ms. Huntington felt that someone was looking over her shoulder. A vocal opponent of the Open Court curriculum at district meetings, Ms. Huntington reported receiving several visits from the superintendent who came to her classroom to ensure she was teaching Open Court.

Ms. Huntington clearly demonstrates how control over her work has not been perceived as a positive addition of the standards movement. Several teachers referred to a loss of flexibility or creativity. For example, Ms. Davis said, "As a teacher, you lose flexibility. You're no longer flexible, and I can see that with Open Court. There's more time constraints. You have to get through this, you have to get through this unit or something" (para. 274-276). And Ms. Villanueva describes her declining satisfaction with teaching by saying:

When I first started teaching, I thought teaching was just going to be about me and the kids and just fun, fun, fun and I am finding out everyday that okay I have to do this, that's something outside of the classroom, I have to fill out this paperwork or I have to this or I have to test the kids on this. I have to follow this so a lot of times, it takes the joy out of teaching. (para. 104-109)

In fact, Ms. Villanueva repeated the phrase "taking the joy out of teaching" numerous times (in references to accountability related mandates) throughout her interview. The frequency of this comment is cause for concern given that Ms. Villanueva is a beginning teacher who may be particularly vulnerable to leaving the profession (Ingersoll & Smith, 2003; Johnson, 2004). Yet, it is by no means a condition only affecting beginning teachers. Fourteen out of 17 teachers made negative comments about increased external direction. Overall, the majority of teachers spoke of external direction over their work in the language of constraint and restriction.

In sum, the vast majority of teachers interviewed described changes in their teaching practice associated with standards-based accountability policy. Teachers describe today's kindergarten curriculum as focused on academic skills, particularly on reading, with an expectation that students will meet standardized performance goals. In addition, there is some evidence that kindergartens are becoming increasingly interdependent with the primary grades as first grade curriculum content is pushed down on kindergartens and teachers use student performance data from the tested grades to inform their instructional planning. Finally, teachers report engaging in both more formal assessments and test preparation activities in order to comply with assessment requirements imposed on kindergartens by school districts. Teachers further report that these changes in curriculum and instruction result from school district policies which exert greater external control over their work. Consequently, teachers engage in practices such as testing and academic instruction despite concerns about the developmental appropriateness of these activities. External control is exerted through curriculum pacing guides, reporting requirements (e.g., test scores collected by school districts), mandated use of highly structured curriculum packages and direct monitoring. Overall, teachers express negative attitudes about their perceived shrinking discretion.

DISCUSSION

What and how much children should be expected to learn in kindergarten has remained a contested issue since the institutionalization of kindergartens in public elementary schools. Historical analysis depicts an enduring tension between early childhood educators seeking to preserve a developmental, child centered kindergarten curriculum and parents and policymakers pushing to increase the academic content of kindergartens in an effort to jump start students' academic preparation (Dombkowski, 2001). This study suggests that standards-based accountability policy is contributing to pressures that push kindergarten curriculum toward more academic content and recast the goal of kindergartens as preparation for the primary grades. Yet, the ultimate impact of standards-based accountability policy on the enacted kindergarten curriculum depends on teachers' responses to policy pressures.

Previous research on teachers' responses to curriculum policy emphasizes the degree to which teachers play an active role in mediating external curriculum policy demands (Cohen & Ball, 1990; Coburn, 2004; Spillane, 1999). In addition, teachers are depicted as having a high degree of discretion over instructional decisions (Ingersoll, 2003). By contrast, kindergarten teachers in this study report the intrusion of strong policy controls over their curriculum and instruction. Similar to the curriculum policies of the 1980s and early 1990s, California curriculum standards specify the intended kindergarten curriculum. However, local policies now add a layer of direct accountability for teacher compliance with curriculum goals. Teachers' descriptions of curriculum pacing plans, highly structured reading programs, reporting requirements, and direct surveillance suggest that external policies may be shrinking the zone of discretion teachers have over their classroom practice. While the tension between academic and developmental kindergarten models is not new, imposition of greater external controls exacerbate this tension and may ultimately force teachers to enact an academic kindergarten model.

Much of the research on teachers' responses to accountability policy emphasizes the influence of high stakes testing on teachers' instructional practices (Hamilton, Stecher, & Klein, 2002; Herman, 2003). However, kindergarten students are not subject to state standardized tests and therefore, are not held accountable for student outcomes by the state. By examining kindergarten teachers' experiences, this study extends the literature on standards-based accountability policy to an untested grade. My findings suggest that school districts have crafted local accountability policies that include kindergarten classrooms, such as imposing testing requirements on kindergarten students. Teachers in some districts described extensive assessment requirements that may have an even greater impact on their instructional practices than state testing because they mandate testing at multiple points throughout the school year. In addition, teachers highlighted other accountability mechanisms, such as the implementation of highly structured curriculum packages with compliance monitored by the school district, as affecting their practice. Thus, standards-based accountability policy has an effect on untested grades such as kindergarten through localized accountability pressures from school districts. These findings suggest the need for a more nuanced approach to studying the impact of standards-based accountability policies which include investigation of the full range of state and local accountability practices.

This study raises a number of issues to be considered in future research. The study's findings arose from analysis of data that were not collected with the particular questions in mind. The fact that change in practice emerged in the majority of teacher interviews without direct solicitation adds to the validity of the patterns found between interviews. The advantage of a bottom up investigation of the impact of policy is the emergence of discoveries such as the impact of accountability policy on kindergarten teachers (Elmore, 1979). However, it is important to emphasize that this study only reports on teachers' perceptions of changes in their practice. Consequently, future research should directly investigate the instructional choices teachers make in the context of pressure to pursue an academically focused kindergarten curriculum. Observation of teachers' classroom practice is warranted for a fuller understanding of how state curriculum policy and local accountability mechanisms play out in the classroom.

Finally, this study has implications for our understanding of the relationship between accountability policy and teachers' career satisfaction and commitment. The majority of teachers in this study expressed predominately negative reactions to the direction kindergarten education seems to be heading. Teachers raised concerns about removing the parts of the curriculum that are motivating for students to learn and teachers to teach. Teachers emphasized the conflict between academic content and students' developmental readiness. And teachers spoke of rising direction over their work in the language of restriction and constraint. These comments indicate that there are concrete ways in which accountability policy is implemented that relate to teachers' feelings of satisfaction with their work. The implications of control oriented strategies must continue to be explored with an eye toward giving teachers greater flexibility to implement mandates in ways that allow them to feel efficacious.

ACKNOWLEDGMENTS

The author thanks Judith Warren Little, Betty Malen, Bruce Fuller, Soung Bae and Sandra Park for their helpful comments on earlier versions of this chapter. Data analyzed in this chapter were collected as part of a larger study conducted by Policy Analysis for California Education (PACE) and funded by the Noyce Foundation.

NOTES

1. I joined the research team in January, 2002, and participated in data collection at two schools and all subsequent data analysis and reporting.
2. All district, school, and teacher names in this chapter are pseudonyms.
3. I am grateful to fellow PACE researchers, Judith Kafka and Sandra Park, who engaged in initial analysis of the kindergarten data with me. Their initial excitement about kindergarten teachers' experiences with accountability policy inspired me to pursue the work represented in this chapter.

REFERENCES

Archbald, D. A., & Porter, A. C. (1994). Curriculum control and teachers' perceptions of autonomy and satisfaction. *Educational Evaluation and Policy Analysis, 16*(1), 21-39.

Beatty, B. (1989). Child gardening: The teaching of young children in American schools. In D. Warren, (Ed.), *American teachers: Histories of a profession at work.* New York: Macmillan.

Bidwell, C. (1965). The school as a formal organization. In J. G. March (Ed.), *Handbook of research on organizations* (pp. 972-1019). New York: Rand McNally.

Coburn, C. E. (2004). Beyond decoup ling: Rethinking the relationship between the institutional environment and the classroom. *Sociology of Education, 77,* 211-244.

Cohen, D. K., & Ball, D. L. (1990). Relations between policy and practice: A commentary. *Educational Evaluation and Policy Analysis, 12*(3), 331-338.

Cuban, L. (1992). Why some reforms last: The case of the kindergarten. *American Journal of Education, 100,* 167-195.

Dombkowski, K. (2001). Will the real kindergarten please stand up? Defining and redefining the twentieth-century US kindergarten. *History of Education, 30*(6), 527-545.

Elmore, R. (1979). Backward mapping: Implementation research and policy decisions. *Political Science Quarterly, 94*(4), 601-616.

Hamilton, L. S., Stecher, B. M., & Klein, S. P. (2002). *Making sense of test-based accountability in education.* Santa Monica, CA: RAND.

Herman, J. L. (2004). The effects of testing on instruction. In S. H. Fuhrman & R. F. Elmore (Eds.), *Redesigning accountability systems for education* (pp. 141-166). New York: Teachers College.

Ingersoll, R. (2003). *Who control's teachers' work? Power and accountability in America's schools.* Cambridge, MA: Harvard University Press.

Ingersoll, R., & Smith, T. (2003). The wrong solution to the teacher shortage. *Educational Leadership, 60*(8), 30-33.

Johnson, S. M. (2004). *Finders and keepers: Helping new teachers survive and thrive in our schools.* San Francisco: Jossey-Bass.

Jones, M. G., Jones, B. D., Hardin, B., Chapman, L., Yarbrough, T., & Davis, M. (1999). The impact of high-stakes testing on teachers and students in North Carolina. *Phi Delta Kappan, 81*(3), 199-203.

Kubow, P. K., & Debard, R. (2000). Teacher perception of proficiency testing: A winning Ohio suburban school district expresses itself. *American Secondary Education, 29*(2), 16-25.

Lazerson, L. (1971). Urban reform and the schools: Kindergartens in Massachusetts, 1870-1915. *History of Education Quarterly, 11,* 115-142.

Little, J. W. (1990). The persistence of privacy: Autonomy and initiative in teachers' professional relations. *Teachers College Record, 91*(4), 509-536.

Lortie, D. C. (1975). *Schoolteacher: A sociological study.* Chicago: University of Chicago Press.

Smith, M. L., Edelsky, C., Draper, K., Rottenberg, C., & Cherland, M. (1991). *The role of testing in elementary schools.* Los Angeles: National Center for Research on Evaluation, Standards, and Student Testing.

Spillane, J. P. (1999). External reform initiatives and teachers' efforts to reconstruct their practice: The mediating role of teachers' zones of enactment. *Journal of Curriculum Studies, 31*(2), 143-175.

Stecher, B. M., & Barron, S. I. (1999). *Quadrennial milepost accountability testing in Kentucky.* Los Angeles: National Center for Research on Evaluation, Standards, and Student Testing.

Weber, E. (1969). *The kindergarten: Its encounter with educational thought in America.* New York: Teachers College.

Whitford, B. L., & Jones, K. (2000). *Accountability, assessment, and teacher commitment: Lessons from Kentucky's reform efforts.* Albany: State University of New York Press.

Weick, K. (1976). Educational organizations as loosely coupled systems. *Administrative Science Quarterly, 21,* 1-19.

Woody, E., Buttles, M., Kafka, J., Park, S., & Russell, J. (2004). *Voices from the field: Educators respond to accountability.* Berkeley: Policy Analysis for California Education.

ABOUT THE AUTHORS

Ann Allen is an assistant professor in the School of Educational Policy and Leadership at The Ohio State University. Her research interests include the democratic governance of public schooling and the intersection of schools and community. She earned a PhD in educational policy from Michigan State University May 2005.

Amanda Datnow is an associate professor in the Rossier School of Education at the University of Southern California. Her research interests include educational policy and politics, with a particular emphasis on the professional lives of educators and issues of equity.

Laura M. Desimone is an assistant professor in the Department of Public Policy and Education, Vanderbilt University. Her area of specialization is the study of policy effects on instruction and student achievement. Her work focuses on comprehensive school reform, standards-based reform and teachers' professional development and their effects on teacher's classroom practice and student achievement in mathematics, science, and reading. She also studies policy implementation and improving methods for studying policy effects.

Wayne K. Hoy is the Novice Fawcett Chair in Educational Administration at The Ohio State University. His research interests include school properties that enhance teaching and learning.

Anita Woolfolk Hoy is professor of education at The Ohio State University. She studies teachers' thinking and beliefs, particularly teachers' sense of efficacy, and the role of educational psychology in the preparation of teachers. Her research has been published in journals in education, educational psychology, and teacher education. She is editor of the journal, *Theory Into Practice*, and author of *Educational Psychology* (Allyn & Bacon), moving into its 10th edition.

Melinda Mangin is an assistant professor of educational administration at Michigan State University. Her research interests focus on school leadership, school reform, and education policy, particularly within the context of low socioeconomic status schools. Her most recent publication is a 2005 article titled "Leading Coherent Professional Development: A Comparison of Three Districts" published in *Educational Administration Quarterly* with William A. Firestone, M. Cecilia Martinez, and Terrie Polovsky.

Cecil Miskel is professor emeritus. During his career, he was a professor and administrator at the University of Kansas, University of Utah, and most recently at the University of Michigan.

Vicki Park is a research associate with the Center on Educational Governance at the Rossier School of Education at the University of Southern California. She is a former classroom teacher whose research interests include urban school reform and teacher preparation.

Jennifer Lin Russell is a doctoral candidate in the Graduate School of Education at the University of California, Berkeley. Her research uses organizational sociology to understand the relationship between educational policy and teachers' practice, career satisfaction, commitment, and self efficacy.

Thomas V. Shepley completed his doctoral work in policy and administration at the University of Michigan in 2003. Since that time, he has served as an administrator in the Baltimore City Public School System and is currently serving as principal of Mount Washington Elementary.

Robert Slater is a professor of educational administration and human resource development at Texas A&M University.

C. John Tarter is a professor of Educational Administration at St. John's University in New York. He teaches courses in organizational theory, politics of education, and educational leadership. His research interests are organizational climate, decision making, and school leadership.

Mario S. Torres Jr. is an assistant professor of educational administration and human resource development at Texas A&M University. His research interests include school law, policy and politics. His most recent publication is a 2004 article entitled, "Best interests of students left behind? Exploring the ethical and legal dimensions of United States federal involvement in public school improvement" in the *Journal of Educational Administration*.

Tamara V. Young is an assistant professor in Educational Leadership and Policy Studies at North Carolina State University. Her primary research interests include interest groups, coalitions, issue networks, and social network analysis.

Printed in the United States
62904LVS00001B/43-45